CUBA: Dictatorship or Democracy?

Working with a team of sociologists and writers, a Chilean journalist, Marta Harnecker, has assembled documentary evidence of a new form of grassroots participatory democracy that permeates almost all aspects of life in Cuba today. The book consists largely of taped interviews and recordings of peoples assemblies, union meetings, Committees for the Defense of the Revolution (CDRs) sessions and peoples power delegates elected under the new constitutions of February, 1976.

The importance of this book extends far beyond Cuba itself. It provides a blue print for how democracy can work in a socialist society no matter where it may be. Sandra Levinson, director of the Center for Cuban Studies, writes

> "it is a book which deals beautifully with one of the most important questions raised in this country about Cuba, and, more generally, about socialism, i.e. are democracy and socialism compatible? It deals with this question in a style that makes it accessible to every reading person . . . . . .in a way that shows democracy a part of every day life. It is a book about real people dealing with their own democracy."

This is a new, extensively revised edition of a book which has already appeared in seven Spanish editions as well as French and Portugese translations.

LAWRENCE HILL & CO.
520 Riverside Avenue,
Westport, CT 06880

Cuba: Dictatorship or Democracy?

Cuba: Dictatorship or Democracy?

Edition Includes Account of National Experience of People's Power

Edited and with an introduction by
MARTA HARNECKER

Translation into English by *Patrick Greanville*

Lawrence Hill & Company
WESTPORT, CONNECTICUT

Library of Congress Cataloging in Publication Data
Main entry under title:

Cuba, dictatorship or democracy?

   Translation of the 5th ed., rev. and expanded, of
Cuba ¿dictadura o democratia?
     1. Cuba--Politics and government--1959-
2. Political participation--Cuba. I. Harnecker,
Marta.
JL1016.C813   320.97291   78-24775
ISBN 0-88208-100-4
ISBN 0-88208-101-2 (pbk.)

Fifth edition, revised and expanded, 1979

English translation from the Spanish copyright © 1980
Lawrence Hill & Co.

ISBN: clothbound edition: 0-88208-100-4
ISBN: paperback edition 0-88208-101-2

Library of Congress Catalogue Card Number: 78-24775

1 2 3 4 5 6 7 8 9 10

Lawrence Hill & Company, Publishers, Inc.
Westport, Connecticut 06880

Manufactured in the United States of America
Designed by Rainstone Designs
South Salem. NY 10590

To the Cuban People—
True Authors of This Book—
on the Twentieth Anniversary of
Their Revolution

M. H.

CONTENTS

PREFACE

This is not a theoretical book. The "objective" Western commentators, unable to deny the accomplishments of the Cuban revolution, have relied on minimizing its significance, claiming that the progress in health, education, housing, and social welfare has all been achieved at the cost of "freedom" and "democracy." This, then, is a non-"objective" book: we wish to show how the Cuban people live their revolution.

With this goal in mind, we have chosen to let the people speak for themselves rather than present an analysis of our own. Eighty percent of this book is a literal transcript of recordings made at assemblies and meetings held in factories, Committees to Defend the Revolution, and people's courts, and of individual interviews, particularly with voters and delegates of the local governing bodies of People's Power in the provinces of Matanzas, Santi Spiritu, and Havana.

In today's Cuba the people debate the laws, dispense justice, approve economic plans, and militantly defend the gains of the revolution.

From the time of Marx and Lenin, Marxian theory has held that the dictatorship of the proletariat is the highest form of democracy. A democracy no longer the instrument of an exploitative minority becomes the expression of power of the immense majority, whose members are finally able to confront their problems resolutely and face their common destiny of liberation. For these reasons, we have wanted the very people who now govern Cuba to show us, directly or indirectly, the manner in which they use their power.

Cuba is not yet a communist society. It is a small, underdeveloped country that for 20 years, has been the target of vicious, deliberate, economic aggression. In 1959, it broke the bonds of dependency connecting it with imperialism once and for all; it then set out on the long, difficult march toward socialism and communism.

Cuba lies just 90 miles due south of the United States. Faced with the constant threat of attack by counterrevolutionary groups trained, financed, and armed by the U.S. government, it has been forced to allocate a large part of its resources to defense, thereby diverting these funds from areas that could otherwise have proven socially useful.

Cubans are a people who, in the process of constructing socialism, must free themselves from the economic and ideological backwardness of centuries. It is now a nation which faces ever greater responsibilities after losing a significant portion of its professional and technical classes. This is why, as we listen to the Cuban people discuss their problems throughout this book, we hear frequent and severe criticism aimed at specific problems. This should not alarm us because, in sharp contrast to what transpires in many other countries, in Cuba problems are discussed to be resolved. Constructive criticism is not the expression of impotence but, rather, the awareness of power and the will to exercise it.

The early reportorial work presented here was carried out by a team of Chilean journalists (Camilo Garcia, Alicia Donoso, Bartolome Hernadez, Manuela Rodriguez, and Marta Harnecker) during May and June, 1975, primarily in Havana and Matanzas. This reporting comprises the entire first part of the book, plus three chapters of the second (*Public Accountability: A Typical Case; In the Rural Zones; The Armed Forces and People's Power*).

Approximately a year later, in September, 1976, a new phase of reporting was initiated, again in the province of Matanzas, using as a focus the evaluation of People's Power by some of the principal leaders of that political experiment.

Finally, the most recent material was gathered by me between April and June, 1978, after extensive research and interviews in the provinces of Santi Spiritu and Havana, a full year after the installation of People's Power in these areas. Much of this material appeared during May and June in the magazine *Bohemia*. The author is responsible for most of the second part of the book as well as for the final editing and introduction.

Marta Harnecker
Havana, October, 1978

PREFACE TO THE REVISED EDITION

The first edition of this book appeared in 1975, at the time of the First Congress of the Cuban Communist Party when the average citizen's direct participation in the affairs of state extended solely to Matanzas Province. This participation was in the nature of a political experiment.

The second edition, revised, expanded, and published eighteen months later, drew attention to the modification being introduced in local government as a result of the experiences of People's Power. These modifications were later incorporated in the new Cuban Constitution, enacted by popular referendum on February 24, 1976.

Instead of altering the original text, we decided to use footnotes to indicate new developments and to write an epilogue, titled "A Year Later," in which we set forth the principal changes. We also took care to show how the major governmental bodies, as specified in the Constitution, operate: the National Assembly, the State Council, the Council of Ministers, the People's Supreme Court, and the Comptroller's Office.

In the epilogue, we meet again some of the leaders of the Matanzas experiment, Alexis, Reinaldo, and Laureano, from the executive committee of the Cardenas regional assembly (a committee subsequently eliminated by the new politico-administrative division) who, on the basis of their own experience, attempt an evaluation of the whole process.

Today—with seven Spanish editions, one in French, another in Portuguese, and a forthcoming edition in English, we have thought it advisable once again to update the book to incorporate the experiences of almost two years of People's Power at the national level. This has entailed a complete revision of Chapter 5, "The People in the Affairs of State," which now includes significant new informational materials and grass-roots reportorial work done in the provinces of Santi Spiritu and Havana. We sincerly hope that our efforts will contribute to a better understanding of the Cuban revolutionary process.

Marta Harnecker
Havana, October, 1978

INTRODUCTION:
THE STORY OF A POWER

> "...not a road for capitalists and imperialists but a
> road for the people, for the workers, for the peasants, a
> road for justice."
>
> Fidel Castro
> July 26, 1970

Those of us who have written this book have pieced together a record of
the manner in which the Cuban people live their revolution, culminating
with the experiences of People's Power.

At this point, we would like to present a brief outline of the history of
revolutionary power in Cuba, as seen through the eyes of its top leaders.
It is they who—through speeches given in the thick of critical events or
in later addresses—can best help us identify the turning points of this
history, and the actual implications of People's Power, now being carried
out throughout the nation.

The Triumph of the Revolution: An Event of Continental Significance

"The triumph of the Cuban revolution was a historical event of conti-
nental significance, an extraordinary challenge to yankee imperialism—
to its political, economic, and military might. Indeed they were not
prepared to tolerate the peaceful development of our revolution."[1]

The victory of the Rebel Army over Batista was only the completion of
one phase. It was a political process that anticipated not only the defeat of

the mercenary army, allowing the people to seize its weapons, but which also incorporated a revolutionary line—the transformation of society to benefit the vast majority and to deliver it from all forms of economic thralldom. Under these circumstances, a confrontation with the national exploiting classes and a frontal collision with imperialism could not be avoided.

A long struggle was thus initiated. The ruling classes and imperialism did not rely solely on their armed might but also on their great economic power and a culture and political ideology which, inculcated over the centuries, helped to keep people subjugated. In the speech quoted above, Fidel Castro said: " . . .once the weapons were secure in the hands of the people, it was necessary to wage a great battle in the field of ideology, in the field of politics. It was necessary to dismantle bourgeois culture, for at the end of the military struggle the enemy still possessed extremely powerful weapons: those of ideology and political custom rooted in our midst; economic superiority and, still more formidable, vast military capabilities.

"And our people joined this political and ideological battle, mobilized against its cultural backwardness, faced up to its illiteracy, confronted its ignorance, until it developed the solid, socialist revolutionary, political consciousness it now exhibits.

"The enemy did not stop at the use of political weapons; it also utilized its economic superiority, attempting to stifle, to strangle our people with a blockade and other forms of economic aggression. Our young Revolution, our people, possessing little economic experience and denied a majority of the relatively few technicians it once had, was forced to wage the difficult battle of the economy.

"Meanwhile, along with the political and economic battles, imperialism mobilized its armed offensives. Almost from the very first months of the Revolution, we saw acts of sabotage, counterrevolutionary action, infiltration of weapons and agents, the development of armed counterrevolutionary bands which would later surface in nearly all of our provinces . . . and the training of mercenary troops which eventually invaded us at Playa Giron.

"Yet there was always a graver peril, graver than the counterrevolutionary bands, graver than mercenary aggression: the danger of direct assault by the armed forces of the United States."[2]

Imperialist tactics were an important factor in the development of the Cuban Revolution. In the wake of each blow, a necessary countermeasure was adopted and, in this fashion, the revolution progressed rapidly. The first ten years of the revolution are years characterized by the struggle for survival in the face of internal reaction, external aggression, and the imperialist blockade. This battle consumed the greater part of the nation's efforts and energies, and a major portion of its human and material resources as well.

The Absence of a Strong Party

The long struggle began without the presence of strong revolutionary party. In 1959, there were basically three revolutionary groups: the July 26th Movement, the Revolutionary Directorate, and the Popular Socialist (Communist) Party. The combined membership of these three organizations totaled a few thousand. In addition, the July 26th Movement was divided, as a result of fundamental internal dissension. These political differences were not overcome until the first months of the Revolution when the right wing of the movement—represented by Urrutia, Miro Cardona, Hubert Matos, David Salvador, and a few others—was destroyed.

After this victory, the remaining cadres, with Fidel Castro by now their indisputable leader, were forced to confront the tasks of organizing the new government and the means of production. This major task prevented them from devoting time to the consolidation of a revolutionary party.

But how had it happened that the Popular Socialist Party (PSP), the Communist Party of Cuba, had accepted the leadership of Fidel Castro?

"It did not require much historical perspicacity" affirmed Carlos Rafael Rodriguez, old PSP militant and current member of the Cuban Communist Party Secretariat, "to recognize that with Fidel the Revolution had finally found the commander it lacked for more than half a century, the leader who could at once tackle the political and ideological tasks of a Josè Marti, and the military duties discharged earlier by men like Gomez* and Maceo. Our people, though weakened in their faith by the repeated betrayals of so many unprincipled caudillos and demagogues understood immediately, in the wake of Moncada and the Sierra, that the hour of emancipation had arrived.

"But for those who saw the achievement of independence as only the first step, for those who had struggled over decades so that the liberating Revolution would open the path to another one, much deeper and definitive, one that could guarantee the well-being of workers and peasants and eventually lead to socialism, the course to adopt was not easy

---

*Josè Miguel Gomez (1858-1921). President of Cuba from 1909 to 1913. General in the successful revolution of 1895. (A liberal, he died in exile in New York City)

"The books affirmed, the theses of the international movement proclaimed, that the transition to socialism from national liberation could only be achieved under the guidance and hegemony of a working-class party armed with the ideology of Marxism-Leninism. It was, therefore, rather easy to be swept away by these arguments of a sectarian and dogmatic schematism had we failed to note that the road to socialism had *already* been opened by exceptional means, and that the disputes over theoretical hegemony were simply a-historical and absurd.

"We did not fall into that error. But, because there are various books by foreign authors sympathetic to the (Cuban) Revolution which still contain wrong interpretations of this phase, we would like to declare that the main credit for the correct and enlightened interpretation of this unexpected peculiarity in the Cuban revolutionary process is due to Blas Roca. For the first time in the history of the movement, after the rise of the Third International, a communist party accepted a political leadership other than its own in the struggle for socialism. It was an unforgettable day when, with Blas Roca as leader of our ranks, we all presented ourselves before Fidel Castro as simple soldiers working in a common cause wherein he was to us, as to the rest of the pro-revolutionary Cuban people, the Commander-in-Chief."[3]

The First Steps Toward a Unified Political Organization

Two years after the seizure of power (which took place on New Year's Day, 1959), an effort was made to give a unified structure to the three parties mentioned earlier. This resulted in the creation of the Integrated Revolutionary Organizations (Organizaciones Revolucionarias Integradas, ORI).

Ernesto Che Guevara reports that the revolutionary leadership, while leaving him in charge of this project of unification, was thinking about an organization of "rigorously selected cadres" firmly attached to the masses, an organization "at once centralized and flexible" which could draw upon the experience gained by the Popular Socialist Party during its many years of struggle.

It was a difficult period, at the height of the blockade and with the massive exodus of professionals and technical personnel in full swing, precisely when they were most severely needed for the management of expropriated industries and businesses.

It was also a time when measures had to be introduced to curb the practice of "guerrilla tactics"[4] in the public administration, an approach whereby individual spontaneous initiative took precedence over collective planning. These measures resulted, before long, in excessive bureaucratic centralization.

It was in this context, and against the advice of the senior members of his own party and Fidel, that Anibal Escalante, a leader of the PSP and organizational secretary for the ORIs, fell into sectarian deviations in his attempt to control the budding "unified" organization.

"This opened the door—due to sectarian tendencies in the PSP and because many honest comrades believed that Anibal was applying a collective line that included Fidel's own—to a dogmatism and sectarianism according to which even PSP deserters were to be preferred, merely on account of their former membership in the [Communist] party, to veterans of the Sierra."[5]

Thus began a "dark, though fortunately brief, stage" in the development of the Cuban revolution. Mistakes are made in the methods of leadership; the party loses some of its "essential qualities of identification with the masses," its correct application of "democratic centralism," and there is a lessening of "the willingness to personal sacrifice." Relying at times on veritable tricks of legerdemain, inexperienced and unqualified individuals are placed in leadership positions, a result, as often as not, of their uncanny ability to shift with the political wind.

"The ORIs lose their function of ideological engine—and the ability to control the productive apparatus—becoming an administrative organism; under these circumstances the danger signals from the provinces, calling attention to existing problems, are lost, for those charged with evaluating the performance of administrative officials were precisely the core leadership who filled the dual role of party functionaries and public bureaucrats."[6]

These sectarian deviations were detected in time and on March 26, 1962, the so-called first Escalante trial was held, in which Fidel denounced these tendencies, citing abundant examples, and proceeded to attribute blame for the tendencies on a number of PSP cadres and especially on Escalante, organizational secretary for the ORIs. The following day, Castro declared that "the seriousness of a revolutionary party is basically measured by the attitude it shows toward its own errors." Bearing in mind that the enemy could take advantage of such public airing, he nonetheless decided to go ahead with it convinced that only a policy of open debate can insure the permanent eradication of such tendencies. Fidel believed that the manner in which the Cuban Revolution developed explains in great part how these errors originated and underscores the role played by the masses in their detection: "Our political consciousness is raised when the masses—not only the leaders, but the masses—take note of these mistakes."

Sectarianism manifested itself in the belief that the only revolutionary cadres, those entitled by right to fill all posts and functions, were the "senior Marxist militants," which in Cuba at that time could only be a militant of the PSP, as this was the only Marxist party before the Revolution.

But in the opinion of Fidel Castro, this formula was not leading to the emergence of a true party, but of a patronage-dispensing machine. "Comrades, we were creating a yoke, a straightjacket. We were not promoting a free organization of revolutionaries but an army of regimented, domesticated revolutionaries."

Fidel is without doubt the great architect of the unity of the Cuban people. Right from the start he opposed sectarianism, while working for the unification of all revolutionary sectors. He struggled with equal determination against the "sectarianism of the Sierra" as well as against that of "the old Marxist militants." He constantly exhorted the people to participate in the process: "Those who didn't have an opportunity to fight [in the Sierra or in the urban struggles] should not lose heart. The future is fraught with opportunities, and history remains to be written, for the Revolution has just begun and we have a long way to go."

In his criticism of ORI, Fidel insists that one of its signal errors was the failure to integrate the masses. "The other organizations—the Directorate, the July 26th Movement—what were they? Were they organizations with an old, structured militantcy? No, they were organizations which enjoyed great sympathy among the masses, but the masses remained an unruly torrent spilling all over them. That was the case with the July 26th Movement and with the other organizations as well. But if we are going to attempt integration and we don't integrate the masses, we will be inevitably falling into sectarianism, and that is exactly what happened."

The Militant: "The Best of the Best"

But how do we integrate people into an organization which is, by definition, the vanguard of the masses?

Early in the process, Fidel Castro devised a method that would be fully applied only in 1965, when the new Communist Party of Cuba was forged. The method consisted in "grouping within the Party the people's finest, the best of the working class. . . ." That is, the requisite for belonging in the vanguard is to be "an exemplary worker." Further, the party member must accept the socialist revolution, and lead a "clean political life." Fidel insisted that, even though the masses would not ultimately select the members, it was indispensable to take their opinion into account before making any choices. It is very important, he stressed, that those who belong to the revolutionary core enjoy "the full support of the masses, and exceptional prestige among them."

This struggle against sectarianism, which often implied a harsh criticism of PSP cadres, could have deteriorated into another form of sectarianism. Castro prevented this, however, and made sure that unity was not jeopardized. "The Revolution is more important than our individual contributions; also—and this is basic—it is more important than all the organizations which may have operated in the field. . . ."

Parallel to this public criticism by the head of the Revolution, a process of internal purification was initiated throughout the ORI cadres. This started with a College of Political Education, where Fidel proposed that an assembly convene to elect the best students at the school who would be regarded, in turn, as militants of the Party. Thus the first ORI-cadre review board was born. After that, provincial boards were set up to continue the cleansing task. Finally, we arrive at the dissolution of the first attempt at unification of the revolutionary forces, creating, in 1962, the United Party of the Socialist Revolution (PURS).* This party reflects the newly open socialist character of the Cuban process after the invasion at the Bay of Pigs.

From the creation of the PURS until its dissolution in 1965, to open the way for the Communist Party of Cuba (PCC), the organization did not expand. Instead, it purified its ranks. Thus, of four thousand workers at the Ariguanabo textile complex, the largest plant in the nation, only 197 were chosen as "exemplary workers."

Che Guevara left a good summary of the process. "As you clearly recognize and approve, the new members of the United Party for the Socialist Revolution emerging from this work center are men and women who can fully rely on their fellow workers for unanimous support. The nuclei being formed at this moment, the Party organizations, will count, from now on, on ample backing, and will consequently abandon the underground work, of an almost conspiratorial nature, which typified their actions for so long.

*Partido Unido de la Revolución Socialista.

"From the shadowy life of clandestine cells, often compelled to elect operatives in mechanical fashion, often without sufficient evaluation of a candidate's qualifications, a transition is being made to a new system whereby the people will decide in the first place who can qualify as an exemplary worker and a party member."

And he adds:

"Anyone aspiring to a position of leadership must be able to confront or, rather, expose himself to the verdict of the people, and remain confident than he has been elected a leader because he is the best of the best, because of his fine performance and spirit of sacrifice, and because of his steadfast efforts in the vanguard of all daily proletarian struggles necessary for the construction of socialism."[7]

The same year (1963), in another speech, Che Guevara spelled out the political complexion of the coming order:

". . .It will not rely on the bureaucratic or mechanical directive, the order imposed from above through narrow and sectarian control, reflecting a discipline more akin to dead letter than to living example, nor will it be inordinately beholden to the prestige of theories and past history . . . .The Marxist must be simply the best, the most honest and well-rounded of human beings, *but always a human being*; a militant of a Party which lives and vibrates with the masses; a guide who blends into concrete directions the sometimes obscure wishes of the people; an indefatigable worker; a toiler capable of giving up his hours of rest, his personal tranquility, his family, even his life for the Revolution, but who is never estranged from the warmth of human contact."

Birth of the Cuban Communist Party

And so, finally, the Cuban Communist Party (PCC) was born on October 3, 1965, with a central comittee in which, according to Fidel Castro, ". . .There is no heroic episode in the recent history of our country not represented there; no sacrfice, no combat, no epic deed— military or civilian—not represented there; and no revolutionary or social sector without representation . . . ."

The new party came to life as the stage characterized by different revolutionary factions and origins drew to a close. "We have arrived at a fortunate juncture in the history of our revolutionary process," said Fidel, "in which we can declare that there is only one type of revolutionary and, since our Party must speak not for what we were yesterday but for what we are today and will be tomorrow, the most appropriate name for it is the Communist Party of Cuba."

It should be borne in mind that at one time in Cuba mere possession of Marxist or Leninist texts constituted criminal evidence. Today these ideas are the patrimony of the entire people.

"Who could have told those lackeys, those judges, those apologists for reaction...who was to tell them...that these ideas would someday unite the people, and that once armed with these ideas our Revolution and our people would become invincible?"—Castro asked, ten years after the founding of the Party. He continued: "One day the people stood up against tyranny, found unity, and triumphed, but it was essentially the working people, the peasants, the students. These different forces blended into one as streams which, born of separate fountainheads, flow toward a great river, the powerful river of the Revolution.

"Thus we saw the unification of all our revolutionary forces! And together we waged the final battle!

"If, a long time ago, the Party of Independence fought colonial power and confronted the reactionary ideas of the time; if, in the days of Mella, revolutionaries had to clash with a powerful empire, the bourgeoisie, and the Cuban landowners associated with it, a whole infernal machine of lies and propaganda, plus the henchmen of Machado; if, after that, the Cuban patriots still had to confront the Batista tyranny, there was yet another great battle to wage after January, 1959: the battle against Yankee imperialism, determined to destroy the Cuban Revolution.

"And, in addition to all this, another struggle, equally difficult, loomed on the horizon: the battle against prejudice; the battle against anti-communism, sown over decades by all conceivable means. And that final battle against imperialism, against anti-communism, against reactionary ideas, against the Bay of Pigs mercenaries, the bandits of Escambray, against the CIA saboteurs—that battle was waged by all of us together, revolutionaries of different origins! First coordinated and later unified, but unified under the principles of Marxism-Leninism!"

Fidel concluded with these words: "We shall always carry in our hearts the day in which, some time after the seizure of power by the Revolution, and following a process of unification by the revolutionary forces, Blas Roca gave into our hands the glorious banners of the First Communist Party of Cuba."[8]

It was only after 1965, that the new method for the selection of party cadres, originally proposed by Fidel toward the end of 1962, was strongly implemented. Through this approach Cuba has been able to build a party with cadres solidly supported by the people. The weaknesses in the construction of a revolutionary organization built from scratch may still be many, but no one can possibly doubt today the strengths of a party born in the very bosom of the working masses, capable of directing, without need for concealment, all the mass organizations, simply because its militants are firmly recognized as the best of the best.

Idealist Deviations

But—are there no flaws in this party? Of course there are, but they must be analyzed within their historical context, while we bear in mind that the revolutionary leadership has always been willing to eliminate them.

Already by February 17, 1959, early in the process, Fidel Castro declared: "The Revolution faces obstacles ahead, cannot accomplish things to perfection, perpetrates errors, yet it also exhibits an invincible will to improve itself and conquer these errors."

One of these errors, acknowledged by the leaders, was to fall into idealist deviations. Yet, if the Revolution incurred this type of deviation, it is equally true that it was extremely difficult for the (young) process to be rigorously scientific about is productive potential, given the acute shortage of technical personnel capable of correctly diagnosing problems in certain specific fields. On the other hand, the revolutionary tension and the necessity to allocate enormous human and material resources to the defense of the Revolution against constant attacks and threats by imperialism, coupled with the need to overcome underdevelopment, compelled the leadership at times to embark on tasks beyond the nation's reach.

Such was the case with the 1970 ten-million ton "zafra," or sugar-cane harvest, which, as Raul Castro himself admitted, reflected " . . .extremely ambitious goals under the circumstances, a fact which led to some negative consequences amply analyzed by Comrade Fidel."

In effect, Fidel recognized as much, with extraordinary frankness, on July 26, 1970, when he declared that, despite the huge efforts made by the Cuban people, the anticipated goals had not been fulfilled, and the concentrated effort in the sugar-cane cutting process had caused dislocations elsewhere in the economy.

"I repeat," said Fidel to the people assembled in Revolution Square, "that we were unable to win the so-called 'simultaneous battle.'

"And, in truth, the heroic effort to increase [sugar] production, to raise our purchasing power, caused a dislocation of the economy, a reduction in production in other sectors, and, in general, an increase in our difficulties.

"Naturally, the enemy made much of the fact that the ten-million ton *zafra* caused such dislocations. Our duty was to make sure that such a forecast didn't come true. But we weren't able to accomplish this.

"Our foes claim that we have our difficulties, and in that respect they are right. They assert that we have problems, and they are right. They say there is dissatisfaction, and they are right. They say there is angry impatience in our midst, and, again, they are right.

"As you can see, we are not afraid to admit when our enemies are right."

And he added:

"It is easier, a thousand times easier, to annihilate the Bay of Pigs mercenaries, in a few hours perhaps, then to solve the problems of a single industry. It is easier to win 20 wars than to prevail in the battle for [economic] development."

He then pointed up the main battle confronting the people: "It's a battle in the area of economics which we must wage together with the people, for only the people can win it."

Turning Defeat into Victory

In that moment of bitter defeat, Castro recalled that, in the face of setbacks sustained on that memorable July 26, in the wake of the defeated assault on the Moncada barracks, the Cuban people had thought only of returning to the struggle, of starting all over again.

"The enemy rejoices in and pins his hopes on our troubles. We said they were right in this, in that, in whatever they want. But in one thing they were wrong: in believing that the people, faced with difficulties of the revolution, would end up by eventually choosing the road of counter-revolution. Ah! In that you were absolutely wrong, imperialist gentlemen! In that you were dead wrong! In that no one will admit you are right at all, not even one iota!

"For you can't understand the people, fathom their depth and moral integrity, their courage . . .

"The people will never stand for being told lies! Trust in the people can never go unrewarded! Trust in the people is never misplaced!"

The setback in the ten-million ton *zafra* signaled a turning point in the development of the Cuban Revolution. A serious process of self-criticism identified the weakest points where joint action by the leadership and the people must be concentrated.

During the closing months of 1970, all of 1971, and the early part of 1972, a great effort was made to update backward economic areas, revitalize mass organizations, and, above all, permit the masses a greater degree of participation in matters of production.

Starting in 1972, efforts were also made toward streamlining the mechanisms controlling the Party and the State. The Council of Ministers was restructured and, in November of that year, its Executive Committee was set up.

In January, 1973, a revamping of the Party's Central Committee was carried out, clarifying and redefining the functions and interrelations between the Party bureaucracy and that of the State.

These measures enabled the revolution to take a great leap forward in the area of economics, resulting, in 1974, in the first experience of direct popular participation in the affairs of state, the experience of the so-called People's Power in Matanzas Province.

Everything Cannot Be Centrally Administered

One of the great lessons learned from the 1970 *zafra* fiasco was the realization that it is impossible for a socialist State to manage everything centrally, and much less in an underdeveloped country such as Cuba. Fidel Castro emphasized this point in his speech of July 26, 1970.

"It is no longer possible to direct the social production simply through a Council of Ministers . . . . Why? Because social production depends today on the social administration of public resources.

"In the old regime, industry, the schools, and even the hospitals were under private administration. But today is no longer yesterday. Before, all a citizen could expect from the State was a post office, a telegraph office. It didn't even cross his mind that housing and other matters were also the responsibility of the State. Today, the citizen thinks that he must expect much from the State, and he's absolutely right. That is precisely a collectivist mentality, a socialist mentality. Today everything is expected from the administrative apparatus and, above all, from the political apparatus that subsumes it. Today people don't have to fall back on their own means alone, on their own strengths, as in the past.

"The fact that the people expect a great deal is in agreement with the socialist consciousness developed among them by the Revolution. Poor performance in any service—and I'm not referring here to those problems beyond our reach, but to those well within our power to remedy and which drag on unresolved—may affect thousands.

"It is impossible today to direct and coordinate this entire apparatus. It is necessary to create a political structure capable of tying together the different sectors of social production . . . ."

Two months later, on September 28, the 10th anniversary of the creation of the Committees to Defend the Revolution (CDRs), Fidel offers an insight into the role to be played by the masses in the process of decentralization.

"The revolutionary process itself has been demonstratng the short-comings of the bureaucratic method, as well as the failure of the 'admin-istrativist (sic) approach.' "

After underscoring the errors made by identifying the Party with the State administration, by allowing the weakening of mass organizations, Fidel Castro pointed out that by relying on these organizations, the workers' movement, the CDRs, the youth organizations, students, the peasants, the Revolution has "the foundations for the ensuing steps, which foreshadow a much more direct participation by the masses in decision-making and problem-solving, as well as a multifaceted input everywhere, and especially in the context of problems affecting them in their home territories.

"Because anything that happens anywhere, in any block, in any public service (community) center, from a distribution center to a school, a bakery, any service of any kind—if this functions poorly, it is bound to affect directly the people living within its boundaries and receiving these services.

"And if any industry performs badly, it affects the economy of all the workers."

He elaborated further: "Undoubtedly by sheer administrative meth-ods it is impossible to solve any problems, and much less in a collectivist society."

Then, bearing in mind that Cuba is an underdeveloped country, he asked: "Who can match the efficieny, the reliability, the sheer excellence of the people in the tasks of supervision?

"Our Revolution takes place in a country with an underdeveloped economy, with primitive production in every sector. A revolution in a well-developed country would encounter great production centers every-where. In a mature economy a great number of small grocery stores, candy stores, bake shops, small cleaning establishments, would long since have disappeared. Yet these represented the level of our productive forces: many small shops, jerrybuilt workshops, with all kinds of services fulfilled by artisans and craftsmen.

"Imagine a bakery on a block, servicing a neighborhood, and an administrative apparatus controlling that shop from above. How could it control it? But can the people be expected to be indifferent to the performance of this bakery? How can they remain indifferent if the administration is good or bad? How can they be indifferent to whether or not there is privilege, negligence, even callousness? How can they be unconcerned over the manner in which the shop discharges its social service? How can people ignore the problems of hygiene in such a place? And how could they remain indifferent to the problems of production, absenteeism, quality and quantity of the product? Of course, they are not indifferent!

"Can we possibly create a more effective method of control than the people themselves? Is there a better method of inspection? No! We can corrupt the man in charge of a production micro-unit, we can corrupt the man who inspects it, we can corrupt the whole world! But those who cannot be bought, those who can't afford corruption, are those affected by it, those at the receiving end."

According to Law 1269, the organs of People's Power are "empowered to conduct the business of government, manage economic units in charge of commodities and services, undertake new construction and repairs and, in general, develop those activites required to fulfill the social, economic, cultural, recreational, and educational needs of the community where they exercise their jurisdiction."

For example, People's Power supervises schools, polyclinics, hospitals, sports facilities, cinemas; the procurement of meats, fruits, and vegetables; restaurants, bakeries, dry-cleaning establishments; local buses and taxis, and the maintenance of local highways and roads.

But in addition to its function as the supreme state organ with regard to the units under its supervision, People's Power must also concern itself with the smooth functioning of production and service units still under the control of central organs and ministries. This is the case, for example, with farms and agricultural plants directed by the state; the sugar complexes; the national factories producing for the country as a whole; export facilities; national transport; harbors; tourist facilities, and so on.

The point is that not all the 5,597 units of production and service under the jurisdiction of People's Power in that area are operating at the provincial level.

The decentralization of the state apparatus which characterizes People's Power signifies the greatest possible decentralization of state functions, concentrating the biggest share of economic and social functions at the lower level of the state structure, that is, at the municipal level. Those activites judged overtaxing to the administrative and overseeing capacity of the municipal assembly are only then returned to the higher echelons.

Let us give one illustration to clarify the way in which activities are distributed among the various levels. In the province of Matanzas there are innumerable roads, streets, highways, utilized by all kinds of vehicular traffic. The *municipality* exercises jurisdiction over the streets or local roads; the *province* has jurisdiction over the various highways linking various regions within the province, and the *state* is responsbile for interprovincial highways. The same division of responsibility applies to the means of transportation, and related matters.

"The lower echelons," Raul Castro explains at the closing of the seminar held for the Matanzas People's Power delegates on August 22, 1974, "are subordinate to the higher ones but operate autonomously within the normative and legal framework set up for them, and should not be subjected to constant inhibiting supervision by the higher authorities. This system streamlines the task of adminstration and renders it more responsive to the demands of the moment, helps free the higher cadres and, above all, the national authorities, from a heavy, voluminous burden which they could not carry effectively anyway, while permitting them the freedom to concentrate on questions more clearly in line with their competence."

The People: Main Protagonist

Fifteen years went by in Cuba before the first experience of People's Power was permitted to extend itself to the rest of the island; it took that long for the lessons of Matanzas to be duly reported and absorbed.

But does this mean that the people were absent, till then, from the revolutionary process?

Not at all. Indeed, if the revolutionary leadership has been able to overcome all obstacles and emerge victorious, it is largely because of its identification with the people, and the unlimited trust it enjoys throughout the nation.

After the *zafra* fiasco, knowing full well he was being heard by a people badly bruised and frustrated in their self-esteem, Fidel said: ". . .only with the people, with the conscience of the people, with the know-how of the people, with the drive of the people, can these problems ever be overcome." He then elaborated for the benefit of thousands of Cubans who listened to him attentively in the wake of one of the nation's greatest disappointments: "When 17 years ago we made an attempt to take the Moncada fortress, it wasn't to win a war with a thousand men, but to *start* a war, and wage it, and win it with the support of the people. When years later we returned with a handful of revolutionaries, it wasn't to win a war with a handful of men. We had not yet gone through the extraordinary experiences, the extraordinary lessons, we have gone through over these years, but even then we knew quite well that the war would only be won *with* the people. For this reason, it was waged and won with the people!

"When this Revolution, only 90 miles away from the powerful and vicious imperialist fortress, wanted its freedom, wanted to be sovereign, and prepared itself to challenge that empire, undertaking a truly revolutionary road, not a road of capitalists and monopolists, but a road of the people, a road of the workers, a road of the peasants, a road of justice— many voices claimed the task was impossible what with heavy cultural, political, and ideological influences we lived under! But we believed that this battle would be won with the people. And it was waged with the people and won with the people!

"It is thus that [the Revolution] has survived till this day."[9]

"Possibly, there is no other case in history," affirms Raul Castro, "in which a revolution, the leaders of a revolution, have enjoyed such massive, committed support from the people, such overwhelming confidence and enthusiasm, so splendid a unity as that offered by our people to its Revolution, to its leaders, and especially to the beloved, indisputable head of the Cuban Revolution, Comrade Fidel Castro."[10]

Democracy Did Not Begin with People's Power

Another mistake is understanding the meaning of People's Power is to think that democracy in Cuba began only in 1974.

The Cuban State, like any state—bourgeois or socialist—represents a dictatorship of some classes over others. During these years it has been, without doubt, a dictatorship directed, by the workers and the previously exploited, to the task of smashing internal and external counterrevolutionary acts. In this new state, the army has became one with the people. Once the revolution was victorious, the army—which had been used in every conceivable way to oppress its own class and kind—turned its energies to the defeat of those who had, while in power, utilized it to repress the people.

But if the Cuban State has acted like a dictatorship toward the counterrevolution, it has been—even without the presence of representative institutions—an essentially democratic state. Over all these years, it had represented and defended the interests of the workers and of the Cuban people, avoiding the adoption of any important revolutionary measure without first consulting the vast majority of the people through a variety of mechanisms.

In his address at the closing of the seminar for People's Power delegates held on August 22, 1974, Raul Castro described the Cuban State as follows:

"When a state such as ours represents the interests of the workers, whatever its structure and form, the result is bound to be a far more democratic type of state than any other before in history, because the state of the workers, the state that builds socialism is—under any and all conditions—a state of majorities, while previous states have been instruments of exploiting minorities.

"The bourgeois-feudal state which had existed in Cuba before the coup d'etat of March 10, 1952, with its 'representative institutions'—the Chamber and the Senate with their periodic elections—was infinitely less democractic than the Revolutionary State, for it was the tool of imperialists, of their monopolies and enterprises in Cuba, and of their local allies, the native and foreign bourgeois, and the great landowners. It was an instrument of coercion, with its army, police, torturers, gangsters, jails, and law courts, all pitted against the interests of the great national majorities.

"For the sake of the people, the Revolutionary State rescued the riches of the nation from the claws of imperialist and exploiters.

"It converted the private property of a few (owners of the means of production) into the property of all.

"It wiped out widespread unemployment and opened possibilities of work for all; it eliminated illiteracy and made education free, hence within the reach of all; it made access to health care easily obtainable and free, a right of all, with old age no longer the cause of anxious concern.

"The Revolutionary State organized the people, gave them weapons, and taught them how to use them in their own defense. The masses have participated in the discussions of all important matters affecting the Revolution, especially of its major laws, and now [our people] begin to participate in the discussion of economic plans up to the level of production- and service-units."

Raul Castro thus summarized the democratic character of the Cuban proletarian state. This democracy, however, has little in common with bourgeois democracy, a point underscored by his brother Fidel:

"We do not claim to exercise bourgeois democracy precisely because it is a great fraud, nor do we think in terms of bourgeois democracy; we think in terms of *workers'* democracy, of proletarian democracy, in which the rights of the exploiting classes have been effectively suppressed, as well as those of imperialism. That is the way we have conceived it and that is the way we apply it.

"Naturally, we call our system a democracy because, in the first place, it rests upon the entire people; second, because it offers full participation to the people, as has never happened before in any other type of human society; third, [it is a democracy] because there is an open and permanent debate, engaging the whole people in the enactment of all essential measues. Here the laws are discussed with the masses, and passage of a bill involves not only the step of democratic consultation with them, but also an educational process for the majority of the people . . .

"Here there is no fundamental law, no important measure, *not* discussed with the entire people . . . Thus the 'dictatorship' is that of the immense majority of the people. That is why it may be called with equal truth dictatorship, workers' democracy, or People's Democracy."[11]

In connection with this point, it is interesting to observe how the experience of bourgeois democracy left its mark on an older woman. (The woman's husband was in prison during the Batista regime.):

"The dictionary says many things. The Yankees also speak of democracy. But it is a word that upsets me a little. It has been so misapplied, even when used by us, that it still sends shivers down my spine. I'd rather hear the word *socialism*, and would like that word to give place rapidly to *communism*.

"Yes, the word *democracy* still gives me shivers. It is as though they asked you: 'Do you like a fence?' For me, through association of ideas, a fence is not, say, a beautiful, Spanish, wrought-iron fence, but a fence that means prison. That is the way it is imprinted on my mind . . ."

People's Power Perfects The Revolutionary State

The term People's Power, used in Cuba to denote the process of institutionalized mass participation in the business of government, may lead to some confusion. Some may think that, only after the masses picked their delegates and these began to exercise their prerogatives, was it fitting to speak of the existence of popular power in Cuba.

"Look, in my opinion"—says a member of the Executive Committee of the Municipal Assembly of Matanzas—"the people have been in power here since 1959, since the triumph of the Revolution. The class struggle was tremendously violent: we witnessed a mercenary invasion and an internal clash of classes during the early.stages of the process. But the people, with power in their hands, decided their own destiny. . . . The First Declaration of Havana, the Second Declaration, were submitted to the people assembled in the Plaza of the Revolution. The people have always been masters of their fate. (An example of this is the discussion of the Family Code, among other legal measures). People's Power is a way to institutionalize the State, since we are already in a positon to do so. Furthermore, it is a way to perfect our democracy. Democracy has existed ever since the triumph of the Revolution."

The establishment of representative institutions marks a major turning point for the Cuban revolutionary process. Yet this development does not imply that the people now find themselves for the first time in a position to participate, or to exercise their democracy. In the speech already quoted, Raul Castro answers the question in this manner:

"Our State has been, and is, an essentially democratic state, a state of the humble, for the humble, and by the humble; a state *of* all and *for* all the workers. What the creation of representative institutions signifies, then, is the perfecting of our State, the rounding out of its definitive structures, and the strengthening of our democracy."

It should be noted that the critical step being taken in Cuba is not overdue. To take root, People's Power requires a set of social, political, and economic conditions which did not fully exist until recently.

The first years of the Revolution were typified by rapid far-reaching changes. Necessity required an agile state apparatus, a nimble organization that could effectively direct the dictatorship of the people against counterrevolution and imperialism. And only by concentrating in its hands legislative, executive and administrative functions, was it enabled to make the quick decisions that the circumstances required.

Thus, thanks to the concentration of power at the top of Revolutionary leadership, it was possible to fulfill the tasks imposed by the struggle for survival adequately—the passage of revolutionary laws, the expropriation of imperialist-held assets, the liquidation of internal reaction.

Furthermore, the problems of Cuban underdevelopment were so acute —especially in the area of resource self-sufficiency—that a failure was almost expected in certain essential tasks. This could have promptly discredited People's Power in the eyes of the masses. It is also essential to take into account the rather low cultural level of the Cuban people at the time of the revolutionary victory.

At that point, the Revolution still lacked an even more critical element: the existence of a strong party of the proletariat, and mass organizations capable of assisting People's Power to fulfill its programs.

A CDR militant from Havana explained to us in simple terms the evolution of the process:

"Early in the Revolution we had to work, do things, in a particular way since the revolutionary state was a young state and did not enjoy the options it now has. The people, coming from a system totally different from the one we have today, had to be educated, had to be prepared to exercise power through new institutions. Today the Revolution has matured to the point where the people can elect, block by block, district by district, zone by zone, all the way up to the national level, those who will be delegates to People's Power in their name. The experiment in Matanzas is the opening stage of a process of national institutionalization (of the Revolution)."

Beginning late in 1970, a concentrated attack on the remaining obstacles to direct popular participation in governmental affairs was inaugurated.

The institutionalization process, however, did not pick up momentum until 1972, when the economy finally showed signs of sharp recovery, and the measures adopted to fortify the mass organizations began to work effectively. After that the course of events accelerated.

Late in 1972 the Council of Ministers was restructured and an Executive Committee created.

During 1973 the judicial system was revamped, and the XIII Congress of the Cuban Federation of Workers held, thereby enormously strengthening the labor movement which would henceforth assume a fundamental role in the management of the economy.

In that same year, the whole apparatus of the Communist Party was overhauled, clarifying its operational mechanisms, defining the limits of its role and responsibilities, and establishing a clear separation between the functions of the Party and those of the State.

And toward the end of that year, the preparations to try a People's Power experiment in Matanzas were initiated.

From Bureaucratic Centralism to Democratic Centralism

In an article in *Cuba Socialista*, February, 1963, Che Guevara wrote: "Our Revolution was in essence, the upshot of a guerrilla movement that sparked an armed struggle which culminated eventually in the seizure of power. The early phases of the Revolutionary State, as well as those of our first administrative organs, were strongly colored, for this reason, by the fundamental tenets of guerrilla tactics as a way of governmental administration. 'Guerrillerismo'* echoed throughout the various administrative and mass organizations its earlier experience or armed struggle in the sierras and fields of Cuba, manifesting itself in an attitude of respect only for the major revolutionary slogans—often interpreted in numerous and differing ways.

"Thus the way in which a particular problem was tackled depended entirely on the idiosyncrasy of each leader. . . . After a year of painful trial and error, we reached the conclusion that it was essential to overhaul our work style and state apparatus thoroughly along rational precepts, utilizing the planning techniques developed by sister socialist republics.

"As a counter-measure, we began to set up the large bureaucratic institutions that typify the first stages of socialist construction, yet our zeal was excessive and a whole series of organizations, among which we may count the Ministry for Industry itself, evolved a policy of such heavy centralization that it discouraged nearly all forms of independent initiative. This penchant for centralization may be explained as a result of shortages of middle-echelon cadres, coupled with the anarchic spirit that prevailed before, both of which made for a reaction which placed extraordinary emphasis on the literal implementation of directives . . . In this manner, our Revolution began to suffer from that peculiar malady called bureaucratism."

Eleven years later, despite the efforts of the revolutionary leaders, the malady has been only partially overcome.

Raul Castro said on January 2, 1974: "We are convinced that the struggle to curb all manifestations of bureaucratism will be successful, and the needs of the population better cared for, to the extent which the masses participate in the affairs of state. The Revolutionary State will grow stronger, more democratic, and more solid because of this participation."

The direct participation of the masses in the running of the nation through the organs of People's Power is, then, an effort to eradicate *bureaucratic centralism* which existed in many state sectors, and to substitute *democratic centralism*, the fundamental principle of all proletarian organization.

But how is this principle of democratic centralism applied to the organs of the state apparatus?

---

*"Guerrilla approach," individual bureaucratic initiatives in the solution of problems, often blind to the need for coordination and system in the organization of administrative tasks.

In the first place, through elections by the masses themselves of those who will discharge their duties at various levels of national life. Second, through periodic accountability sessions held by delegates and leaders of executive committees before the community that elected them. Third, through the power invested in the electors to recall any delegate proven remiss in the fulfillment of their mandates.

Only through actual, direct participation of the masses in the governing of society, only through enlisting their wisdom, experience, and creative initiative, is it possible to streamline the administrative machinery.

But, for this participation to be real, it must be remembered at all times that the actual holders and repositories of supreme authority are not the elected delegates or members of executive committees, but those who elected them.

In a speech delivered at the Seminar on People's Power on August 22, 1974, Raul Castro said:

"In each electoral precinct, maximum authority is not vested in the [elected] delegate but in the body of electors: it is they who invest the delegate with the mandate to represent them in their problems, complaints and viewpoints, and it is they who can revoke this mandate at any time if the delegate should fail to perform according to expectations. Because of this, it is the delegate who is held accountable to the electors and not the other way around; it is the majority of the people of each precinct who hold supreme power, primary power; the power of the delegate is derived from, bestowed on him or her by the masses.

"In the case of municipalities, maximum authority and rank remain vested not in the elected executive committee, but in the municipal assembly of delegates that chose the members of the committee to implement its resolutions and policies between assembly meetings, and it is the assembly which reserves for itself the right to modify the committee whenever necessary and to whatever extent it deems appropriate. As a result, it is the executive committee that is held accountable to the municipal assembly, and not vice versa.

"In similar fashion, while the president, vice-president, and secretary of the municipal executive committee are elected by members of the committee itself, their appointments must nonetheless be ratified by the assembly; as a consequence, they remain accountable to the latter in the implementation of all resolutions and policies agreed upon by these two organs of People's Power at the municipal level.

"Accordingly, because the president, vice-president, and secretary of the municipal executive committee are subordinate to the executive committee and the municipal assembly, and because the executive committee as a whole is subordinate to the assembly, and the assembly is, in turn, composed of delegates elected by and accountable to the masses of voters in their respective precincts, it is the masses who ultimately hold the supreme power and can wield it to function as active protagonists in the governing process within an institutionalized framework of initiatives and decision-making.

"If the pyramid were built in an inverse manner, and the executive committee were subordinated to the president of municipal People's Power, and if, in turn, the assembly were subordinated to the executive comittee and its president, and if the masses of each precinct were beholden to their delegate, then real primary power would not, in fact, be vested in the masses but in the president and the municipal executive committee, and each lower rung in the pyramid would possess less power, less freedom to initiate and make decisions. When we finally got to the bottom of the inverted pyramid, that is, the masses, these would be found to hold no authority or rank whatsoever, relegated to the role of passive pawns of the process, silent executors of decisions taken in the upper echelons.

"And what we have explained about the municipal situation acquires greater importance as we go up the ladder toward the higher echelons. This is particularly true for the professional members affiliated with People's Power executive committees at the regional and provincial level whose members are not, in their entirety, chosen in their [respective] precincts by the masses, but chosen by the delegates of the masses who make up the regional and provincial assemblies.

"The regional executive committee is elected by the regional assembly to implement its resolutions and to handle all governmental matters between assembly sessions. As a consequence, the executive regional committee is subordinate to the regional assembly and is accountable to it. The same arrangement holds true at the provincial level."

The Party's Leadership Role

The Party is the highest leading institution in Cuba and as such it directs and controls the state and the mass organizations. But to lead is not to supplant. This is how Fidel Castro described the role of the Party in a speech, July 26, 1970:

". . .we cannot make the Party Secretary into the factory manager . . . nor can we make the manager into the secretary of the of the Party, because, if he is dedicated to the tasks of production, it is an absorbing function in itself. And while industry works with machines, the Party works with human beings. Therefore it follows that the responsibility of the Party in that area cannot be direct but must be indirect. It is the Party that must point up any deficiency, any malfunction of an administrative nature; but it can't tell the administrator how to do his job. We must establish as clearly as possible the functions for which the Party cells are to be held responsible, and those which fall within the purview of the manager or, better still, pertain to the problems of management."

This distinct separation between the tasks of the Party and those of administration in the industrial sphere may easily be translated to the state apparatus at all levels. The Party leads the State, controls or monitors its performance, and implements its approved directives and plans; thus it stimulates, propels, and contributes to the better functioning of the whole state machinery, but on no account is it permissible or correct for it to substitute for the State.

How is this achieved? Through which mechanisms does the Party direct the machinery of the State?

It accomplishes this through the preparation of general directives on the basic questions affecting the economic, political, cultural, and social development of the nation, as well as the methods to be followed for their resolution; by monitoring the performance of state bureaus and orienting whatever corrective measures are undertaken, but without invading the administrative domain or substituting its own judgements for those of the administrators or managers; through such support and assistance it can help the state apparatus thanks to its own organization, methods, and resources; through the Party militants who work in the state bureaucracy, and who implement Party decisions while explaining these to non-Party members; and lastly, because, for the foreseeable future, it will be inevitable for the majority of the Party leadership to act as top figures in the state hierarchy.

On the other hand, the Party must insure the maximum development of mass organizations.

"The role of the Party is not to substitute for the mass organizations but to direct this phenomenon, this process, to be at the helm of this formidable revolution of the masses," Fidel declared on September 28, 1970, before thousands of the CDR cadre. "If the Party becomes the mass, it ceases to be the Party, it ceases to be the vanguard, it ceases to personify a selective process."

Now, the Cuban Communist Party discharges its function of leadership of both the state apparatus and the mass organizations not by oppression and force, but by moral authority before the masses, and due to the clarity with which it articulates their interests and aspirations. Its effectiveness derives, above all, from public trust earned by example. For party members can be found in the vanguard in all tasks.

The Party is something the Cuban people already feel as their own. Born in its very womb—since its members cannot be admitted without the masses' approval—it is watched over with the care a mother gives her child.

This control exerted by the masses over the Party has always been encouraged by the revolutionary leadership. As Fidel aptly summarized it in his speech of September 28, 1970: "In addition to the active work, in addition to the zealous overseeing of the direction of the Party exercised by the militants, it is necessary for the mass organizations to assist the Party in this task [of vigilant introspection] to ward off any manifestations of corruption, any sign of privilege. In other words, the masses must watch the Party and make sure that it is exemplary in everything, thus justifying its role of [legitimate] vanguard."

This direct participation by the people in the affairs of state, this proletarian state led by a Marxist-Leninist Party intimately connected with the people from which it springs and upon which it relies for its control and accountability—is this dictatorship or democracy?

M. H.
Havana, August 10, 1975

Notes

1. Fidel Castro: Speech given at the close of the war games commemorating the XV Anniversary of the Revolutionary Triumph, December 30, 1973.
2. Ibid.
3. From the speech by Carlos Rafael Rodriguez at the conferring on Blas Roca the degree of Doctor Honoris Causa of Juridical Science, on September 26, 1974.
4. Ernesto Che Guevara, *Cuba Socialista*, February, 1963.
5. Letter from Carlos Rafael Rodriguez to Marta Harnecker, November, 1972, replying to an article concerning the history of the Cuban Communist Party published by M. Harnecker in the magazine *Chile hoy*, no. 10, August 19-24, 1972.
6. Ernesto Che Guevara, Preface to *The Marxist-Leninist Party*, 1963.
7. Speech by Che Guevara at a workers' assembly in May, 1963, to introduce 'exemplary workers.'
8. Speech commemorating the Fiftieth Anniversary of the first Cuban Marxist-Leninist Party, August 22, 1974.
9. Speech by Fidel on July 26, 1970, at the Plaza of the Revolution.
10. Seminar of August 22, 1974, chaired by Raul Castro.
11. Press conference by Fidel Castro and President Echeverria in Havana, August, 1975.

Part One
The People's Participation

1 INDUSTRY: A CENTER FOR DECISION MAKING

A Discussion Meeting

"This box is fine. The flaps are on the correct side, no problems. And here is a box with both flaps folded the wrong way. The inside panel is on the outside and the outside panel is in. That means that the spools on the machine were on backwards. This shows a complete lack of concern on the part of the worker responsible for corrugating the carton."

Although it is scarcely a subject that merits a discussion meeting dealing with the technical economic plan of 1976—the main reason that some ninety workers from the shop that produces corrugated cartons at the "Sergio González" factory (the plant turns out cardboard containers and paper bags) have gathered in the social hall—the question keeps popping up. The day before, more than three thousand boxes had been produced with defects that made them useless. The news had spread throughout each section of the shop, and there was now a general feeling of dismay.

Roberto Fernández, the plant manager (whom the workers call "Robertico")—who presides over the meeting together with Comrade Díaz, head of the accounting department, Comrade Fernando Schapman, the union's secretary general, and Comrade Pastor Fundora, shop foreman (the four are also the Party's top officers in the factory)—addresses the worker charged with operating the machine responsible for the defect: "Elio, do you have an explanation for this?"

"Sometimes the rear panel is on backwards. But the front one is the one that must be watched because that's where the identifying stamp goes," a slender worker with light-colored eyes calmly replies.

"That's no explanation!" the manager snaps, visibly annoyed by the answer.

He went on: —"I'd like to ask the workers here, if some money were missing from your envelopes and we answered you in this manner, what would you say? You have to paid, right? Now I'd like to ask a second question: Has any machine operator been harmed; has anyone been hurt in the pocket?... We, that is all Cuba, from the beginning of the Revolution until rather recently, have had an incorrect perception of economic questions, knowing that we were the owners of everything, that our jobs were guaranteed, that neither Mr. Dodge nor any of the other Americans who ran this place could come around any longer... men who saw to it that when we dropped a press, we were kicked out of the factory.... As this doesn't happen any more, well, we tend to forget easily; we lose sight of it all. We are a bit forgetful of work in this revolutionary process. We put all our thoughts into the future. Yet we don't see that the things we do today jeopardize, or rather delay, that future. We are going to make full use of this meeting to meet this question head on. Because...how many times have we thrashed out these problems before? Is today the first time? Is this the first time it has been brought up."

A pause punctuates each question. The manager proceeds only after making sure that the workers are sufficiently motivated to answer them.

"No, it isn't the first time, gentlemen. The fact is that we don't express here—in our daily work for which we are being paid the same zeal that characterizes the fulfillment of our revolutionary duties. That hurts us. Besides, this problem hasn't come up with the new workers; instead, is has come up with the old workers, with workers who, in the other system, didn't have any job security, any economic guarantees, any of the liberties we enjoy today. We are not going to permit this any longer.... When the workers are required to pay for the raw materials they damage, they'll be careful soon enough. And the time when we used to say, 'assign the inept to sweeping' is over. Anyone will be glad to sweep with 250 pesos in his pocket. But sweeping is now going to bring only 81 to 95 pesos."

Since 1974, a normative work procedure has been introduced in Cuba that seeks to pay each worker according to his or her output. Every worker has a guaranteed minimum salary, but anyone who produces more can earn more. Formerly, the worker who worked hard made as much as the worker who didn't. The situation discouraged workers who tried harder. The new procedure was adopted during the Thirteenth Congress of the Confederation of Cuban Workers (CTC) in November, 1973.

"We are going to take certain measures," the manager continues "not in this meeting but in the production meeting, because this has got to stop. We have insisted on it on more than one occasion. . . .We are in agreement with the technical department that we must raise quality— especially when we recall that our own minister, Commander Che Guevara, asserted that *quality* is respect for the people. Today we enjoy better conditions, we have better machines, better personnel after one more year of factory operation . . . ."

José, a young black worker, breaks in: "I agree that the operator is to blame for the defect. But tell me one thing: aren't the people responsible for quality control supposed to be checking the cartons as they come off the press? What were they doing these past days? How did three thousand cartons get by like this without their noticing?"

The manager makes an effort to keep his emphasis on the responsibility of the corrugator.

"I'll explain how the system works. Let's make no mistake about this—quality control is a problem that should also concern the machinist. The inspector from quality control can only check statistics. He's not being paid to produce better quality. If you read the appropriate job descriptions, you'll see that the quality control people are concerned only with recording the number of first-rate pieces, and of noting those which are defective. If we go back a bit, in this very factory, the manager, or shop steward, or—what was he called?—the plant manager, used to make the rounds, and the only thing he picked up was the first box run off by the machine. He picked it up, checked it with the operator, and anything that happened later was the operator's responsibility. We want to keep the facts straight! To believe that it is the inspectors who must watch over quality, and not the operator shows that we are in bad, bad shape. That's as if you told me that you didn't observe the output standard because the person responsible for norms doesn't let you in on the results. It's quite the same. The standards man—what does he do? He checks the average output, the time and the number of units so he can later transfer these figures to his records. The quality-control man checks quality only and exclusively so that the factory may have some idea of why quality is dropping, at what point it is deteriorating, whether or not it is a problem of the punches . . .what kind of problem it is. . . .In short, he finds out where the problem lies so that we can begin to tackle it . . .you understand?"

José, feeling by the words of the manager, that he has not been fully understood, insists: "Look here, I don't mean that the compañeros are not to blame at all, but I see one fellow after another going around, standing before the machines, picking up a carton, looking at it. But they pick up the boxes just to look at them . . . to see if they're OK . . . and if they pick a lemon instead of a box . . . ."

"The responsibility for the lemon lies with the operator," the manager interjects.

"Let me finish, let me finish," insists José, bothered by the interruption. "I think the responsibility lies with the machinist *and* the team. There's one who comes with a bucketful of water, another who gets the starch, another who looks at the carton, but it seems as if no one ever notices anything. Now, it's quite obvious the machinist was at the moment asleep at the wheel for it's perfectly clear when a spool is rightly placed and when it's upside down. That I know. . . . It's clear that the fellow was asleep on the job."

"I'd like to point out to Comrade Vega"—says a voice from the back of the room, "that the best quality control there is, in any shop, is the operator himself, together with the other members of the team. They're the best control."

"What I'm saying is," José went on, "I am putting this spool on all wrong, and Alfredo is watching me and says nothing, well, he's to blame, too . . . you understand?"

"Wait, wait," "Robertico" exclaims, "I don't want this discussion to get off the track. The main blame rests with the operator. There is secondary blame—you brought this up—but I'd sooner you didn't dwell on it so much; that's why I make the comparison with the standards man, because, if not, quality would have to depend solely on the quality control. And if I'm an operator, I can then wash my hands of the matter, collect my full salary, and maybe even get a bonus—all for a bunch of garbage."

After making clear that the principal responsibility for quality rests with the operator, the manager is prepared to admit that the people in quality control are partially responsible for the job, too.

"Now, the morning shift has inspectors, and the comrade was right next to the machine all the time, asleep. He *must* have been asleep because the three shifts all produced damaged cartons . . . . Now we're not going to play with the economy this way, no sir. . . . we are going to weigh the responsibility of each person, we're going to analyze it, and we're going to take it before the meeting to be discussed by the workers. But let it be clearly understood—because this is the main point—that it is the operator who determines quality, not the person from quality control."

The topic has sparked many discussions in small groups in the audience. Before going further the manager decides to recapitulate the situation concerning the corrugating operation.

"The corrugating machine had mechanical problems which have now. been corrected, but the raw materials still present grave problems which will be totally solved next year. Besides, there's the problem of quality control. Unfortunately, we don't have the manpower as yet to afford an inspector on each shift. We can put an inspector on the first shift because we know it has the bulk of the work force . . . but we must bear in mind that the person primarily responsible for quality is the operator; it is he who knows how the equipment works, the specifications to make it run to turn out an acceptable product. On more than one occasion, and I'm not mentioning any names, we've loaded the corrugating machine without any regard for work rules. The paper can't be inserted here, it's got to be passed through the wringer, yet . . . it's been done any number of times, any number of times, compañeros, and we all know it. There's a violation of work rules. Who's to blame? Is it a violation or not? There, we have sixteen violations of work rules"—he points to a document on the table—"before the work review board last year. Measures are taken . . . discussed, adopted. Yet what we've got here is negligence, pure negligence."

"Look, what you say is right," says José, calmer now, "yet you're talking about violations, and I was talking about the problem with the machine. Didn't anybody notice? I mean the fact the operator must pay for the whole thing . . . . I'm going to steal a cow and sell ten pounds to my neighbors, and twenty pounds to Cheito, and when the police show up I'll just tell them, look, Cheito bought twenty pounds from me. They won't take me to jail alone, they'll have to drag in everybody. The same here, the operator has the largest share of the burden, but the others who ate the cow must pay, too."

At that point the union secretary, a black comrade of impressive height, intervenes in defense of the corrugators.

"You have expressed to me," he says, looking over toward where they are sitting, "that you're working under a certain amount of tension, because when the spool runs out, you have to change it very quickly, due to an objective problem caused by the lack of a spindle that loaded up the refresher spool (it has been some time since the spindle in question broke). To fulfill the norm, you have to switch the spool more quickly, and on account of this you can't pay attention to whether or not the carton is properly placed. I think here may lie the explanation for this."

The corrugators nod in assent with the explanation offered by the union leader.

Someone observes that the spindle should have been replaced a long time ago, that it has been four months since it broke.

"I'm only suggesting," the union official explains, "it is possible that, as a result of this situation, the compañeros, trying to meet the norm, may be putting the spool on however it fits. But I'm not blaming maintenance."

The manager, addressing the meeting and, as is customary with him, pausing after each question to secure enough participation by the workers, declares: "In any event, there's an anomaly. Aren't we in agreement about that? And there are responsibilities, isn't that correct? And heeding the words and the sentiment of all the workers, we're going to conduct an investigation in depth, because, in truth, the responsibility falls on several shoulders. We're going to investigate this question exhaustively, and delimit the responsibilities. We're going to clarify them, with respect to the machines, and with regard to the leaders. We're going to conduct a broad inquiry, and we'll welcome anyone who wishes to participate, because if we continue now with this, we'll be talking about the spool's spindle for two years . . .and, to wrap it up, the reality is that some boxes came out badly made, and the one to blame, in small or large measure, is the operator; and the one to blame, in small or large measure, is the fellow who should be controlling the whole thing, and, also to blame, in small or large measure, is 'Robertico.' What we should do is discuss this in a meeting."

Lázaro, a compañero of approximately thirty years of age, dressed in overalls, steps forward and grasps the microphone: "About the problem of quality, there's a fundamental problem that arises on account of personnel shortages. I'd like to inform the comrades that in the old days—and this doesn't mean it should be this way now—I was a sweeper in the paper bag department . . .And at that time there were no inspectors. I was the inspector, because I picked up the bags as I swept and observed how they were coming out. Today we have inspectors, and we're spending money in the search for raw materials necessary to turn out the quality expected of our factory. It just happens that . . .what we're doing is so much rubbish! Rubbish!" He raises his voice. "And before, uh? The sweeper had the control duty, and there weren't so many inspectors or whatever. What's needed here is a bit more awareness. Whether on the part of technology or comrade Elio, right? He's one of the veteran pressmen in the factory. We must exercise more care, because this involves the money belonging to all the workers . . .because what we make here is utilized by all of us together. It's not a question concerning a lone individual. And it's embarrassing that after so many years of revolution we should still be stuck with a problem like this. We must look after the Revolution that is so great and which belongs to us all!"

The workers applaud him heartily.

The manager insists upon the need to watch production: "Before the triumph of the Revolution there were methods of control employed by the capitalists. We've been able to witness the different methods, and it's possible that we've made some mistakes in economic matters—and when we say mistakes, we're talking about all of us, right? Because, in the last analysis, we're all part of the government, isn't that true? It's the people who govern, and determine at each particular point what is to be done . . .and therein rests the greatness of our Revolution. . . .What you were saying about the controls, Lázaro, that's a question we can't settle here at the factory, it must be analyzed by governmental agencies. The Revolution requires us to say: so much has been spoiled through bad cutting, and we should tackle this problem forthwith: so much has been damaged through bad folding, and we should apply ourselves to this; so much has been lost by inept corrugation, and we should see that this is set right . . .thus we must be vigilant."

Next the manager touches a sensitive nerve among the workers, whom he knows well. An important portion of his time is spent with them on the shopfloor.

"I know you don't particularly like the inspector because you think he doesn't do any work. You are disturbed by the fact he may come around, pick up a carton, examine it, fold it, and say nothing to you."

"We benefit from quality control, but we'd like the fellow to do the job he's supposed to," José says, "because there lies the problem of Héctor Ramírez. Three shifts have gone by—you understand?—and not a single compañero was told whether or not the inspector actually detected the badly made cartons . . ."

"Look, just so you'll understand, José," 'Robertico' says, "either we change the methods or we replace the people."

"No, it's not necessary to change the people, no, no, no."

"We go on with the same people?"

"We go on with the same people, but working, because we work hard."

"Well, then, that contradicts what Lázaro says."

"No, Lázaro is another matter, because he is addressing a situation in the past, you understand?"

The manager sums up the situation: "To recapitulate, let's see if we can reach a consensus. Lázaro proposed the elimination of inspectors and transferring their function to the operator. López suggests that no, we shouldn't eliminate them, but simply increase the number, since there are some shifts without them, . . .and in addition, they should watch what is being produced. Logically, the blame should still fall on the operator, but they would also share in it. Which way do we go?"

The workers pronounce themselves in favor of keeping the inspectors, but demand that they also collaborate with the operator, if production mistakes are to be eliminated.

The meeting is drawing to a close. It has taken four hours. Seventy-five percent of the workers have attended. Some of the absentees are sick, others on vacation, and some must tend the machines while production continues.

The meeting had opened with an explanation of the plan for 1976.

Figures proposed by JUCEPLAN* are displayed on a sizeable blackboard, both in units and in value. These figures are called "target figures." The union, for its part, through talks with the workers, had arrived at an estimate and, assisted by the factory's management, formulated other figures that appeared on the blackboard as the figures advanced by the factory, which in this case were lower than those of JUCEPLAN.

But the presentation did not solely concern the two sets of figures to be discussed; it also included a backward look at how production had increased since 1971, the year when light industry began discussing production plans with the workers, thereby anticipating by a few years the same measure recently adopted at the national level. In addition to this, target figures for the first six months of 1975 were also displayed on the board. It was these figures, reproduced below, that monopolized the debate.

In the chart it is abundantly clear that the figure for production units proposed by the factory is lower than that of JUCEPLAN: The former is 17,759.000 units, and JUCEPLAN's 20,611.800, or more than two million units below the target figure.

If we look at the columns more closely we realize that the figures proposed for 1976 are the same as those which had been advanced for 1975. There is a logical explanation for this. The JUCEPLAN figures are formulated according to a series of investments anticipated for the factory. Among these are an increase in storage capacity, the building of a new press, and the paving of interior corridors. (The corridors, badly riddled with holes, now make the transfer of materials within the workshop more difficult.) If these goals are met, then the workers are willing to meet the targets proposed by JUCEPLAN, but in the absence of the improvements the workers can only commit themselves to the same figure as the year before.

*Junta Central de Planificación (Central Planning Authority).

Statistics Relating to the Production of Cartons

(The figures for "units" and "value" are given in thousands of units and thousands of pesos, respectively).

	Cartons	National	Export
1970			
Units	9,289.2	7,919.6	1,369.6
Value	2,720.4	2,107.9	612.5
1971			
Units	13,709.9	10,348.3	3,361.6
Value	4,253.3	2,672.8	1,580.5
1972			
Units	15,119.5	10,098.6	5,020.9
Value	5,449.2	2,830.7	2,618.5
1973			
Units	16,476.7	10,321.3	6,155.4
Value	6,351.1	2,902.2	3,448.9
1974			
Units	17,269.5	9,588.8	7,680.7
Value	6,715.4	2,526.7	4,188.7
1975 Plan			
Units	17,759.9	8,759.9	9,000.0
Value	6,951.3	2,149.7	4,801.6
First Six Months 1975 (estimate)			
Units	8,742.5	4,317.5	4,426.0
Value	3,420.5	1,059.2	2,361.3
Target Figure 1976			
Units	20,611.8	10,940.2	9,671.6
Value	7,385.8	2,226.0	5,159.8
Figures Proposed by the Workers, 1976			
Units	17,759.9	8,759.9	9,000.0
Value	6,951.3	2,149.7	4,801.6

NOTE: The following investments had not been carried out, negatively affecting the plan: 1) Expansion of working space and installation of new press; 2) Warehouse for finished products; 3) Warehouse for raw materials; 4) Paving of factory corridors; 5) Hydraulic forklifts.

Thus, in reality, the plan is born among the workers. Management assists them in the discussion of the Plan, on account of its over-all view of what the industry can accomplish in a coordinated fashion, and offers its opinion to the assembled masses. The workers analyze all the facts in the meeting. And ultimately it is they who either approve or change the figures.

The Role of the Workers in the Discussion of the Plan

With the meeting over, we gather with a group of workers, among whom we count workshop operators, management personnel, and Party officials. The conversation drifts toward the workers' participation in the planning of production.

"The first thing we have is a basic proposal," the manager explains to us, referring to the discussion of technical-economic plans. "This proposal is then taken to the industry level; from the industry it goes up to the appropriate ministry, in our case the Ministry for Light Industry, and thence it goes to JUCEPLAN. This organization then works out the so-called target figures. These are then passed down the line again to be discussed anew by the workers, who ultimately settle on the figures they believe themselves capable of producing, taking into account conditions existing at the factory. The workers say, for example, we are going to produce such and such a quantity of paraffin-coated wrap. They know the meeting to discuss the plan is nearing, and they begin whipping out their pencils, figuring the whole thing out. . . .

" 'Yes, but we can make that amount only if we have the cooling equipment installed,' they say to themselves. These and other points are studied by them and taken before the meeting."

"This way of debating the plan is quite recent, isn't that right?"

"This began in 1970. After the report by the Prime Minister on July 26, the shift was significant. Because prior to 1970 this just didn't exist, this business of giving concrete figures, of taking the plan to the people, so they could analyze it, dissect it, and put it all together again as they wished. . . .Before 1970 it was done, but in a different way, a simpler way. Management had an obligation to advise the workers each month of the requirements of the plan—what was needed, what had to be produced, and so on. There were meetings, but they were simpler, not of this magnitude, nor prepared with all kinds of analysis. They were departmental meetings, where the workers made a moral commitment to the needs of the product being manufactured. And the management was charged with informing them via blackboards of how the goals were being met. There was always participation. What we didn't have was this kind of discussion. Now the worker has a share in the economic affairs of his factory. What is sought now is no longer the patriotic appeal, the revolutionary sloganeering after a figure, but a compañero who can analyze what is going to be done, and why. In those days it was *Patria o Muerte!* as we used to say. Now this stage of *Patria o Muerte* is being left behind, thanks to good economic planning."

"And how do you arrive at those figures you submitted at the meeting?"

"We have a whole series of [economic] histories showing the performance of particular production lines over the years, starting with 1971. Then, on the basis of that accumulated experience, that is, equipment capacities, the number of work shifts per year, the labor force available, and so on, we formulate the figures. Besides, the Junta [JUCEPLAN], compiles the needs at the national level, that is, what's needed from this or that industry, and that's how the plan begins to develop. The next thing, then, is the target figure, which is passed down the line, but that figure can be changed by the workers. That's what happened here. The problem in the corrugating shop is that a large area is needed to move these products. We've reached our limit, and if the space is not enlarged —Well, it's like a home with three rooms. You can fit in three bedroom suites, but you can't squeeze in five."

At that moment, Compañero Fernando Schapman, the union secretary, speaks up: "How could anyone foresee at the beginning of the Revolution that some day we'd have this kind of meeting? And that we'd have counterrevolutionaries. All this is a process. We have reached a stage where . . .the workers truly participate, no? In the decision-making process, I mean. In the old days, of course, we encouraged the workers to produce, produce, and produce, but oftentimes we didn't know whether we had the raw materials to carry out the plans we had just described. Today this kind of mishap doesn't occur. The state goes to where the workers are, or to the representatives of the workers' movement, and a comprehensive analysis is introduced of what is feasible and what isn't, and of the difficulties that have to be overcome. Then you begin to get feedback from the workers, those things you may have heard when you visited here. They may tell you, for example, 'If the new machine can do it, I can do it. But can you give me assurances that the supply of raw materials won't be interrupted? Because it's happened before that the materials sat in the warehouse while I wasted two hours of work. Do you know what it means to waste two hours?' They tell you things like that and plenty more. Discussion of the plan advances in that manner until a commitment is reached: the workers make a commitment to produce a definite amount, along the lines of *Patria o Muerte!* but after analyzing all the details, and knowing what they'll be able to accomplish under better conditions, because as the years go by we're building better resources. Formerly, well, we had nothing. Those truly were conditions of *Patria o Muerte!* But to accomplish things in that fashion matters had to be dumped in the laps of the vanguard, that group of workers with an excellent record of work and loyalty to the Revolution. Thus the masses were being left behind, were not being drawn into the tasks at hand. It was therefore necessary to find some way to involve them, to make them participate, a unique way of making them responsible for the tasks posed by the Revolution."

Fidel recognized this problem in his speech of September 28, 1970, some months after the great drive to produce 10 million tons of sugar cane had ended in failure: "At this time we are engaged in a great effort to develop our workers' organizations to the maximum. Why? Because, unfortunately, over the last few years, they have lagged behind, not through any fault of their own, but because of errors on the part of the Party, of the political leadership of the country. And was this done deliberately? No! It came about in an unconscious manner, as a result of certain idealist notions. For, concerned with the creation of a vanguard workers' organization, we fell into the error of neglecting the general workers' movement."

In the beginning, plans were drawn up by the experts, and pertinent figures were simply passed down to the masses. The role of the leadership consisted, at that time, in convincing the workers, by propaganda campaigns, of the necessity of making the required effort.

But such plans were deeply flawed, Armando Hart asserted on May 12, 1969, because "the masses, the workers, did not participate in the plan. Yet it was necessary to get the workers to take part. Very often the heads of administrative and production units applied correct management policies, but the workers did not recognize them as their own, and hence they had no practical value. Under capitalism, a management that did not depend on the workers could still function as a managerial force, because capitalism utilizes the simple and cruel device of dismissing those who failed to toe the bourgeois line. . . .But under socialism a management that does not rely on the masses, which does not seek the people's participation, fails. It is not an efficient management. The difference between a communist manager and another who is not lies precisely in the fact that the communist manager must get the workers to participate, to share in the tasks of management. If he does not achieve this, he will not succeed as a manager."

"Robertico," the manager of this factory producing cardboard containers, has taken this lesson to heart.

The Party in the Factory

The conversation, which initially revolved around economic plans, now turns to the question of the Party.

We know that Robertico Fernández is a party member, apart from being the plant manager, but what was he before?

"Before the Revolution I was working with a typesetting outfit associated with the daily *El País*. At the outset of the Revolution, light industry was socialized by the government. I took part in three such 'interventions.' After that, I myself was appointed an 'intervenor,'* and then was sent to school. First we were in charge of a labor force and then we went through different administrative positions until we got around to forming this unit. Then, more study."

"What are you studying?"

"Economics, at the Institute of Economics. Study is fundamental. The country can't be developed with a low cultural level. Today, having only a sixth-grade education here is to be illiterate. A middle level is the minimum. There are educational facilities for different levels. For example, secondary courses for workers which enable them to go on to the Workers' College, and thence to the university. Here anyone who doesn't study truly has a problem, and not a problem connected with work, either, because there he's given every opportunity. During the early years of the Revolution we made a mistake in that respect; we worked too much. We don't solve anything by working sixteen hours a day and not improving ourselves. We should work fourteen hours, and improve ourselves the rest of the time."

"Is there a model worker in this group?"

"Yes, Pastor Fundora," Carlos says, a worker. He is referring to the shop foreman.

"Could you tell me on what grounds he was chosen a model worker?"

"Well, look, he and I go back twenty years. In my view his attitude has been correct since the victory of the Revolution. He was a union leader in this very plant. We had to struggle together against the bosses. He's a vanguard worker. He does volunteer work, and a number of qualities make him stand out among the masses."

"When did they sponsor you, Compañero Fundora?"

---

*A government-appointed manager of nationalized industry.

"About two months ago."

"And since when have you been the shop foreman?"

"For about a year."

"Could you say anything else about the compañero?"

"I've also known Comrade Fundora for many years," Lázaro says. "I was a union leader with him. One story that comes to mind in connection with the compañero involves a Mr. Alma—"

"Who was he?"

"A workshop foreman. This was a factory where many workers applied for work, but it only hired those with some kind of pull. There was a group of 'stand-by' workers, and other temporary workers, who sometimes made only seven or eight pesos, and sometimes nothing. I was among them. One Christmas season when each worker was taking home a hefty bonus I got a meager one that I still keep. It was all of 9 pesos 60. Seeing that, I said to myself: 'Some Christmas you are going to have!' But soon enough the Revolution triumphed, and Mr. Alma continued doing his job: running personnel, saying: 'You're on,' 'you're leaving.' This was at the beginning of the Revolution, when we still had a lot of private industry. The story goes that one day Compañero Fundora grabbed the sheet of paper Alma was brandishing and told him: 'From now on, you're not dismissing a soul from this place. From this moment on, all the workers are going to work. This is a Revolution, and we can't allow people to go unemployed.' And he opened the doors, and all those who were waiting outside came in to work. In addition, Compañero Fundora has gone to cut sugar cane with us. His brigade set an example, and almost made it as a Millionaire Brigade.* For all these reasons I support the choice of the compañero as a model worker, and member of the Party, as he will make one more good revolutionary comrade the Revolution can count on. What more can I tell you!"

"And there were no reservations?"

"Yes, some," Roberto says.

"Do you recall any?"

"No, not really."

At that point the subject himself speaks up.

"Well, after being chosen by the meeting as a model worker, a process conducive to joining the Party ensues. This requires that you prepare an autobiography. I did make a mistake in writing it and put down that I had been a member of an organization with, well . . . a rather dismal record from before the Revolution, when, in fact, I had only collaborated with it, and withdrew when I realized its true character. Later on, this

---

*A brigade that has cut a million *arrobas* of sugar cane—about 25 million pounds.

was analyzed, and the opinion was that a person who had shown such lack of judgment could not be admitted into the Party."

"Then this isn't the first time you've been named a model worker?"

"That's correct. This incident, which hadn't been clarified sufficiently the first time around, held me back. This time, however, the question was discussed by both leadership and the masses."

"I was wondering why you had been put forth as a model worker only two months ago when you have so many revolutionary qualifications. Now I understand the reason."

"There are workers here who work with the CDRs,* who do volunteer work, who are in the military units, who go to harvest sugar cane . . .and who, for all these reasons are selected in the meeting, but a compañero can still say: 'Look, pal, I don't accept,' " the Party secretary explains.

"But what reasons could he possibly have for not wanting to accept?"

"Because he doesn't want to bear the responsibility of a Party member, because he doesn't want to have his life investigated. That's why free choice is the basic principle in these matters."

"Look, twice I was selected a model worker," Lázaro breaks in, "but I couldn't make it into the Party ranks, although I'm not giving up hopes that some day I'll make it, and I would like, when I die, to have them toss the Party card to me in the coffin."

Everyone laughs at Lázaro's way of putting the matter.

"Could you explain to us why you couldn't make it as a Party member?"

"When by biography was studied by the *conjunta* [a review board of Party members charged with evaluating a candidate's dossier.—Ed.] they told me I had to master certain things. And problem number one was my temper. You saw me as I took part in the meeting. I'm very impulsive, quick-tempered, I have trouble controlling myself, and though I've made some progress, I still have a way to go. Various other things like that. But, really, what they tell you is the truth, the greatest truth you can ever hear. And when you come out, you come out in high spirits instead of becoming depressed. The point, however, is that you must attempt to overcome the problem."

"And why weren't you elected a model worker in the last meeting?"

"Well, I completed my term in the trade union and was sick for a few months, but I'm still not giving up hope. Some day, I don't know whether near or far, I expect to become a Party member."

"Did any of the compañeros present here today participate in the review board?"

"Yes, I did," Roberto responds.

*Committees for the Defense of the Revolution.

"Lázaro, would you mind if the compañero explained to us the reasons why you were not accepted by the Party?"

"Not at all. Go ahead."

"Better if he explained it himself," Roberto says tactfully.

"There are times when we concentrate on a particular job and neglect others," Lázaro begins, "and one of the things they raised with me was the low level of schooling I had. When I began at the factory, you could say I was almost illiterate. I had barely finished second grade. I kept on till the sixth, but after that I let go. I became a union leader after the Revolution and dedicated myself to this task, dropping my studies. I also dropped out of the Defense Committee (CDR), and as I had too many duties I raised the possibilitiy of resigning my post. These were some of the comments I received and, to tell the truth, I found them to be accurate. I had to overcome these things. Now I'm going back to school because I must resume my studies. If I don't study, I'll be left behind. If I had perservered, I'd already be in the Workers' College or climbing the steps of the university, like may compañeros who were illiterate before the Revolution and who today attend the university. There are old compañeros who had never studied before and who today are doctors, fifty years old and older. Ah! But they made the sacrifice! You can rest assured that the compañero who's selected as a model worker by this factory has been analyzed for his attitude toward work, that he's ready to tackle anything. . . .And that's why I wasn't chosen. As they say in the vernacular, "Give it to me straight!" Because someone doesn't belong in the Party ranks if he doesn't want to get off his ass. . . .I came out extremely happy that day. They asked me: How do you feel? I answered them: Perfect. I thank you for telling me this. 'Robertico' was selected by this process."

"I, too, was chosen a model worker and could not become a member of the Party on the first try," Roberto adds.

"Why not?"

"Because of ups and downs in my work. I made it up to the national level, but then, because of flaws in my performance I was demoted to a regional administrative unit."

"How do you explain that failure, when you now seem to be so enthusiastic about your job?"

"I imagine it's a problem of development, of training, of study, of talent. That was a very high level for me, though when I say that I'm not trying to justify my conduct at the time."

"But did you feel insecure?"

"Of course. Yet if we bear in mind that I filled that job for three years, I should have accumulated the experience . . ."

"Is there another Party member here?"

"I. I was fortunate enough that when they analyzed me for the first time, I passed at once. I had no problems with the review board." The man who has spoken is Luis, foreman of the drum shop.

"In what year?"

"In 1969, in this plant. On September 9, 1969."

"You remember it well!"

"Certainly. It's like being born again!"

"Indeed!" Carlos says, laughing.

"He's a very special case," Roberto points out. "He was a factory owner."

"Really?"

"He was a capitalist!" Carlos exclaims in jest.

"A capitalist? Never!" Luis says gravely. "I come from humble origins. My parents were workers, peasants. My father died during the capitalist era, in extreme poverty. I started working in the packaging industry. I got to be a shop foreman in the age of capitalism. Afterwards, I became a manager, in another factory, and was being paid quite handsomely. But realizing the exploitation that went on, and the increasing demands of the boss, I decided to leave. I had my savings, fifteen hundred pesos, and a brother-in-law had a comparable sum. I said to him: 'Listen, let's set up a little business. I'm tired of being exploited and I know how to run a factory.' In that manner we set up, without any capital, a small industry."

"Of what kind?"

"Cardboard containers. Then the Revolution came and the little factory was already a going affair. It had about twenty thousand pesos worth of machinery."

"And how many workers"

"About thirty, all relatives. It was a family affair. About that time an ex-boss of mine suggested that we set up a factory in Oriente and that I could run it. So I became involved with two factories, one in Havana and the other in Oriente. But as soon as the Revolution arrived, I became a militiaman, because I sympathized with the Revolution. I never had capital. What I did have was the initiative to develop a factory, but never with the intention of being a capitalist—because I didn't have it in my blood, you understand? After becoming a militiaman, the year 1960 came around and I enrolled my fifteen-year old son as a militiaman, too.

And as he was taken with the battalion for the 'mop up' operation in the Escambray,* I was acting as chief of transportation in Oriente, receiving the incoming weapons and distributing them throughout the country. And I wasn't allowed to go to the Escambray. Then I raised the question with Tony Perez. I told him that the only favor I asked was to be allowed to go with my son on the mop-up of the Escambray because if I have trained my son politically and given him to the Revolution, it's logical that I succeed with him or die with him if there's any dying to do, even though we didn't think much of dying but of fighting the enemy. So they let me go. And after the Escambray came the Bay of Pigs. I was assigned to go to Holguín, as this was the spot where the invasion was expected. We stayed in a field for about a month and never saw the enemy. Then, when we learned about the victory, we were very disappointed that we didn't get to see any action. When we got back, I remember it was the first of May, my partner had taken off for Miami. I turned the factory over to the state at once, but industry wasn't getting much attention in those days because there were too many problems. That's why they gave me a job with Public Works for a while, until I was transferred to Havana and returned to the shop I had here. I immediately went to see the manager and told him I wanted to give the factory away and work in it in whatever capacity they thought appropriate. He put me in charge of my own firm. But after that I was moved through different shops till in September, 1965, they assigned me to head the drum shop in the plant, which is my specialty. I'm sixty two years old."

"In this plant there are 640 workers. How many Party members are there?"

"Nineteen," the Party secretary answers.

"How many vanguard workers?"

"About 140."

"How is the vanguard worker rewarded?"

"A monthly citation is presented to the three most outstanding workers in each workshop. In addition, the CTC* has a variety of vacation plans, tickets to theaters and nightclubs. For all these things each union chooses the best workers. And it also happens that when the compañeros spot a fellow worker showing signs of exhaustion, they propose his name for a month's rest at full salary, without his losing vacation days normally accrued, or having to pay anything, anywhere."

*Sierra from which CIA-supported counterrevolutionaries and bandits struck back at the revolutionary government.
*Confederation of Cuban Workers.

"Sometimes there's a problem when one or more workers request the benefit of such a measure," 'Robertico' says. "If there are ten petitions and only three places— well, previously it was the management and the union which made the choices, but as we can make mistakes, the matter now goes up to the workers' meeting so they may decide who deserves the rest. It is the workers who have the last word."

"And if a Party member begins to falter in his performance what can the masses do?"

"When a Party member loses his standing with the masses, a whole schedule of sanctions begins to be applied. But rather than allowing the masses to come to suspect there's something to be desired in the member, the Party leadership will already have taken the matter in hand, and analyzed him with regard to the areas where improvement is necessary. In case there's no Party representative in the factory, the workers take the question to the sectional Party representative, and advise him of the complaints they have about the Party member.

"And you, compañero? You're a union official. Are you also a Party member?"

"No."

"I don't understand how a leader chosen by the workers, and enjoying their respect, cannot be a Party member. . . ."

"Well," Fundora says, "it happens that he was chosen a model worker.

"And why didn't he get to be a Party member, too?"

"I didn't want to be analyzed. I had problems."

"When were you elected secretary of the union?"

"In 1970, but in fact I was never at the factory itself, as I was often taken to work the *zafra*. In those days the call-ups were frequent. Four here, ten there, and so on."

"It seems there's been a great change in the tasks of the union since 1970. Can you tell us anything about that?"

"Well, the tasks were much more limited before. Everything was centered on the activity of the vanguard workers, on call-ups for different purposes. The union had little to do with the question of production. Now the union plays a central role in production, in the drawing up of economic plans for industry. Management furnishes us with a series of facts and data that we take to the workers for discussion."

"You must be extremely busy with all these assignments. When you're elected a union official, do you quit your job?"

"No. We work an average of five hours a day at our customary jobs, and the rest we devote to the problems of workers, to questions relating to production. Every day we have a brief conference to discuss problems of production with management officials and Party leaders."

"Compañeros, now that the problem of linking salary to output is being debated, does it happen that you, as union representatives, have to face a great many salary complaints from the workers?"

"No, no one complains about the minimum salary. Their only concern is with getting paid fairly for their work, according to their productivity."

"Tell me, compañero. Now that there are more products being freely distributed, have you stopped the practice of distributing scarce goods among the better workers, as it was done before?"

"No, that system continues. When there are more products of that kind, more flow into the factories, but distribution still goes by merit. There is a committee chosen by the workers themselves—the union representative does play a part in it—which determines the manner in which the distribution will be carried out, but the decision must be ratified by the meeting later. In this way we try to avoid any unfairness in the allocation of goods."

The Party and the Rank-and-File Workers

In a lithographic plant in Havana, in the wake of the discussion of the 1976 technical-economic plan, we meet with a group of workers, among whom we find union leaders, management workers, Party members, and common workers. The conversation again focuses on the Party.

"Compañeros, in the meeting where the model workers were elected, was there any nomination by some comrade which had to be withdrawn after discussion?"

"Yes, there were two cases," answers the secretary-general of the Party. "One concerned a worker who didn't wish to accept. The other, Manuel, had a low scholastic level and was not making any effort to improve himself. Logically, this disqualified him, because one of the conditions for being a model worker is that he or she should continually strive to improve his or her education, especially in this process wherein Fidel has said that to have a sixth-grade education is to be illiterate. . . . It's necessary to improve oneself ideologically as well as culturally. This allows us to accumulate a lot more political 'savvy.' "

"How many workers were proposed as model workers during the last meeting?"

"Seven. The workers choose the best from among the best. If a worker nominates a compañero and some other worker feels that that compañero is not the best, he asks for the floor and explains his objections. For instance, it has happened that we haven't considered exemplary a compañero who took a nurse as a bride then prevailed upon her to stop working and devote herself to homemaking. *That compañero is practicing machismo.* He thinks he's the one who's supposed to bring home the bacon and that she must be a houseslave devoted entirely to him. These are questions the workers understand. It is not correct for a compañera to resign her job on account of marriage. But if the compañero overcomes this fault, he may be proposed again in a future meeting. Everything can be overcome, and the Party cadres are particularly willing to assist these comrades in this area. The important thing is to identify the problems in time. One person may not know a thing about the compañero, but another one may."

Another worker speaks up: "I was nominated but did not accept because being a Party member involves a whole series of responsibilities that, for personal reasons, I cannot fulfill. A boxer can't get into the ring if he's just coming off a bout with flu. That's the kind of situation I find myself in. I'm waiting to recover a bit and return to the arena."

"Was any compañero here elected a model worker on another occasion?"

"Yes. Efraín" the Party secretary says, motioning toward a worker who is now a member of the union bureaucracy. "He was elected in 1970."

"And why wasn't he elected a Party member?"

"Because of his jocular temperament."

"But how come? Is it by any chance a crime to have a jovial disposition?"

"My character, besides being jocular, was also superficial. I didn't have the seriousness before the masses that is required of a Party member. . . .I didn't know how to distinguish between a time for seriousness and a time for play. . . .But now I've overcome that."

"Then how do you account for the fact that you were not chosen a model worker at the recent meeting?"

"In that meeting several workers came to see me to find out whether I'd be interested in being nominated. I said no, as I still preferred to wait a while and make sure I've got this thing licked, and then move to join the Party. Besides, at the moment I have too many family problems, a sickness in the family. They are not the ideal conditions to take a step forward, the step required to really go to the fore."

"Compañero, you're a union official and you're not a model worker?"

"No, it's not necessary to be a model worker to become a union officer. The union leader is elected by acclamation. He must have a number of qualifications: he must be a good worker, not a goof-off, display good social conduct in the factory, etc.; all these are lesser requirements than those for a Party member. In the case of union leaders, there's no second inquiry. In the case of a model worker, the masses nominate him but the Party investigates his personal background and may decide he is not deserving of Party membership."

"Does it happen here, among the Party leaders in this factory, that the secretary-general is an ordinary worker and the managers ordinary Party members?"

"In our case, the secretary of the Party, right here, is also the manager, and acting shop foreman," Efrain answers.

The secreatary-general explains for the leadership: "In the beginning, in order to consolidate the Revolution, the revolutionary vanguard was chosen to direct the economy. Because of their knowledge, their preparation, Party leaders had to fill managerial positions. Now, with the new methods, we are trying to eliminate this completely. The Party official must be an ordinary worker, and at least a third of the leadership in the factory must be workers directly connected with production. And you will see that in many places an ordinary worker is the secretary-general for the leadership and the manager an ordinary Party member."

"What was your work when the Revolution came to power?"

"I was a lithographer . . .a skilled worker."

"With what level of schooling?"

"Only the fifth grade."

"Could you explain to me why the Party insists so that the leadership be composed of ordinary workers when it knows better than anyone else that a significant portion of management is of working-class origin?"

"There is a very good reason behind it, and I have experienced it better than most. I think it's one of the best directives passed by the Party. I feel this way because it was our duty to see to it that the economic directives were adhered to, and this sometimes made it impossible for us to evaluate our performance with the necessary detachment of an ordinary worker. For although the managing officer may be a compañero with great revolutionary understanding, it is still difficult for him to be fully aware of the workers' concerns, and so he's not likely to move with the requisite speed and determination to find solutions to their problems. Sometimes, of course, solutions are delayed on account of the position the compañero occupies in the state bureaucracy. And even though my own service is not unrelated to the workers because of my own character, it is still no less true that the managerial routines steal precious time that, were it spent closer to production, might allow me to serve the workers' aspirations better. And that's the reason the Party and the government have decided to eliminate, to the greatest possible extent, the political-administrative dichotomy, so that administrative duties of the Party might be carried out in full accordance with the required excellence."

"You, compañero Efraín, are not in the administration. Could you tell us how you look upon this measure?"

"I believe it's a fine measure, since sometimes we get mixed up. I mean, we don't know whether we're talking to a management officer or a Party leader. If, on the other hand, he's only a political operative, it will be easier to know how to approach him. A Party secretary can't discharge his duties well if he's in the administration too, because, in fact, the tasks are too many. . . ."

Union and Management under Socialism

"In a country like ours the workers' consciousness is shaped, the revolutionary consciousness. Before the triumph of the Revolution we had to struggle against the capitalists. Asking, asking, asking, without ever getting satisfaction of our demands. Now our dual function, as unionists and revolutionaries, is to defend the interests of the workers and also to defend the interests of the state, because we are a part of the state, we are a part of our country's economy. We must see to it that the economy keeps on growing. The Revolution affirms that this, every-thing, is ours, and it is true. It doesn't mean it is ours and we can take it home. No, no. This is ours to produce for the commonwealth. That's why we must increase our productivity, so we can grow still further. The goal of the union is to defend, as always, the interests of the workers. So it is assumed that we are the countervailing force to the management side. But our administration is revolutionary and the role, therefore, becomes one of making sure that they, too, manage well a business that belongs to us all. There's not a single worker here who doesn't have a real under-standing of what he's doing and why. Previously, in the capitalist era, the worker worked for his own benefit and tried to escape such unjust circumstances. Now, no longer. The concern is for the interest of all. Formerly, a union local was a place run by a bunch of four or five people who lived off the workers. Not so now. In today's local we have every-thing. A worker can drop in anytime. There he has his library, his recreation place, all that."

This is the vision of a union leader in Matanzas Province.

"You, the workers, do you feel you are the power. Do you know you are the supreme power in the land?"

"Look, listen closely. I'll give you some examples. We have a work plan in our union. It comes down to the work center, and it is the workers of this center who analyze it, offer suggestions, pass resolutions, and so on. And that's how it evolves. The same applies in the economic sphere. In the capitalist countries, as far as the factory is concerned, there's a plan and it must be carried out. And whoever isn't helping its implementation either shapes up or ships out. Here, economic plans are passed down the line to the work centers. The workers discuss them, analyze them, approve them. Suggestions are made; something that may be incorrect is rectified; something obscure is clarified. That is concrete. That is power. With the laws, the same procedure. At present, we are discussing the new socialist Constitution of our Republic. It is being discussed right here in the factory. And the workers make contributions. Imagine, those who drew up this proposal. . . .It's something conceived at a high level. And yet it comes down to the work place so the workers, the people, may contribute to this Constitution. Here everything is discussed, all the laws. Every time the Revolution enacts a law, it comes first to the workplaces. Suggestions are made, even modifications. Even though compañeros in the national leadership possess a high level of expertise, we still make suggestions and modifications, and they're heeded. That is the great and rich experience we have as revolutionaries. We truly feel like masters of our fate."

"And what have the workers gained by the Revolution?"

"A great deal! Everything is guaranteed today. The salary, the social conditions, the environment, the economic situation—for the agricultural worker as well as the intellectual worker. Today in our country we make no social distinctions between an intellectual, a technician, an engineer, and a laborer. Here a worker can be a leader of the country. Not so before. In the old days a worker died still bound to his job. He couldn't do anything remarkable or become somebody. We see with pride how the top leaders of our nation come to our place of work. They get in there and they share with the workers. They come to see how they feel, what problems they may have. That's socialism. Previously, many landowners, many rich people, many powerful men lived here, and the only thing they cared about was their own welfare. When the Revolution came, some stayed behind, and they lived thinking the Americans would invade us, that they would kill us, so they could resume management of the country, running their businesses, and so on. That crowd couldn't care less if the people paraded naked in the streets, went without shoes, without food. Today in our country we don't have needy cases. In the capital we used to have four or five poor neighborhoods. Here we had little girls who were unable to educate themselves, and because they were hungry, they sold their bodies. I remember that we used to see U.S. aircraft carriers here in our harbor. The sailors would come ashore, and there would be pandemonium. They didn't respect anything. And no one could complain because, naturally, the old rulers benefited. Today things are different. I can assure you that if we are attacked at some point by the imperialist power, even those Cubans with the least developed consciousness, even those who think least of the Revolution, will ask for weapons to help defend it. In those days I was working six hours a day, and was interested only in putting in my time and going home. Today we are indefatigable. Because we have to go forward and time is running out."

"You have a manager. How do you get along with him?" we later ask of the union secretary at the "Frank País" fertilizer plant in Matanzas.

"Quite well, he's very good. He's a person just like us, one more worker. If he makes a mistake, then we are to tell him, talk with him, discuss things, ask him to explain something. If there's something the union thinks is not right, a meeting is called and the matter is clarified. Everyone speaks his piece. If the workers have some criticism to offer, they say it openly. But our managers are revolutionaries. Maybe here and there one might find a misunderstanding, but everything is eventually clarified. Here the union section—there are ten of us—meets twice a month with the Party and management, and we discuss the plans, what we've done wrong, what we think needs to be done, and so on. And if at any time there's something that requires haste, we simply hold a meeting, and presto!"

Next we talk with the manager.

"How does management get along with the union?"

"There's no disagreement with the union. We always meet to discuss, to see the problems from management's stand-point, to comment on good or bad policies affecting performance. Once a month we have a session with the factory managers, and if management is at fault somewhere, we offer the criticisms there: how we must act, how we must treat the workers. Any suggestions are collected there, too. For example, the union is the authority that mobilizes the workers throughout the nation, constantly gathering their concerns and transmitting the same, through reports, to the managers."

"How long have you been a manager?"

"Two and a half years. Before, I used to work in the fertilizer industry. I began with a pick and shovel around 1959, before the triumph of the Revolution. When the Revolution came, I continued working at the same occupation. I arrived here, at this factory, in 1968 to work as an aide to production. Later on, I became head of a production brigade. After that, I was appointed a manager by the management. Now, if I fail, if the workers are dissatisfied with my performance, they can throw me out. They can get together and demand it, after an analysis of my handling of affairs, of course. Finally, they can get together and petition a higher organization, if they're not happy with the attitude adopted by the plant manager. An analysis is conducted to determine the extent to which the workers are right. If this is so, and the workers' charges prove correct, the manager is let go, and a new one takes his place."

"Without the Revolution, could you have become a manager?"

"Not a chance!" he laughs. "I don't know where I'd be if the Revolution hadn't arrived. If I were still alive, I'd be struggling, as in the days of Batista's dictatorship. Besides, I'm black. Imagine how it would be. Being black was always worse. There was terrible discrimination. In Havana there were areas like El Vedado and Miramar, where not everyone could get in. In those days I worked in construction, as a mason. I suffered a great deal, personally. And that was true for the majority of the people. That can't be forgotten. It's still fresh in my memory. That's why the participation of the entire people in the tasks of the Revolution, with such devotion, baffles other countries. These are countries where the authenticity of our revolutionary mobilizations of the people is still doubted. That's why the preceding explanation is apt. We suffered, and now we are building for ourselves."

"You, compañero, have you been able to study?"

"I have, but with difficulty. The time I was talking about before, it was very difficult. When I was fourteen, I had to quit school to help my parents. Then I started working, devising ways of live. Because of that I couldn't continue my studies. After the triumph of the Revolution, we joined in all the tasks. But there were many things we didn't know: what a socialist revolution was, what it meant. . . . We went on working hard, but, at the same time, we tried to keep improving ourselves. Yet it was hard, as there were so many things to do. But now I've resumed my studies. We workers can work, and after the day's over, we can study at night. We can all study whatever we like. And our children can do it better and for free. Our fundamental line is self-improvement [through study], because in that manner we can increase our participation."

"Tell me, compañero, how do you see these elections in Matazas?"

"Before, we used to vote with a machete. Yes, that's the way it was. Not now. The people went to vote freely for the candidates they thought best for the district. The people themselves elected the candidates. Those elected have no privileges of any kind. The only privilege I'd say the delegate has is to be entrusted with one more revolutionary task. He goes on living where he always has lived. He may get a house later on, if he earns it, because of his work at the factory or whatever, but on the same basis as the rest, and he'll have what others have. With the creation of

People's Power, fundamental changes have taken place. It's the people themselves who are guiding their destiny. It's not that it wasn't this way before. I mean before People's Power. But now everything is easier, and everyone does things, not just the delegates. For example, the state has a great many important matters to solve and can't attend to the problems of a rural area containing, say, five hundred people. It's not possible for the state to control everything, fix everything . . . .But the creation of People's Power makes the state's tasks easier. It can examine and solve a series of problems through the people, directly. They can build streets in their zone, in the district, build a high school, a vocational institute, a house, a cinema, a barbershop: in other words they accomplish certain things the state, as such, cannot. It can only supply the guidelines . . . . The people themselves carry them out."

"And the Party—what can you say about it?"

"It's difficult to be a Party member. One has to be mindful of the revolutionary tasks, behave impeccably, set an example. One must strive hard, for the very workers who choose are the masses who decide who can be Party members. They elect the model workers, and after that there's a review. That's really something! One must grow, study always, and continue to be an example. The Party is the greatest thing the Revolution has. The Party gives everything for the sake of the people's happiness; it orients us, it guides us, it watches over us. It is our greatest source of pride."

2 THE PEOPLE'S JUDGES

Justice before the Revolution

"Around 1950 I was a district attorney in Santa Clara, Las Villas, and there was a civil governor in that area who was a regular bandit. His name was Santiaguito Rey. One day a complaint was filed against this character for forgery of documents. It seems he had falsely certified some folks as having rendered certain services so they could expedite obtaining their retirement papers. As a prosecutor, I began an inquiry, appointing an honest man from the region, an investigator for the police, to gather the facts. Knowing full well who Santiaguito Rey was, I instructed the investigator not to restrict himself to the violation at hand, but to get whatever he could on Rey. About a week later the investigator turned up with all kinds of information on the governor's crooked deals. It was dynamite! There was a conscientious investigator! Keeping mum, I prepared the indictment. I even did it myself, did not turn it over to my secretary. And one day, early in the morning, I sat down and processed it. Can you imagine? He was a very influential man! So I sent the summons notifying the governor of the charges against him, and by four o'clock of that same day I had been transferred to Guantanamo, in Oriente Province.

In Santa Clara I lived thorugh a similar experience. There was this unfortunate soul who owned a little plot of land on the outskirts of the city, but with the natural growth of the region, the plot fell into the area earmarked for Santa Clara's expansion. Suddenly a construction company turned up alleging that the plot in question was the property of the state before the war. They sued the poor wretch, asking that he return the property. That suit came to me because I was then a local municipal judge. I went down to the place to verify the plantiff's allegations, and saw that the situation had nothing to do with the stated claims. In that area there was an aqueduct built during the first American intervention in Cuba. It stood as a natural boundary that could not be obliterated. I prepared a written report incorporating the facts I gathered. It seems, however, that one of the clerks spotted it and blew the whistle for the outside world. One afternoon, as I was sitting at home, three members of the superior court came to pay me a visit—very affable, very talkative. They didn't know me, but they knew my name all right. It was Coya this, Coyita that, we like you so much, etc. . . . And I, suspecting something, was wondering all the time: 'What is it they want from me?' It wasn't long before I found out. Soon enough, one of them, Miranda by name, leaned over and said: 'How come you are here, my boy, with your talents! You're a genius!' And I asked myself: 'what is this guy driving at?' And it went on: 'Let's see, my boy. What are your plans, your aspirations?' I replied: 'Look, Doctor, none at all. I worked hard to get my degree, and when I descended the university steps with that diploma under my arm I had ten cents in my pocket. Today I earn two hundred pesos. I've gotten ahead some, don't you think?' But he insists: 'But, dear boy, you can't be satisfied with that . . . Coya, let me tell you why we are here. . . . It seems you are handling some matter relating to a plot of land in these parts, and, frankly, we are interested in this matter.' I said: 'Well, Doctor Miranda, you got here a little bit late because I've already written my decision, and the plaintiff lost.' 'But, Coya,' he said, visibly upset. 'couldn't we possibly look into the matter?' 'No, Doctor,' I said, 'I'm very slow and only know how to do things once.' They got up and left without even saying good-bye. I lived only two blocks from the court-house. I went there immediately, picked up the dossier, and returned home. And that very night I set down my verdict in the matter. Next morning I got to the courthouse early and transferred it onto the books. A few hours later I learned I had been transferred to a small peasant village. The whole thing can be summed up, then, as follows: When the Revolution came to power, the judicial system was corrupt, but not to the last man, because exceptions like myself did exist here and there."

These are the words of a middle-aged man, about fifty, who became a lawyer by great personal effort, since his family had only modest means and could not finance his education. Thanks to his excellent performance, he obtained a scholarship that exempted him from tuition. But in 1937 he was almost forced to quit because university loans were exhausted and free tuition was no longer being granted.

"They didn't want to let me take my exams because I hadn't paid the registration fee. After elbowing my way up to the dean, a demagogue who liked to pose as a progressive, I said to him: 'It seems to me that you never had the misfortune of being poor. . . .' Eventually I got to take my exams."

Today, compañero Coya serves as a judge with the Cardenas court. To him the Revolution has meant the freedom to apply the kind of justice that he could never apply before under the pseudorepublic,* and still less under the Batista dictatorship. He is one of the judges who achieved total integration with the revolutionary process.

If this was happening at the municipal level before the Revolution, when the municipal courts were getting 130 pesos to pay the salaries of the judge and sheriff and for the materials needed, what was happening in the higher echelons?

In a country with a population slightly above six million, there was a Supreme Court composed of forty-three members, an enormous number if you consider that the United States has only nine, and the Soviet Union twelve.

A justice of the Supreme Court earned a thousand pesos a month before the Revolution—that is, a thousand dollars a month—and he worked from one to four in the afternoon, Mondays through Fridays. He was entitled to a two-month vacation annually, in addition to two weeks off at Christmas and Holy Week.

Besides this Supreme Court, there were provincial, regional, and municipal tribunals, and prosecutors attached to each.

When Cuba was turned into an American neo-colony at the turn of the century, so-called correctional courts were set up at the municipal level. These heard trivial offenses: drunkeness, marital disputes, and so on. One judge alone decided the punishment, and there was no appeal. The judge could impose sentences of up to six months, and he had a jail at his disposal. These judges were deeply hated by the people.

The first judge of one of these correctional tribunals in Havana was an American who spoke no Spanish and had to rely on a translator to carry out his duties. These tribunals were an important weapon for Batista. All the police had to do was file a complaint, and the person in question was sentenced forthwith, without any prior investigation of the offense.

*A reference to the supposedly republican form of government in Cuba during the period from 1902 to 1959.

There were also the so-called emergency tribunals, which dealt with political crimes. In Havana there was a special courtroom with five judges entirely devoted to this. They were practically paid appendages of the government and its repressive system. In the provinces, the same court which heard common criminal offenses was tranformed into an emergency tribunal when circumstances required it.

From the time of Machado, these tribunals fuctioned continually as organs of political repression, without appeal.

The Selection Process after the Triumph

When the Revolution triumphed, a law was passed striking down statutes making judges unremovable. The emergency courts were suppressed. All Supreme Court judges were removed. As magistrates a new group of persons was appointed; their fundamental characteristic was that they had not been Batista supporters. Also removed were many administrative judges and prosecutors. The rest of the judges remained in their posts.

In the beginning, all these judges sided with Fidel and the Revolution, but as soon as the Revolution began to take measures that hurt the interests of the ruling groups, such as rent reduction, expropriations of the landed estates, and so on, a movement against the revolutionary government began to take shape among the members of The Supreme Court.

They attempted to defend the sector affected by the revolutionary measures, granting generous compensation to the estate owners, and so on. This process came to a head toward the end of 1960, when the revolutionary leadership found itself compelled to undertake a new purge. This time the purge encompassed not only the Supreme Court, but also the regional and provincial courts. In this manner the remaining counterrevolutionary judges were eliminated, even though the judicial system went on functioning as usual. Its structure was not changed.

The Party eventually appointed a commission headed by Blas Roca to investigate a new Constitution for the nation. Part of this assignment was to work out a new law for the organization of the courts and the prosecutors' offices, to modify some penal laws and to draw up new rules of criminal procedure; in sum, to develop for Cuba a whole new judicial system in better accord with the principles of the Revolution. Members of various tribunals and faculty experts took part in this project. By the end of 1972 the job was finished. The result was not solely the product of deskbound ponderings; its principal inspirational source was the practice of justice during the ten years of the Revolution.

The People's Courts

"I address the judge of the First District to advise him that citizen Mauricio Ojeda was found to have stolen a pulley from an oil well project near Jordan, and for the theft I put him at the disposal of the People's Courts. That is all I have to say."

The secretary, having read the complaint by the plaintiff, continues: "With regard to the reason for which he stands accused in connection with the pulley so defined, the defendant states: On the occasion in question a man by the name of Manuel came to my house looking for fertilizer and was carrying something in his truck. I asked him: 'What's that?' He told me it was a pulley used to compress manure. When we finished loading up the manure, he pulled the rope out of the clamp and asked me if I wanted to buy it. When I asked him how much he wanted, he said: 'Five hundred pounds of fertilizer.' And that's how the pulley came to be in my possession. That is all I have to say about this matter."

These are the accusation and the plea by the defendant in one of seven cases tried on a Wednesday night in the Martí municipality, a rural area in the Matanzas Province.

Despite torrential rains, the room, about thiry feet long by thirty feet wide, is overflowing with people. Most stand. Only a few are sitting. At one end of the room the tribunal can be seen composed of three judges. One conducts the proceedings, while the other two join in the interrogation and deliberation. On either side of the tribunal, facing each other, sit the plaintiff and the defendant. The former is a regional policeman who found the pulley in the defendant's home. The latter is a young man, of peasant stock, who doesn't appear overly perturbed by the situation, if one is to judge by the smirk on his face.

Both characters have been summoned to appear by an elderly man with a high-pitched voice who acts as clerk of the court. He sits facing the bench, with his back turned to the audience.

With the charge read, as well as the defendant's deposition, the judge who is presiding over the session, a man of medium height, slender, bespectacled, about forty-five years of age, addresses the policeman: "Are you prepared to confirm what you deposed?"

"Yes. His brother had a similar pulley, and upon questioning he confessed the truth. We knew it had disappeared from the drilling site."

"You were aware, then, that two pulleys were missing?"

"Two pulleys and several other items."

"Was it possible to confirm that the pulley in question was the same one missing from the well?"

"It was, because both pulleys were identical. The brother had kept his there at home."

After asking the plaintiff to sit down, the judge turns to the defendant, asking him whether he has any legal animosity toward or friendship with any of the judges. Only when he has given a reply in the negative does the cross-examination begin.

"Have you heard the complaint? Do you wish to make a statement?"

"Look, what I have to say is that I exchanged that pulley for fertilizer with a truck driver whose name I don't know. That's some time in the past. . . .That's all I have to say."

"You live in the area close to the excavation. . . ."

"Right next to it."

"When going home, mustn't you cut across these roads?"

"Yes."

"Did you know that there was an oil well there?"

"Everyone knows that."

"You never stopped in? You didn't have any friends at the site?"

"No."

"You didn't know either that two pulleys were missing?"

"I didn't know a thing."

At that point the People's Court president yields to one of the other judges so he may continue the cross-examination. An elderly man, and rather portly, he is dressed in white, which causes him to stand out among the other judges, who are dressed in work clothes.

"The truck driver you mentioned, does he belong to this locality?"

"No."

"How is it, then, that he got to your place looking for manure?"

"Someone must've told him."

"Did you know what a pulley was, the use it is put to?"

"No, not me. . . .When he offered me the thing, I said: 'What do I want that for?' He told me it would be useful to move engines, pull pipes out. I asked him how much he wanted, and he said one thousand *puntos* of manure. And I said 'O.K.', not thinking that—"

"You didn't know the truck driver?"

"No, I didn't know him. I only know he came around looking for fertilizer."

"And without knowing him you got involved in this transaction?"

"Yes, well—without thinking I was going to run into problems. I though the pulley was going to help me lift heavy weights."

The judge, insisting: "So you didn't know the truck driver?"

"No, I'd never seen him before."

With the conclusion of the interrogation by the second judge, the president of the tribunal offers the floor to the last member of the bench, a little man, somewhat elderly with the look of a peasant.

"Did you . . .at any point care to find out where he had gotten such an object?"

"No, never."

"Now, look here . . .in the specific matter of the fertilizer, the compañero who picks it up must show you an authorization. This time it wasn't that way. Besides, you state the truck driver appeared lost—"

"Yes, looking for manure."

"So he got there by accident?"

"Yes."

"And so you went ahead and got involved in the transaction, just like that?"

The defendant falls silent.

The president of the court asks the defendant whether he has anything else to say. When he says no, the president asks him to sit down and then addresses the audience: "The information we have concerns two missing pulleys. The strange coincidence is that one of the missing pulleys is identical to another one found in the house of the defendant' brother. This brother was honest and acknowledged the theft, but the defendant asserts that the pulley in his possession, identical to the other one, was purchased from an unknown truck driver."

After these words the president recesses the hearings, and the judges file into an adjoining room to deliberate. After a few minutes they return to the main room, and the president orders silence and delivers the verdict: "We find the defendant guilty of the crime of theft. In the name of the Cuban people he is hereby condemned to pay a fine of sixty pesos. If the defendant agrees with the penalty, he may stop by this court on Monday morning at eight o'clock to effect payment. If he disagrees, the law grants him the right of appeal, which must be filed before next Saturday at noon."

This is the last trial of the evening. Several cases were heard earlier: that of a woman who sold stale fish, that of a couple in the process of getting a divorce who were quarreling about the property settlement, and that of a peasant charged with allowing his sheep to graze on the lands of a neighbor.

When the hearing is over, conversation continues with the members of the People's Court.

The judge who acted as president is, in fact, the tribunal's vice-president. He had to sit in for the president, who is recuperating from an illness; like the rest of the judges, he is a worker who must discharge his judicial tasks after working hours.

The only requirement from the standpoint of cultural qualification, is that a judge have at least a sixth grade education. After their selection the judges are given specialized courses that equip them to perform their new tasks.

"This is a small county. Don't you get into hassles by being too well known among the neighbors you have to judge?"

The vice-president replies: "If the court renders a fair verdict, there is no problem."

"But you say, at the opening of each trial, 'If you have an enmity or significant friendship.' What happens if the defendant says yes?"

"Well, in most cases this doesn't happen. When we realize a complaint has been filed against a friend or against someone toward whom we feel a strong enmity, we ourselves request that we be replaced by other judges. On the other hand, the fact that we know our neighbors so well enables us to pass fair sentences. For example, look at the case of the pulley theft. Didn't you notice the kind of questions we were aking? He lives near where an oil well is being drilled. It's no mystery to the defendant that all those tools belong to the work site . . . .He's no fool. That's why everything he said sounded illogical. Everyone knows that work tools are disappearing from the work site. He lives nearby. His brother is found with a pulley identical to the one in his possession; his brother admits the crime. If we ask him what route he had to take to get home, it is because we know he must pass by the place. Besides, the spot where he lives is a bit out of the way, in the backwoods, and has no electricity. The only place you can find that is at the drilling site. We know he goes there to play dominoes, listen to the radio, talk. . . .But confronted with all these facts, the defendant insists he bought the pulley from a truck driver he doesn't know at all. Now, that's pretty naive, because it is very difficult for us here in Cuba to engage in barter without knowing the person. Besides, five hundred pounds of manure is too little for a pulley. A pulley costs far more that that. For all these reasons the tribunal pronounced the sentence you saw."

"And if the defendant relapses into crime? Isn't the punishment too light?"

"The policy of the People's Court is not to condemn, but to seek a verdict that will really help the person. In this case the matter concerns a first offender. It is neither educational nor rehabilitative to burden the person with a harsh verdict. We must avoid putting him in such a situation as to force his rejection by society. We try to make those who have committed a crime feel they are still part of society, so that a 'readjustment' may be possible. With this philosophy we have seen crime go down in our region. The measures have proven effective!"

"After what you have told us, could you tell us what the principal difference is between an old professional and the people's magistrates?"

"There's a great difference. That can be corroborated by all the judges present here. In the old days the judge had no contact with the people. He locked himself up in his office. We are different. Since we are not professionals,* we are in daily direct contact with the population. And if there's a trial, since you know the place, know what's going on, there are more elements for judgment. The people have confidence in us because we come from the same population. The previous judges, besides keeping to themselves in their chambers, separated from the people, always sided with the rich."

"Can you lose your prerogatives as people's judges?"

"As soon as we commit the slightest offense, for which we are found guilty, we lose the 'public trust,' and lose our right to adminsiter justice. Anyone serving in a People's Court must have an impeccable integrity."

"Was any of you a candidate to People's Power?"

"Three of us were candidates."

"And?"

"We lost."

"Why?"

"Well, the public itself realizes that two functions in the same person may conflict, that both need to be reconciled, and that this implies greater sacrifice. Then, as the election is carried out in the same district, in other words where the person is best known, the majority says: 'Damn it, if I vote for so-and-so, and he's elected, it's going to burden him even further in his present occupation." This I can tell you because I've overheard such comments as 'I'd vote for so-and-so, but, just imagine, he already has this, he has that, etc. . . .' It also happens sometimes that the other candidates are better known, their performance is better known than ours."

"And how was the election campaign carried out here?"

"There was no election campaign here. Here everything is done by meetings. And the people nominate the candidates there. The only thing we do here is get a picture and attach a biographical account to it. The

---

*As of 1979 the law regulating the judicial system stipulates that one of the judges must be a professional.

posters were placed in the stores. . . . We don't think of running an election campaign here as we did before."

"Are any of you Party members?"

Two persons raised their hands.

"How did you become Party members?"

"Well, I was elected as a model worker at my work place. The meeting is democratic. There anyone can put forward his own motions. . . . If I nominate Olivares, for example, I've got to explain why I am nominating him, and we see how others react. . . . Maybe if they know something that goes against Olivares, they may stand up and say: 'Well, look, I understand Olivares is not qualified because of this, that and so on . . .' "

"Becoming a Party member seems difficult."

"It's not easy. . . ."

"And you, as judges, if a Party member makes a mistake, shows a weakness, do you treat him differently from the rest?"

"No, no, no. If a member commits a crime, he's treated exactly like the others, because he fell into an error he should have avoided. Being a Party member is no advantage whatsoever."

The judge in the white suit interrupts him: "I'd say the only advantage we have as Party members is that we are the first in the need to go forward, and of making everything go forward. That's the only advantage, yes . . . that we must always be in the vanguard."

It was Fidel who, during the early years of the Revolution, while visiting Havana University Law School, proposed to the students the necessity of turning over to the masses the search for new ways of administering justice. So experiments and research began to be organized around the best way to handle small offenses commonly observed in the neighborhoods: family quarrels, drunkenness, disputes among neighbors.

After a period of experimentation, the Ministry of Justice decided in 1968 to set up this type of People's Court throughout the nation. Existing in all municipalites, sometimes more than one per city hall, they had jurisdiction to try offenses with maximum sentences of less than thirty days. In very unusual cases they could reach up to six months. As penalties, they used court admonishments, fines, and detention.

The Revolutionary Courts

The Revolutionary Courts were another phenomenon born in the heat of the struggle itself. They emerged during the revolutionary struggle.

They were created in the combat zones. Their chief mission was to punish traitors, deserters, and individuals who committed different types of crimes in specified areas. They were military tribunals. In their operation they relied on a procedural law worked out by the *mambises*, that is, by the liberation army in the war against Spain. This law, called the "Penal Law of Cuba at War" was so well designed that it could be put to use by the revolutionaries fifty years later.

The courts were made up of three officers of the Armed Forces, not necessarily jurists, and a prosecuting attorney. The defendants could utilize civilian lawyers or anyone they chose. Any death penalty pronounced by the court had to be reviewed by a higher court.

When the Revolution triumphed, these courts spread across the country. Their duty was to bring to justice all war criminals and collaborators with tyranny. They discharged their function admirably until their suspension in mid-1959, when the main war criminals were thought to have been dealt with. Pending cases were taken up by the ordinary courts.

However, as only a few months after their discontinuation pirate planes attacked Havana, leaving behind dead and wounded, while acts of sabotage increased throughout the country, the revolutionary leadership was compelled to reintroduce them, but now they had a new function: the trying of counterrevolutionary crimes, that is, the offenses committed against revolutionary authority.

The courts were kept busy, especially with the counterrevolutionaries holed up in the Escambray, true bandit organizations that managed to operate in that area till 1965, and with the Bay of Pigs mercenaries.

Over the years new powers were conferred on these courts. It was necessary that they hear crimes which, though frequent, had to be tried by these tribunals because of their seriousness.

A New Judicial System

"It is not reality that must adapt itself to institutions, but institutions that must adapt themselves to reality." These words by Fidel Castro inspired the reorganization of the judicial system now being tried in Cuba.

Since August, 1977, when the law regulating the judiciary was enacted, the country has enjoyed a unique system that blends the prerevolutionary courts with those that sprang up in the revolutionary process. This system is based on a People's Supreme Court made up of five divisions. The first two divisions—penal and civil-administrative—existed in the preceding system. The three additions comprise a court to hear crimes against national security, a tribunal for labor offenses, and a military court.

The provincial People's Courts have the first four divisions, while the municipal courts have no special divisions and are empowered to try civil, penal, and labor offenses.

All these courts are collegial bodies. It is not a single judge, but a group of judges that passes judgment. Both professionals and nonprofessionals may be found among the judges, the latter frequently being ordinary workers with no particular expertise in judicial matters.

Judges sitting in the provincial and municipal courts are elected by their respective People's Power assemblies on the recommendation of the Ministry of Justice. They are held accountable to the people; that is, every so often they are expected to explain their performance to the electorate. And they may be recalled at any time by those who elected them to that office. On the other hand, there is always a higher court empowered to hear appeals.

The Revolution reserves a place of distinction for its lay judges, for they enhance the judicial process through their experience as ordinary workers and citizens.

Professional judges are elected to serve for five years, but lay judge remain in office for only two-and-a-half years. The latter discharge their duties two months a year in nonconsecutive periods, while being paid the salary they would earn at their regular jobs.

Lastly, there is the Republic's Attorney General whose basic task it is to watch over the observance of socialist legality, making sure that all state agencies and citizens comply with the laws and other orders stemming from revolutionary authority.

More than three million Cubans participated in discussions of drafts of the law revamping the judicial system and of other bills of popular interest.

Thanks to this system these matters received ample attention everywhere, and valuable suggestions were collected from the basic institutions, a procedure that helped to perfect the bills.

The Work Councils

"A few months ago, as we talked with a group of compañeros at one of the sugar complexes in Camaguey, we were informed of a tremendous lack of discipline there. Someone mentioned that severe measures had been taken against a chronic absentee and loafer and that, later, this fellow had been stirring up trouble among the masses, claiming that an injustice had been done him. We were assured by Party comrades that the measure was just, because that fellow was a real goldbrick. I asked them: 'How did you arrive at this step?' They replied: 'The chief of personnel called him up and laid it on him. After that a real sense of disgust pervaded the ranks of the workers, and many started turning to absenteeism also.' I explained to them: 'If the head of personnel summoned the worker and arranged punishment bureaucratically without meeting with the workers or calling the work council together, the punishment did not serve its educational purpose and the man was free to go about his scheming.

"But if, instead of proceeding in this manner, he had assembled the workers, and explained to them the work rules and the fight we are waging against absenteeism, the measure would have been the product of the masses. It would have been turned into an educational force, and that man would have been unable to sow dissension or create unrest. The moral is this: Any disciplinary measure not handed out by the workers themselves, under current social conditions, cannot be made to work. The old order functioned on the basis of terror and its power arrangements. But in a free society, the administrative functionary who prescribes such a measure is simply ignored, because there the people are free and the militia can't come to arrest them.

"In conclusion: the measures of labor justice or labor discipline must be taken by the workers themselves, and they must possess a high degree of political consciousness. And this cannot be developed if political activity has not been carried out previously among the workers. At places where there is a lack of discipline, in the absence of prior political action to raise the consciousness of the masses, it would be absurd and impolitic to impose such measures. First we must create the consciousness, teach the rules of the game, and then let the masses decide on the by-laws and sanctions."

These words, by Armando Hart, are from his speech introducing Party members to the Faculty of Humanities and Philosophy of Havana University on August 2, 1969.

But what are these work councils that Hart mentions in his speech? And how do they operate?

The work councils are agencies designed to dispense labor justice in the factories, and assist in the formation of socialist morality. They operate in the factories and deal with labor offenses and violations such as infractions of the labor code, tardiness, stopping work before the shift is ended, disrespect, abuse by word or deed, damage to factory property, negligence, disobedience to orders, and so on. The possible penalties range from admonishment before the workers meeting, disqualification from filling a specific post, and the loss of work privileges.

These agencies of labor justice came into being in 1964 and are manned by the workers themselves. There are five members—a president, a vice-president, and three associates. A quorum for a hearing consists of three people, and a complaint pressed by a fellow worker or by the management is a necessary precondition for a hearing. As a rule, there is one work council in every enterprise having more than twenty-five workers. But in larger industries it is expected that a council will be available in each department at every shift. In factories with fewer than twenty-five workers, a delegate is appointed to be an associate of the nearest work council, or with one showing the closest affinity with the kind of work being performed at the plant in question. When a case belonging to the smaller plant is tried, the delegate sits with the tribunal, replacing one of the regular judges.

The judges are chosen by direct vote among the workers. The candidates are proposed at a meeting. Their qualifications are evaluated there—the quality of their work, their record of work attendance, whether they have ever been penalized before, and so on. They must have at least a sixth-grade education. At least twice as many candidates as vacancies must be nominated, in this case, ten. With the selection of candidates complete, the electoral process takes over. The workers are instructed to vote for only five names on the ticket, and asked to place two crosses by the name of the person they feel should be president of the council, so that this position can also be filled directly. The electoral process is directed by a committee chosen by the meeting itself.

The preceding facts came up in the course of a conversation with three young attorneys affiliated with the Labor Ministry of Matanzas. Ricardo, the regional officer for the agencies of labor justice in the province, is a mulatto totally devoted to his duties. "How could it be otherwise," he says to us, "when I got a taste of the way things were before the Revolution, when the worker was at the mercy of the capitalist and his lieutenants at the factory, being compelled to submit and grovel before the threat of dismissal and hunger."

"Can you nominate someone on the management side of the enterprise to be a labor judge?"

"No. The members of the labor council can be neither management nor labor officials. They have to be workers pure and simple."

"But management can veto a candidate?"

"As a part of the meeting, yes, just as the Party leaders and the union officers can explain why they think a given companero has the required qualifications. Nevertheless, the meeting has the final say about this."

"That means it can support someone's candidacy against the wishes of the leaders?"

"It can, if the majority understands this particular worker deserves to be a candidate, if the majority feels management is wrong."

"And how long does the work council's tenure last?"

"The term is for three years but the members can be recalled if the masses so decide."

"Are the chosen companeros given any particular training?"

"Of course. The Labor Ministry sets up a series of instruction programs, especially for the work council presidents. They take a course that lasts around thirty days, as interns and quasi-interns, where they receive instruction on the subjects and methods pertaining to labor justice."

"Could you explain to us the actual operation of one of these councils?"

"If a worker shows repeated unwarranted absences, for example, and management demands a sanction or disciplinary measure, the work council receives the complaint and starts the process. It then summons both parties—the worker and management—at a given day and hour, outside working hours. They try not to interfere with production. Once the summonses are served, the case is publicized, since the hearings are open to the public. Any worker wishing to attend may do so. Moreover, the union leaders are invited. Sometimes a great number of workers show up, sometimes less."

"And who defends the accused?"

"Himself."

"And do the workers take part in the proceedings?"

"Yes. When the hearing date is set, it is stipulated that both the worker and management must appear before the bench with any evidence germane to the question at hand. At that point, for instance, the worker can produce a medical certificate he had failed to file on time with management. He can also produce a witness who saw, for example, that he had a son gravely ill, this being the reason he was unable to either show up or advise management . . . ."

"And can management apply sanctions that bypass the work council?"

"Yes, it can, as long as it doesn't involve final termination or moral sanctions. Furthermore, if the worker does not agree with the punish-

ment imposed, he has ten days to appeal the verdict to the local municipal court."

"Can a member of the management be tried by a work council?"

"No, in these cases each institution has its own system."

"What happens if a member of the work council commits one of the
offenses discussed here?"

"The work council of which he is a member brings him to justice,
except that, under the circumstances, he's obviously not going to sit on
the bench."

Reflecting upon what we have seen, there is little doubt that a new
revolutionary judicial system has been born in Cuba.

3 ALL OF CUBA A PARLIAMENT

Toward the Institutionalization of People's Laws

"Ah, Brother! Each of the words in this bill is blood of our blood. . ."

Sixteen years ago, Arturo Menéndez could not swim at the more beautiful Cuban beaches. So he had to frequent the Havana Malecon. He could not enter tourist hotels and restaurants, and a whole series of occupations was forbidden to him. Arturo Menéndez is black, like thousands of Cubans. Today he is a vangaurd worker at the "Giron" bus factory.

One day, on May 28, 1975, he was acting as reader of the draft Constitution before his CDR. His voice almost broke when he came upon the following:

"Chapter V. Equality. Article 40. All citizens enjoy equal rights and are subject to equal duties. Article 41. Discrimination on account of race, color, sex, or national origin is forbidden and punishable by law. The State institutions educate all, from the earliet possible age, in the principle of equality among human begins."

There was no discussion. The right to equality, won with the blood of more than twenty thousand Cubans fallen during the insurrectionary period and the revolutionary war, was approved unanimously by the CDR where Arturo Menéndez is a member. The right existed formally for many years, but only now is it being honored in practice exactly as it was codified in the draft of the first socialist Constitution of Cuba.

During the months of May and June, 1975, no fewer than six million Cubans discussed and approved, in more than 168 thousand assemblies, the draft of the socialist Constitution, the supreme law incorporating all the economic, social and political victories of the Revolution.

From January 1, 1959, when the guns fell temporarily silent—their bursts were soon to be heard again in the battle against bandits and mercenaries—no siginificant decision has been arrived at in Cuba without prior knowledge, discussion, and approval of the people affected. Since the old Capitol closed its doors on the former congressmen, all of Cuba is a parliament, and every Cuban a legislator.

Popular participation in decision-making takes many forms, issuing naturally from the dynamics of a new creative process. The Cuban people supported, weapons in hand, the Revolution's declaration of its socialist character, in April, 1961. In similar fashion it approved the First and Second Declarations of Havana. On every corner of the island there is a Cuban who has something to say, and who is saying it.

Nevertheless, the process of institutionalizing the Revolution begins in Cuba after 1970, accelerating after 1972. With the economic base consolidated, with the mass organizations and the Cuban Communist Party on a good footing, with the economy on the road to rapid development, with the existence of the new Council of Ministers, and the creation of its executive committee, the representative institutions of the state could now be created.

It was then that the people, the revolutionary government, and the Party began to work out a series of legal instruments which might regulate the essential aspects bearing upon the stabilization of state institutions.

Of late, huge strides have been made in this regard. To name a few, a law was recently enacted organizing the judicial system to accord with the development of Cuban society.

In 1974 a Family Code was discussed and approved, a complex of juridical norms that got rid of forever the old residue of bourgeois laws affecting the family and regulated the rights of children, the equality of women, and similar precepts.

The code was prepared by a special commission, technically qualified, juridically wise, and possessed of great integrity. It might have been supposed that under these conditions the new body of law could have gone into operation immediately. But it did not. Inasmuch as the new code concerned each and every inhabitant of Cuba, it was taken down to the grassroots and discussed by the mass and political organizations, principally by the CDRs, the organization which groups all families block by block across the nation. Their suggesions were collected and incorporated into the enacted text.

The draft of the socialist Constitution was discussed in a similar manner.

By emphasizing that no one has been kept from participating in the fundamental questions of the Revolution, it may be affirmed that at the present time the Cuban people participate more than ever in the adoption of decisions and the development of legislation.

But now the people's legislative role has also been institutionalized.

A law is drafted, as a bill, by a special commission. Such a commission is generally composed of members of the Commission for Juridicial Studies of the Party's Central Committee and of government officials and representatives of the mass organizations.

After that, the bill is analyzed, discussed, marked up, and approved by the PCC's top leadership: the Political Bureau and the Secretariat of the Central Committee. Next it goes down the line for discussion at different levels of Party and mass organiztaions. Finally it is discussed by the rank and file.

When the bill finally returns to the commission charged with drafting it, it has been enormously enriched with proposals and additions. Each sector of the people has legislated according to its specific interests.

In this manner, the indispensable precedents for tackling the writing of a new constitution—the socialist Constitution of Cuba—were established.

Background of the Bill

Until 1975, the Fundamental Law of 1959, an updated revolutionary version of the 1940 Constitution,* was still in effect. When the Revolution triumphed, it abrogated the so-called constitutional statutes of the Batista tyranny, substituting in their place the above-mentioned Constitution of 1940, with the revisions needed to reflect the shift in favor of revolutionary authority.

*Cuba, as a republic, had six earlier constitutions: the Constitution of Guaimaro (1869), the Constitution of Baragua (1879), the Constitution of Jimaguayu (1895), the Constitution of La Yaya (1897), the Constituion of 1901, and the Constitution of 1940.

When the CDR national leadership made public, on July 8, 1975, the results of the popular deabte on the bill. Blas Roca, president of the Commission of Juridical Studies of the Party's Central Committee, member of its Secretariat, and president of the Constitutional Commission in charge of the new fundamental law, addressed himself to the present Constitution, and pointed out the necessity for a new one.

"We have," he said, "a Constitution that is the Fundamental Law; it is a fundamental law that made good use of everything that is progressive in the 1940 Constitution. In the speech given by Fidel from the hospital, during his trial for the assault on the Moncada Barracks, he said we would reestablish the Constitution until the people might decide to modify it.

"Some articles of the 1940 Constitution could not be kept. They supported the idea of a Senate, of a Chamber of Deputies, accomplices to tyranny who were later left 'legally unemployed.' The Revolution had to create new institutions to substitute for them."

Next Blas Roca explained the need for a new fundamental law: "The present Constitution, despite all the features that were regarded as progressive for its time, has been made obsolete, as Fidel once remarked, for it answers to bourgeois concepts, and this is the reason we need a new Constitution, one that reflects the socialist society we have built."

The Constitutional Commission of Party and government, composed of twenty members headed by Blas Roca, was created on October 2, 1974, by decision of the Party's Politburo and the executive committee of the Council of Ministers, even though Fidel had stressed four years earlier the necessity of undertaking the project. Its mission: to write, along the principles stipulated by these two institutions, a draft of a new fundamental law of the Republic. On the Commission there were, besides the jurists, representatives of the country's principal mass organizations.

The Commission, which worked with great dedication, went about its business in a totally informal way, putting an impressive amount of effort into the assignment. It showed little patience with formalities and bombast, concentrating on substance. The draft, which had to be ready by February 24, 1975, was finished several days before the deadline.

On February 24—on the day commemorating the eightieth anniversary of the Revolutionary War initiated by José Martí—the First Secretary of the Party and Prime Minister of the Revolutionary Government, Commander-in-Chief Fidel Castro, received the draft constitution from the Commission.

Levels of Debate

On this occasion, Blas Roca asserted that the draft was "a good departure point for the discussion and refinement process to follow, first by the top Party leadership and government, later by the entire people, and ultimately by the Party Congress, from which the definitive text deserving of approval as a socialist Constitution would issue, to be ratified by all citizens through free, direct, and secret ballot."

Fidel, for his part, declared: "Our people will be proud when this Constitution is debated. The Revolution will take a giant historical step toward its institutionalization, toward the termination of the provisional character which still attaches to the revolutionary government."

The Party, as a leading institution of the Revolution through its Politburo and Secretariat, came first in the discussion and modification of the bill.

At a session of the twenty members of the Commission, it was remarked that "almost every article of this draft reflects the hand and thought of Fidel. . . .It was he who introduced the greater number of modifications and clarifications . . .Practically a third of the modifications were introduced as a result of Comrade Fidel's initiatives. . . ."

Forty-five days later, on April 10, on the one hundred sixth anniversary of the Constitutional Assembly of Guaimaro—first fundamental law of the budding Cuban Revolution—the draft was taken to the public, thus opening the way for a full public debate.

On April 23, the daily *Granma*, the official organ of the Central Committee of the Cuban Communist Party, called upon all mass organizations to initiate a process of active discussion in the assemblies and meetings scheduled by them after the twenty-eighth.

The president of the Constitutional Commission had indicated a few days earlier the leadership's intention of turning the draft over to the masses for a general debate: "We believe that at the end of the discussion," he said, "this document will have been significantly improved by the proposals issuing from the masses, and will receive its definitive character at the Party Congress, which will then turn it into a proposition to be submitted later to a referendum of the whole people."

Thus, the draft constitution—a preamble, twelve chapters, and 141 articles dealing with the political, social, and economic foundations of the state, citizenship, family, education, culture, equality, rights, duties, and fundamental guarantees, local agencies of People's Power, tribunals and prosecutors' offices, the electoral system and, lastly, procedures for its own amendment—was discussed first by members of the Party and Communist Youth, and after that by various mass organizations: the Confederation of Cuban Workers (CTC) and its twenty three national unions, the National Association of Small Farmers (ANAP), the Federation of Cuban Women (FMC), and the Committees for the Defense of the Revolution (CDR), the Federation of High School Students (FEEM), and the Federation of University Students (FEU).*

The document was also given—a peculiar trait of the Cuban Revolution— to the different military institutes of the revolutionary Armed Forces (FAR). In addition, the opinion of state leaders and functionaries was sought, with emphasis on those whose activites related to legal or political questions.

On that same April 23, *Granma* advised: "Excellence must be the keynote of the process. To this end it is necessary to observe the calendar of meetings and the celebration of meetings and preparatory seminars, but it must be borne in mind that the role of moderators is solely that of clarifiers of concepts and doubts and *that on no account are they to influence with their judgment the masses, who ought to decide freely what they consider most suitable in every case.*"

Finally, the PCC paper explained that, upon completion of the discussion by the rank and file, "and after collecting the opinions and suggestions of the masses, to be channeled through their national leaderships,

---

*On July 16, 1975, the Commission on Verification and Internal Organization of the Party's First Congress released the official figures for the process, characterized by both its bulk and analytic spirit and by the seriousness with which it was undertaken. From the tabulation we can deduce that:

(a) The Cuban leadership of the Communist Party (PCC) took the matter up at 19,471 meetings attended by 159,853 members.

(b) The Confederation of Cuban Workers (CTC) ran 42,312 meetings throughout the country, with the particiaption of 1,619,675 workers.

(c) The National Associaion of Small Farmers (ANAP) organized 6,157 meetings, with a total audience of 210,499 small farmers.

(d) The Commitees to Defend the Revolution (CDR) mounted 70,812 discussion meetings, with an attendance of 2,064.755 *cederistas*, having a prominent feminine presence.

(e) The Federation of Cuban Women (FMC) conducted 47,958 meetings attended by 1,568.036 members.

(f) No fewer than 361,314 high school students analyzed the project (FEEM), while 20,517 university students also debated the subject in 1,125 meetings organized by the Federation of University Students (FEU).

the Preparatory Commission of the First Congress will make the corresponding modifications before submitting them to the Party. After that the people will again participate, either accepting or rejecting the Constitution by a referendum based on universal, secret, and direct suffrage."

Thus, for almost two months, the draft of the socialist Constitution circulated everywhere: among workers and peasants, block after block in the cities, and penetrating the factories, sugar cane mills, peasant camps, universities, schools, institutions, and military units.

Workshops, meeting halls, workers' social centers, and even the streets and sidewalks—where the CDRs usually congregate—replaced the posh benches of the former parliament, today converted into the Cuban Academy of Sciences.

Lawmaking by the People

A CDR located in the heart of El Vedado, the old, upper-class district of Havana. At the dais the president and the ideological secretary of the CDR, who records the proposals. Between the two, a young *cederista*,* charged with reading, aloud and clearly, the first six chapters of the draft. Pictures of Fidel, Martí, Che Guevara, Camilo Cienfuegos, printed on huge posters, seem to participate in the assembly meeting with the fifty-odd neighbors of the district. It is May 28, 1975.

The reading of Chapter I, concerning the "political, social, and economic foundations of the State," has ended. Hands are raised asking for recognition by the chair.

A worker from the back of the room: "I propose that we give Cuba the official name of Socialist Republic. This was proposed by a tobacco worker from the 'Corona' factory, but I'd like to add something. Although we always speak of a republic, we're really referring to a banana republic. Because, in fact, we never had a true republic in the past. We went from one form of colonial status to another. Indeed, it is only now that we possess a true republic . . .but it is a socialist republic. Accordingly, the text of the Constitution must make it clear that it is a socialist republic."

"The comrade's proposal may be valid, but we have to bear in mind that Article 1 fully explains the socialist character of the new republic." The voice coming from one side of the room belongs to a teacher living in the neighborhood. "There it is clearly stated," he continues, "that 'the Republic of Cuba is a Socialist State of workers and peasants, and other manual and intellectual workers.' Look closely . . .'socialist state.

*That is, a member of a CDR.

. . .' Besides, there's something else. Changing the name would involve a series of costly changes. We might have to modify all kinds of existing documents in the country, birth certificates, the currency, even treaties signed with other nations, I raise this point so as we can consider the difficulties such a change in name might entail."

The debate has begun.

"I don't agree with the compañero," a worker says. "We are no longer just a republic, so I think the name should correspond to the reality. I understand that some day we'll have to call ourselves by our true name and, as a result, we'll have to modify our coins, fix our documents, etc. . . .I believe that now that we are going to approve the fundamental law of socialist Cuba, the name that should govern our republic is Socialist Republic of Cuba . . .and let's not drag our feet on this because we'll have to do it some day anyway."

"Compañero president, may I?"

The interruption comes from an elderly compañero dressed in olive green.

"Of course, go right ahead."

"Thanks. Look, compañeros, we don't have here any traces of capitalism in our midst anymore, apart from a few memories. Everything here is already socialized; everything is already in the hands of the state. And here we have only one party, the party of the workers. So we are in a special position. What are we anyway, since Fidel said on April 16, 1961, that we were socialists? What are we, then? When even our children's songs proclaim it! We are socialists! This is the first socialist Constitution in America. And in memory of our ancestors, as the preamble says, we must acknowledge a change in name for the first time in one hundred years of struggles."

"Look, compañero, I'll repeat it to you from the text," the teacher remarks, and reads from the bill. " 'The Republic of Cuba is a Socialist State of workers and peasants and all other manual and intellectual workers.' Do you really need more than what is already said in Article 1? In our opinion, the change in name is irrelevant. And remember that this was already submitted to the scrutiny of the Politburo where there are men who have studied these problems in depth . . . .This surely didn't escape them."

"But what are you saying, man?" says the worker, feigning surprise. "I also know that even Comrade Blas Roca, who is presiding over the Preparatory Commission, has said something about the name . . .but, let's get this straight, let's put it straight . . .we are here to discuss and introduce our proposals, and one can disagree even with Comrade Blas Roca."

"Yes, compañero, I'm in agreement with that," a young woman says aggressively. "The objection raised by the compañero is unacceptable."

"O.K., O.K., compañeros, it's all right," the teacher says defensively, "but I also believe that socialism is a transient situation, a sociopolitical state of the Republic on the road to communism. We are going to cause an enormous expense by dint of a simple change of name and on account of something transitory. My opinion is that our country should be called Republic of Cuba for a long time."

"How come the USSR puts it in its name—Union of Soviet Socialist Republics," the worker who began the argument asks.

The teacher, showing off his knowledge of the Russian Revolution: "Well, what the compañero says is interesting, but it isn't any the less true that they started their revolution with that name. From the very beginning, from the first decrees concerning the land, everything carried the word 'socialist.'" They didn't have to make costly alterations as we might have to do here."

"But just imagine, compañero," the same worker says undaunted, "that someone said later that we'd have to make the changes some day anyhow. So why not now?"

The discussion is winding down. The room is alive with the din of multiple conversations. Many hands gesticulate, animating the expressed opinions. Here and there voices are raised, but no one else asks for the floor. The president ends debate and asks for a vote on the question.

More than forty arms are raised when he calls for those who agree with the name change. Fewer than ten vote against. As usual, there are no abstentions. Everyone has an opinion.

*****

The 10th of October region is one of the most populous in the Cuban capital. At the CDR No. 26 "Josué País" they have just finished reading the first six chapters of the draft constitution. This time the people have packed the small premises, and the neighbors from the block are spilling over onto the sidewalk. Without a doubt, attendance by women is better, for the debate began early, and the men have not yet finished returning from work.

"Anyone have anything else to propose on this chapter?" the CDR president asks.

"Just an opinion, since everything is so clear," someone says. "It's to support the provision allowing freedom of belief. No one here is prevented from believing, but if they should utilize religion to undermine the principles of the motherland—well, the state should not allow that. Just imagine! We can believe in anything we want, religiously, as we say ordinarily. But the state, as the people's state, should also reserve to itself the right to move against those who'd use religion against the rights of the people."

"Are we all in agreement?" the president inquires.

"Yes!" is the reply from many voices, while some people nod in assent.

Earlier, a construction worker, a member of a microbrigade from East Havana, had read the relevant article: "Article 54. The Socialist State, which bases its activity and educates the people in the scientific materialist concept of the Universe, recognizes and guarantees freedom of conscience and the right of everyone to profess any religious belief, and to practice, within the framework of respect for the law, the creed of his preference. The law regulates the activities of religious institutions. It is illegal and punishable by law to oppose one's faith or religious belief to the Revolution; to education; or to the fulfillment of one's duty to work, defend the homeland with arms, show reverence for its symbols, and fulfill other duties stipulated by the Constitution."

Still earlier, a young girl wearing the uniform of the Revolutionary Armed Forces (FAR), had read Article 44, concerning work in a socialist society. This had sparked an interesting discussion.

The article in question reads: 'Work in a socialist society is a right, a duty, and a source of pride for every citizen. Work is remunerated according to its quality and quantity; in supplying it, attention is paid to the needs of the economy and the society, the worker's preferences, as well as his aptitude and qualifications; it is guaranteed by the socialist economic system, which facilitates the social and economic development, without crises, and which has wiped out unemployment and erased for good the seasonal slowdown called the 'dead season.' Every citizen is obligated to fulfill conscientiously the tasks belonging to his job."

When the reading has finished, a very tall black worker speaks out. He towers over a group of women clustered at the back of the room. "I've got something to propose here. We know that in order to receive the benefits outlined by the law we must work, but there is no article in there addressing the question of penalties against people who do not work, who live as parasites."

A redheaded woman who is holding a copy of the draft in her hands interrupts him.

"There is a law against vagrancy. Besides, Chapter VI, Article 1, says that work in a socialist society is 'a right, duty, and a source of pride for every citizen. . . . ' "

"All right, but since they set up sanctions, for example, against those who might use religion against the state, why not set up sanctions against those who do not work?" the black worker demands.

"True,' the girl says. "Come to think of it, this article doesn't mention anywhere that the person who doesn't work will be punished. As that law already exists, it would be a question of adding it so the person who will not work will be punished in accordance with the vagrancy laws."

"It should be made clear that the sanctions should only apply to those fit and able to work but who neither work nor study,' a voice proclaims from the back of the room.

"Of course, pal. For those who are fit and able," the black worker asserts.

"The socialist law stipulates that he who doesn't work doesn't eat," a young militiaman adds. "Everyone must either work or study. If not, sanctions!"

"Yes, but a clarification is in order, compañero, the girl insists, "because the law punishes the male who doesn't work and exempts the female."

"Then both should be punished, for if women claim the same rights as men, they should be held liable for the same penalties," an elderly worker says vehemently.

"Hold it, compañeros," the redhead says. We still don't have all the conditions allowing a woman to work. Steps are being taken in that direction, though. I think sanctions should not be proposed against women who don't work . . . ."

The black worker, somewhat peeved at being drawn into such an argument: "Well, I'd like to explain that when I made the proposal I wasn't thinking of women. That was something raised by Jaime. I agree, too, that conditions are not yet ripe. . . . What happens is that we're seeing the damage caused by those who live without working. Maybe they are only a few . . . but we have them. Just today, around two o'clock, there was this fat cat, big, strong, and well dressed, trying to steal something from a warehouse!"

A burst of laughter greets the report.

"Look, Ricardo, it says here that work is both a right and a duty. I think your concern is well taken care of," the redhead says.

"Yes, but I'm talking about sanctions," the black worker retorts.

" If we propose that the law punish those who do not work, we should have to make an exception for women, as our country still lacks the ojective conditions which might permit all women to work," explains the girl. "And we can't write into a general law, like the Constitution, a particular question such as the one under discussion. Then, it will seem we have a problem."

"How right you are! In effect, if the objective conditions are lacking, the law can't get involved in this mess. . . .it has to lay down general provisions, and if the proposal raises that problem with women—then down with my proposal!" the black worker exclaims with feeling.

A round of laughter approves the compañero's decision.

When, in July, of 1975, the Commission on Verification and Internal Organization of the First Party Congress concluded the tabulation it discovered that of the proposals advanced by the masses in the almost 170 thousand assemblies held throughout the nation the inevitable topics were changing the name of the republic, the inclusion of an article specifying Spanish as the only official language, and another establishing the peso as the only official Cuban currency, even though, across the country, other amendments were made that reached both into the preamble and the twelve chapters comprising the Constitution.

As long as the popular debate lasted, the communications media guided the discussion methodologically, always under the explicit condition that they exert no influence over the decision adopted by the masses. In an attempt to supply historical and informational materials, the press instituted special question-and-answer sections, while television carried special interviews with members of the Preparatory Commission. The magazines did likewise. Radio stations broadcast daily commentaries by Blas Roca.

The two chambers of the Capitol in Havana would have been unable to accommodate the more than four million legislators hailing from all over Cuba.

4 BLOCK BY BLOCK

Collective Vigilance in the Face of Counterrevolution

"We're going to set up a system of collective vigilance. We're going to set up a system of revolutionary vigilance. And we are going to see whether the lackeys of imperialism can get away with their business as usual, for, ultimately, we live all over the city, and there is not an apartment house, not a block, not a district, not a neighborhood, without ample representation here. We are going to inaugurate, in the face of imperialist campaigns of aggression, a system of collective vigilance in which everyone will know who everyone else is and what his business is in the neighborhood; and what relations he had with the tyranny; and his occupation; and who he hangs out with; and what he is up to. Because if they think they can handle the people, take on the people . . .what a fisaco are they in for! For we have set up a vigilance committee on each block . . .so the people can keep vigil, so the people can be on the alert, and so they can see that when the mass of the people gets organized, there can be no imperialist, no lackeys of imperialism, no sellouts to imperialism, no instrument of imperialism allowed to move freely in our midst."

Fidel Castro pronounced these words on Septemebr 28, 1960. At that time the maneuvers of imperialism to block the revolutionary process were becoming increasingly clear, while its efforts to foster counterrevolution were reaching a feverish tempo. Acts of sabotage and terrorism were occurring everywhere.

"We didn't know where the stones and truncheons were coming from, the whole paraphernalia utilized against the comrades who at that point went into the streets to defend our Revolution," says Ildelina, secretary for the CDR "Miguel Fernández Roig," of Havana.

From that moment on—even though the people had spontaneously created vigilance committees already—the Committees to Defend the Revolution began to be organized all over the country.

From the time they began to sprout to their moment of truth seventy-eight feverish days went by: And on April 17, 1961, the day of the mercenary invasion at Playa Girón, the organization, the people's will, that force of which Fidel spoke, sprang into action.

"At the time of Girón," Ildelina continues "the CDRs 'checkmated' the counterrevolutionaries, the *gusanos*,* since we knew how to detect them on each block, in each house. We immobilized them all. That Fifth Column was stopped by us."

There were scarcely more than eight thousand of them on the entire island when the mercenary invasion came. Yet in a matter of hours they carried out the orders delivered by the commander-in-chief: to redouble vigilance.

By arresting the counterrevolutionaries in timely fashion, the people avoided not only the subversive activities and public disorders contemplated by the enemy within, but also uncovered huge caches of staple goods and foreign reserves stashed away by hoarders and speculators.

Work continued after that, and the organization grew and developed. Civilians and soldiers, workers and housewives, old folks and youth, helped to carry out tasks entrusted to the committees.

"Look," says Ana, the coordinator for District 13 of Havana**—the CDRs are an important tool of the Revolution. It is an organization where you can and do find members of other organizations; you can just as easily run across a member of the FAR as an *Anapista* [a member of ANAP], or a woman from the Federation [FMC], or a Party cadre. Look, all of that in three letters: CDR. Because here everyone is a *cederista*. Not everyone is a member, not everyone is in the federations, but all those willing to stand up for the Revolution are *cederistas*."

After the defeat of the mercenaries at Girón, the CDRs grew in number; by the end of 1961 a hundred thousand Committees with half a million members were keeping watch over the country.

Gusanos, literally "worms," connoting the lowest form of life.
**The District CDR groups ten to fifteen CDRs in a given neighborhood.

At that time, too, watchkeeping was instituted in towns and cities block by block. Every night, patrols of one or two *cederistas* would keep watch, in effect, over every inch of the island.

This type of vigilance lasted till 1969. Today, when the danger of counterrevolution has disappeared, only a block's strategic points are watched, but the state of preparedness continues, with the people easily mobilized to meet any imperialist threat.

In the beginning, the people's vigilance was not confined to their place of residence. Many public functions, demonstrations, shows, such as the cinema and the theater, as well as other activities, relied on *cederistas* to watch over discipline and order. Provocateurs were severely dealt with by the people themselves.

The Tasks Grow

Ildelina goes on to recall moments of intense activity: "There's no task assigned to the CDR by our Commander-in-Chief that the working people, unified block by block, won't implement. We began with revolutionary vigilance. It was the first task, the first assignment from Fidel. Next we were in charge of what came to be called the margarine card, and of various commodities, until ration books were introduced, and so on and so forth."

The commercial viability of capitalist Cuba was based to a large extent on imports from the United States. But in 1960 U.S. imperialism was already brandishing the club of economic blockade against the Revolution.

Edible fats—margarine and oil—controlled by Chicago consortiums, grew scarcer. Most grocery stores and warehouses, for their part, hoarded the goods with the criminal intent of profiteering, of speculating at the expense of the workers' needs.

Then the CDRs entered the picture. To regulate the distribution and sale of edible fats in an equitable way, the revolutionary government ordered a census: this task, "the margarine census," was carried out by the CDRs, thereby regularizing the sales of those products.

At about that time difficulties also began to arise in connection with other basic necessities. Hoarding became prevalent. The CDRs made up control cards and black boards to announce the articles in stock.

But for the regulation of staple goods a general plan was still necessary. Eventually, a plan was devised for ration cards to guarantee each household the necessary foodstuffs. The plan originated in Public Law 1015, enacted on March 12, 1962, which created the National Board for the

Distribution of Foodstuffs. The second decision of the organization entrusted to the CDRs the supervision of food distribution.

This however, was not the only activity the Cuban people began to control.

Massive inoculation campaigns, blood-donor programs, conservation of raw materials, social security, cultural and sports activities, and much more, became the everyday duties of the CDRs. There was practically nothing of consequence in the country in which the organization did not play a role.

"We are a region free of polio," Ildelina says. "Do you realize what this means? In twenty-four hours the people vaccinated all the children here. You already know that Committees, as mass organizations, are the ones that bear the burden of most revolutionary tasks. The Party depends on the CDRs, the Party directs them and it knows that, when it comes to mobilization, it has here the strength of the majority. Because here you find everyone—housewives, workers, Party members, ordinary citizens, people in general. It is a beautiful organization and we're proud to belong to it . . .and we do join . . .are in fact charter members, aware of our responsibility . . .of what we have done and what we have to do. . . ."

Among these innumerable tasks, Ana recalls one that brought so much satisfaction to her area: "Right here, one evening, around the time of the crisis of '62, in a few hours we formed"—addressing her companion— "how many, Edelmira? Eighty? Yes, eighty sanitary brigades. And they were set up with a smile, because no one in this country is afraid of death. Have you noticed how much a Cuban laughs? He's always laughing. That's what infuriates imperialism most. We never cry. We have no reason to cry. The time for tears is gone, and our martyrs have not died to be cried over. To the contrary. We're building. Day by day the people experience some pleasure, some victory. It wasn't like this before. There was much concern over being denied what we had earned with so much blood and sweat. We don't go into the streets anymore wondering who we have to fight. Time has settled these questions. We tied the hands of imperialism. It is there, very close, but tied down. We? Here on our island we work, we struggle, we see to it that every effort is made to put every possible man and woman into the work force to make our homeland great."

Edelmira, an elderly *cederista* who is responsible for health care, has listened attentively to her comrade's words. She adds: "I believe the government could not have accomplished the tasks it is attempting without the Committees. Because it can't muster the necessary manpower. We vaccinate people; pick up pregnant women so they can keep their monthly check-ups; we treat dystrophy sufferers, premature babies, home hygiene problems, gastroenteritis. We see to it that people receive medical attention on time, because the Revolution gave us that, free medical care for all. . . ."

Voluntary work, on the other hand, is one of the features of this organization. (More critical voluntary work mobilizations are carried out by the unions in the factories.) The CDRs earned their distinctive character, beginning in 1961, with the first mobilization of the masses for the *zafra*, the literacy campaigns, and the conservation of essential materials.

Today, every Sunday, hundreds and hundreds of *cederistas* beautify their streets, paint their houses, fix their gardens. Men, women, and children participate in these activities. But, when the Revolution needs them for other tasks, such as going into the countryside to harvest coffee or cut sugar cane, thousands respond.

"Look," Ana says, "the harvesting of tomatoes, coffee, potatoes, anything, always relies on the *cederistas*. We are summoned, and you have to be careful. Because all of a sudden you may have eighteen truckloads of people, with some being turned back because they don't need that many. Because it is the people, the entire people who goes out. So you have to be careful when the order is given, it is not one or two who show up, but hundreds. There's no highway big enough for all of us."

The Structure of the CDRs

"In our CDR we have a president who's in charge overall. He's elected by us, as are the heads of various sections. We have an organization secretary and other people in charge of various vigilance sections, ideological work, culture and education, mobilization and popular order, public health, savings and conservation, CDR-FAR liason, social work, and solidarity." The speaker is Alejandro, a member of Ildelina's committee.

The organizational structure corresponds to the territorial, political, and adminstrative divisions of the state and Party, even though it has two other, lower levels—the district and the block.

At these levels and at the national management level, there is a coordinator, an organizer, and the sections already described, plus a person in charge of social security and external affairs.

The four million *cederistas* in Cuba not only participate but act upon, analyze, and explain in all their complexity problems existing in each neighborhood. And it is from the elderly woman, the common worker, or the young man that the solutions often come.

An Honest Evaluation of Community Services

Every so often an entire neighborhood becomes convulsed with noisy meetings, carried out, as a rule, in the streets. There the performance of various community services is evaluated. These meetings are one of the most important activities the organized Cuban people engage in today. They are part of the new consumption and services section. Convened by the leaders of the respective neighborhoods, they are attended by the residents as well as by those responsible for each of the commercial units in the area.

Anything can be discussed. Cubans on such occasions display no inhibitions about pushing their complaints. But that is not all. They also show their ingenuity by offering solutions and participating in their implementation. From the problem of the mosquito plague to the proposal to set up a coffee shop in such and such a place, everything is open to discussion by the *cederistas*.

"I'd like to say that the sanitation people in charge of the polyclinic should come to fumigate as they did last year, house by house, because, to tell the truth, the mosquitoes are eating us alive . . . ."

So began the services meeting for District 8 of Lawton, a neighborhood on the outskirts of Havana. There, for two hours, more than thirty people discussed and analyzed their problems. The meeting was held at a corner storefront.

A stout woman has opened he meeting. As she explains the problem, the woman sitting next to her nods approvingly and remarks: "I was going to raise the same point."

"Look, compañero," a nurse standing in the wings responds, "I work at the polyclinic, and a fumigation campaign has already begun. The problem is that we don't have enough workers to fumigate house by house."

The people's concern is not difficult to understand. Every so often, owing to the humid climate and the tropical rainfall, a mosquito plague incubates in the ensuing puddles and swamps. This is a constant problem in Cuba, and the topic comes up regularly at almost every meeting.

"We know about our revolutionary government's preoccupation with sanitation, public health, and so on, and we are not onlookers but actors in these campaigns," says a black worker sitting in the front row. "But the compañero is right to press the point" he continues, "lest we go to sleep on our laurels and forget that cockroaches reproduce, that mosquitoes reproduce, and that the campaign must be pursued at all times. It should be one of our chief concerns, right?"

"It's all right to insist on this, but you shouldn't forget that the polyclinic has many activities. We have, for example, a campaign to kill sick and stray dogs. We are short of personnel, and we have to allocate it over several campaigns, not just one," the nurse replies.

"A cesspool is being created on this block. I personally have gone to the polyclinic, and no one came. The excrement is running through the house, and seven kids live there. I'd like to hear some compañero tell me where we can take this matter."

"We're ready to go all the way to the Central Committee if necessary!" says a voice from the back.

All these problems are recorded in the minutes, which are then sent on to higher administrative levels ultimately responsible for an answer.

"We will take due note of your complaint and make the proper inquiries," says the district leader who is presiding over the meeting. Then, addressing the people, he asks:

"Anyone wish to say anything else about the polyclinic?"

A murmuring is heard in the room, but no one speaks up. The leaders then announces that the problem of soft-drink distribution is next on the agenda.

A bit sheepishly, a young female worker says, "Last time I was left without my soft drink. You never know when they are going to distribute them."

The storekeeper says, "We were advised of the distribution too late. So comrades in charge of distribution are not to be blamed. But if the next time they fail to pick up on time, then it's their fault. There's another thing. The soft drink cartons must be left outside the store. There's no room inside, and if the bottles are stolen, it is the people who'll have to pay . . . ."

"I don't get it. If the bottles are stolen, why do the people have to pay for them?" a voice asks from a corner.

"I've got the solution," a white-haired matron says. "With a little bit of wire screening contributed by each of us, we could close off a section of the store's gate. It would have to be closely knit so no one could get his hands through the holes."

The neighbors show signs of approval, and the proposal is adopted. The ensuing ripple of discussion is interrupted by the leader: "Anyone have anything else to say about the store? This is the moment to speak up, because here we have the warehouse reps for the area, and they can answer our questions."

"I'd like to speak about a general concern—the problem of the beer and malt liquor," says a worker in the front row. "The households had a six-pack guaranteed them before. Now, with the policy of putting the beer on the market on a first-come, first-served basis, the supply suffices for only a few people, because if a family has thirty six-packs, and it wants to take another thirty, it can. We don't understand that. The availability of decontrolled goods should not turn into an abuse of the privilege. If I can take fifty and that leaves the rest of the people without beer, there isn't a fair distribution as there should be. There's a distribution based on privilege. The person who has the most bottles and gets there first can take it all. I think we should really look into this policy and see whether or not we're making a mistake."

A few months before, the revolutionary government began to decontrol some products previously sold only through ration books. Because of the blockade a system of rationing had to be imposed in order to insure equitable distribution of consumer goods. Today, the workers are beginning to have access to some of the products already decontrolled. However, the fact that sufficient quantities do not as yet exist to meet the increased demand causes the problems described here.

"The guideline is that they should be sold without restriction," the woman in charge of the store insists. "If a person wants to take thirty cases, he can. For my part, I have instructed my people to sell one six-pack to a person, so if we have thrity, we have enough for thirty people. But if a person insists on fifteen, the storekeeper has to give them to him, because the guideline is for 'unrestricted sales.' "

"That's what the people don't understand," the same compañero says heatedly. "That's the way it's been set up, but the people must be listened to or we're in trouble. There's a general clamor that the arrangement is wrong. So we must begin to reconsider the rule, because, you know, formerly, each household was guaranteed a pack of beer at regular intervals. Now that has been discontinued. But by putting the product on the market without restrictions, and not guaranteeing everyone a certain amount, what we get is a hoarding, and an authorized hoarding operation at that. And this makes for—you know what?—a black market for reselling and profiteering. What we're saying is that this rule has to be reconsidered."

A *cederista* standing at the other end of the room: "I support the compañero."

A ripple of approval runs through the room.

A pregnant woman, who has been talking softly with her friend sitting next to her, decides to intervene: "I'd like to say, with regard to the malt liquor and beer, that they're luxury items and charged accordingly. That's why it happens that beer arrives today and sometimes sits on the shelf for ten days unsold. It takes a special occasion, like someone throwing a party or something, to shell out fifteen pesos for a case."

"Look, we still don't understand," says the worker in the front row. "The people haven't raised the problem of price here, but the problem of distribution. Whether they put it on the market at a peso or five pesos, the problem is one of equal access to the product by everyone. Isn't that clear?

"What has happened is that an equitable distribution has been eliminated and replaced by another that is a colossal mistake. For years we had a fairer, more functional system, yet now, overnight, some bureaucrat has decided on this policy without consulting with the people. That isn't right."

Despite this forcible argument, there are persons who spring to the defense of the new system, such as the corner grocer: "I don't think the matter should be approached in that manner. Formerly we had only one distribution center between Thirteenth and B Streets. There was no other unit in the whole area. But at present we have one beer distributor on each block; we have pizza parlors, where we can take three or four bottles and get beer. What I mean is that distribution has changed completely. I think the compañeros higher up have improved things a lot. We have gained in quality. The problem is that the beer output isn't enough to satisfy the entire population. But the policy of selling it without restrictions comes from above and we should not change it . . . ."

"It isn't that we should change it," the compañero says.

The storekeeper recognizes, however, that the matter has a flaw that should be corrected. "I am the one who distributes the beer and malt liquor here." He continues, "It is true that soon after the decontrol people took five, seven, nine cases. But the last time it came, the price not being the same, most people took only two packs, and as long as it is delivered two or three time a week there isn't any problem. Many times there's beer till the following day, but with malt liquor it's different. As you know, every time a new product is decontrolled, there are long queues, but afterward, as time goes by, things return to normal."

"I don't doubt what the compañero says, but I think this is not going to be solved that way," the worker in the front row insists. "If it is a lack of money that keeps them from wiping out the stock, it means that when they have got the money, they may be in a position to hoard. What I'm talking about is the fact that we have to adjust the distribution guidelines."

The Cuban government has decided to gradually decontrol certain products, to the extent that the country can increase their availability. But the transfer of a product from the ration book to decontrol creates initial problems, which are very rapidly overcome when the public realizes that the products are going to remain on the market, without disappearing.

A young girl, still excited, as she got to the meeting only a few moments earlier: "What I have to say about the dry cleaner's didn't happen to me, because I don't send my clothes to the cleaner's. It happened to my sister with her husband's trousers. She took them for a clean-and-press job. They said they'd be ready in a few days. When she went to pick the trousers up, she saw they were dirtier than before. They were a real mess! They had pressed them but they hadn't cleaned them. I don't know if this ever happened to others, but this is a terrible service."

In Cuba, dry-cleaning establishments are also in the hands of the people. As happens with many services, the demand is greater than the existing capacity to satisfy all comers.

"Is that the No. 16 dry-cleaning shop?" a white-haired woman asks.

"No, not that one."

"Well, No. 16 is the same. I had the same experience with a pair of trousers. When I look them over, I see the marks of small change and everything. I mention it to the compañera, I show her the pants. She goes like this—she shrugs—turns her back on me and walks away. I'm not sending anything else there!"

"I took a clean pair of pants to be pressed and they returned them dirty," the pregnant woman says.

The comment provokes a round of laughter. The leader remarks to the secretary that the representatives of the cleaning establishment should be summoned to the next meeting. Once this subject has been dealt with, the meeting turns to the question of "frozens," as they are called in Cuba. (A "frozen" is a thick milk shake.)

"The machine there has these things," a worker in the front row says, referring to the spouts through which the machine dispenses ice cream. "Chocolate comes out through one, and something white through the other. In the middle there's another thing that gives chocolate combined with the white stuff: chocolate swirl"—that's the name given in Cuba to a mix of the two flavors—"and what I'm saying is that if I want to have only chocolate, why don't they just give me chocolate. Ah! No such luck! It's obligatory to have swirls. Why do we have to have swirls when we want plain chocolate?"

"I got in line the other day to have an ice cream. Then my turn came and no one would wait on me. I told the girl at the counter that I was going to lose my job. She paid no attention. So I had to leave without getting my ice cream," a girl says.

The secretary asks for more details: "What was the name of the person at the counter?"

"I don't know. It was Tuesday, at three o'clock."

The secretary makes a note to investigate the matter further. Then, when no more questions are heard about the "frozen," the meeting turns its attention to the problem of the butcher shop. They approve the fine job the unit is doing. Next is the garbage problem.

"The garbage collector gets as far as the corner of Concepcion Street, but he never sweeps it," a corpulent mulatto woman declares.

"It's our block," a compañero responds from the back of the room. "There's no need for garbage men. The *cederistas* can sweep it."

There is applause from the audience, but also some disapproving reactions.

"That's no solution! The gesture is appreciated but it's obvious that that isn't the solution!"

"We'd have to applaud, then, several other CDRs that also sweep the block."

A middle-aged compañero mischievously offers a few specifics: "The "Alfita" [Alfa Romeo, the first vehicles to reach Cuba from Europe after the Americans imposed an economic embargo] which picks up the garbage passes by our street, but it is as if it was on a grand tour, on a picnic, because it comes around but it doesn't sweep."

"From 10 October Street to Route 200, the sanitationmen, instead of dumping the trash into a can, dump it on the street. In the morning— and I walk by the spot every morning as I go to work—what one steps on is pure garbage. That can't go on!" a compañera exclaims.

The meeting goes on. Other problems are referred to. Everything is taken down by the secretary. Before adjourning the meeting, the president says: "It isn't always enough to try to get bureaucratic institutions to solve our problems. We can raise the issues, but they're left there. It will be different when we have People's Power, as exists now in Matanzas. Can you imagine? People's Power within a half a block! And the freedom to intervene, to make decisions and carry them out without having always to depend on headquarters . . . ."

Going Beyond Critical Analysis

"This is a meeting we convene every once in a while to give the people an opportunity to express their opinions about the services. The spirit of this meeting must be the one illustrated on that poster"—he points to a poster on the wall—"For excellent service! And each comment must be offered in the spirit of helping to make this a reality."

Just as in the previous meeting, complex problems are discussed in the services meeting of Twentieth Street, in the same section of Havana. But this one begins with an explanation by the person chairing the meeting.

"We'll split up the discussion by items. The compañeros can talk about anything they want, but in the spirit of resolving the problems we have. The spirit of this meeting must be not to critize how each section works but, more than that, to try and resolve each of the cases with the participation of the whole group. If a compañero raises a question about a given item, and another compañero corroborates the report, it isn't necessary to raise the same question again. Even though you may have the right to prolong the meeting, we must try to keep it brief, for there are those who must get up early tomorrow to go to work. A record will be kept of the proceedings. The minutes will be sent to the departmental CDR, and from the department to the Party and to those in charge of agencies concerned."

The discussion begins with the first item, La Placita, a small open-air fruit-and-vegetables stall.

"Let them deliver the fruit to the store too, so we can pick it up on the ration card," a feminine voice asks.

"Yes. As the speaker indicates, we can't stand on line for the fruit that reaches La Placita, because we have to watch the children and fix dinner at a given time, so it happens that it is the same persons who are always picking up the fruit delivered. . . . And as it is decontrolled, they carry off any amount they want. If we don't get it through the ration card, we can't get it at all."

A young man with glasses raises the ineluctable problem of garbage: "I'd like to know if it is possible to fix it, the refuse problem, that is, right next to La Placita. I often walk by the place and can testify to the putrid stuff that accumulates there. I don't blame the people who work there, though, but the administration in charge of the problem."

Cubans are always concerned about the cleanliness of streets and sidewalks. It is one of the CDR duties, so, in every meeting, the job is reexamined, along with the block's problems.

A young mulatto woman returns to La Placita. She alleges that it is always the same people who get to buy here, as she has even seen some carrying pineapples away by the sackful. Angrily, she adds that she does not believe a family can eat a whole sackful of pineapples. She asks that the sales be regulated.

The manager of La Placita takes the floor. "I'd like to explain to you how decontrolled and 'regulated decontrolled,' sales should operate, in my view. It is done with fruits in periods of abundance and scarcity, depending on the seasons of the year. The region and the government designated a given spot on each block to market the decontrolled goods, whether fruit, meats, vegetables, or whatever. This is programmed for all distribution units. Ever since I took charge of Block 326, we have cut down on shortages. Fruits, meat, we keep them at their best. Instead of working five hours, we work seven. I am the block administrator, and yet I'm a simple worker, a foot soldier at the bottom of the ladder, assisting the person in charge, who's another compañero. For example, we received on the seventeenth 7,770 pounds of mangoes. I doled them out equitably twenty pounds per consumer. I got pineapples and distributed them at three per person, and so on and so forth. As manager, I have felt the pressures put on by many people who demand a greater quantity. But I am responsible. This sale is decontrolled, but "directed," so that the majority can be served. This is the reason fruit doesn't go anywhere else. Now, about the refuse at La Placita. We are experiencing a serious problem: the shortage of transportation. Our section has fifteen trucks to spread around the different outlets. One or two break down just ferrying workers. By agreement with other compañeros I've arranged for trucks from the Ministry of Public Health to pick up the refuse every day. And we are doing a thorough clean-up job two or three times per week."

Some are not satisfied with the answer, among them the compañera who opened the discussion: "I see that you didn't answer the first question. If it has adequate knowledge of a subject, I understand the government will guide us; for example, it got the draft Constitution before the people so it could be discussed. Now, if in this assembly we raise the problem of the fruit, which must be distributed properly, if this question is raised here, we have to put it on the record. But your answer hasn't been clear."

A murmur of approval can be heard.

"As we said in the beginning," the leader insists, "everything said here is recorded in the minutes. What he can explain"—he is referring to the manager—"as well as what he can't. For the moment, the policy the block representative follows is not to take the fruit out of the place . . . and, let me just say I don't consume any fruit myself. . . ."

"I'd also like to raise the garbage problem," says another grocer. "And I'd like to ask a few questions. Aren't comrades who work in the city administration in charge of refuse collection? Aren't they supposed to collect the trash from each shop? Because if it isn't that way, then we know why we have so much rot around us. I ask the question because I'm a storekeeper, and they don't pick up my trash either. And I'd like to know whether there's a body in charge of this task, if it has the obligation."

"There is an organization charged with picking up the garbage," the leader says. "But it has its difficulties. It had to pick up the refuse not only from La Placita, but also from the grocery store, the houses, and so on and so forth. No matter, it should be picked up. And, incidentally, at the beginning of the session I mentioned something that must be the mood for all of us here. It is true there are difficulties. But here in the area, on our own, we can resolve many of them. Among us we have many compañeros who are truck drivers, and sometimes their trucks are sitting idle in front of their homes. And we also want to observe the resourcefulness displayed on other occasions by the CDRs. So I'm appealing to the comrades present here to cooperate more fully with the truckers, so when you get a chance you can help pick up the garbage. You can ask for authorization from the enterprises where you work at anytime and pick up the refuse that exists there."

The idea is approved by acclamation.

Various everyday problems continue to be brought up by the audience. The grocery, the butcher shop, the queues—everything is taken up in the services assembly in hopes of an answer or a solution.

"Beginning with this meeting," the leader announces, "in addition to the measures pursued by the CDR, the minutes will be sent to the Party sections so that they may double-check the solutions to the problems in their meetings. So while it is true that we may not have an immediate solution to some of our problems, the new procedure will help in their resolution. This doesn't mean the Party is a magic wand, either, that tomorrow it'll come by with a new grocery store, but it is one more road toward the solution."

Before offering the floor again, he introduces the area's most distinguished *cederista*, as well as the most exemplary *cederista* family. There are distinctions bestowed by the CDR upon those individuals or families that stand out for their attitude, their commitment to the Revolution, their steadfastness vis-a-vis revolutionary duties, and a whole series of other qualities.

The session continues. A construction worker, still wearing his hard hat, has the floor: "We would like to raise a question that concerns us all here. In our district we don't have a department for, well, how do you call it? The place where they sell ice cream. And our district has lots of children. How could we get one of those?"

"Another thing, compañero," a pregnant woman says, switching to another subject. "How could we get a bigger meeting place, hopefully with loudspeakers, for our meetings? You can see how crowded it is here. It would be a greater incentive to participation by the *cederista* members."

"Compañeros," the leader answers proudly, "because of the size of this group, not just because of its size, but also because of the effort we're going to make to solve the problems raised, I suggest that the next session be held on the street. That would be one way to make it large, with loudspeakers, chairs, and all. Now, with regard to the petition you drew up"—he is referring to a construction worker—"I wanted to read to you a proposal just in from the Vista Alegre district. It reads as follows: 'To whom it may concern: We the *cederistas* of Vista Alegre district, would like to apply to you for an INIT establishment [coffee shop], since the closest establishment is on Dolores Street and Route 16, and that means we have to catch a bus when we want to go there."

The leader shows the text around, written in longhand, with the signatures of the petitioners. He resumes reading: "We would appreciate it if you would take our proposal under advisement and assign an establishment as soon as possible. To make your task easier, we would like to mention that a site exists at 958 Dolores Avenue, between Twentieth and Twenty-first Streets, and that it has been vacant for two months."

They also mention that they can fix the place with voluntary labor. The leader announces that the application has already been filed with the appropriate bureau and that it was favorably received, with work to commence as soon as the materials are delivered.

The session would not have been complete without somebody raising the eternal mosquito problem. A compañera carrying a child in her arms touches upon the question: "Compañero, I'd like to speak about the mosquito problem. The plague these days concerns all the neighbors. For besides being a nuisance, they can cause an epidemic. What I'd like to know is whether the polyclinics in other areas have health brigades who fumigate periodically, because this isn't done here. And it must be the polyclinic's duty to see that an epidemic doesn't spread. I say this because I'm a health worker and our polyclinic is constantly seeking ways to keep the pests at bay."

The bread problem, the unnecessary queues, everything is brought up. And everything is put down in the minutes in order to compel an answer at the next session.

The Necessity of Decentralizing Decisions

A young Communist asks when the next meeting will take place and why the present session was delayed. The leader explains: "Now, look, you may have seen that a few months ago we didn't have assemblies. I say this so you can understand what's going on. Approximately two months ago we were directed to reintroduce this type of meeting with the area's residents. But after consultation with the neighbors themselves we came to the conclusion that no meeting should be convened right away as we hadn't received a reply to a series of inquiries and concerns raised by the local residents. For the assembly should have some sort of answer to these matters. There are problems that simply won't have any answer because events may intervene that put the questions beyond the power of the appropriate agency. But there are problems that can be resolved, such as the question of the garbage, the coffee shop, the grocery store. . . . We don't gain much by setting up meetings every month if solutions and answers are not forthcoming at that time. But we do hope that by the next session we'll have a reply from the state agencies as much for public health as for the block residents in the matter of La Placita, etc. And at the beginning of the meeting we'll read a report with the solutions to the problems raised here. But we must also bear in mind, in some cases, we can also pursue these matters personally. For example, by having a word in person with the manager of the bakery, or by directly investigating the problem of the water. We represent the great *cederista* mass, and as these are its problems, we should endeavor to solve them, not just listen to them. Anyone wish to add anything else?"

The room has slowly begun to empty. Loud comments are made.

"I'm so eager to see People's Power right here in Havana. They say that things are going much better in Matanzas."

The problem is that there are things that inevitably get stuck in the bureaucratic machine. The people send up their list of concerns but they do not confront the officers directly in charge. So things may just sit there.

But with People's Power, if someone doesn't do his job, the people can recall him. It is a system that will improve the society, that will improve the Revolution. Today people are put to work in the public agencies, and among these people one finds the good, the bad, and the indifferent. But with People's Power they will be accountable to the people, who will be empowered to say to them: "You haven't done your job properly! Please go home!"

Part Two
Government by the People

5 ELECTIONS OF A NEW TYPE

People's Power came to the province of Matanzas as a political experiment two and a half years ago. The experiment was formally began during the elections of June 30, 1974, and it came to an end on September 30, 1976, with the Sixth Provincial Assembly held in Matanzas, the capital city.

A few days later, on October 10, the entire Cuban people went to the polls to elect its representatives. At that time the new sysytem of government, now perfected and enhanced by a successful pilot project lasting almost a thousand days, was adopted for the whole country.

Without Bayonets or Guns

Fidel summed it up well on July 26, 1974:

"For the first time elections have been held in Cuba with neither bayonets nor guns at the school gates. And this is logical, because these were not elections to plunder, it was not a brawl to share in the spoils. These were elections of the revolutionary people, organized by the revolutionary people, and for the service of the revolutionary people, with the participation even of the Pioneers*—who helped to organize these elections—and with an enthusiasm on the part of the masses truly without precedent in the history of our country.

"These elections are for real. And they had a huge scope. Why such a scope? Some may have wondered, at the beginning of the revolution, when the capitalist class still existed, along with the landowners and the

---

*School children's mass organization with uniforms and institutional style similar to Boy Scouts, but designed to introduce the young to socialist values, duties, rights, etc.

rest of the exploiters, whether we were going to call for elections that extended to all the right to vote and be elected. No. We couldn't have done that. We conceived the Revolution as the rule of revolutionaries, the dictatorship of the proletariat, that deprives the exploiters of these rights; but the fact is that we don't have big landowners any more, we don't have big industrialists, big traders, big importers, big owners of sugar mills. They exist no longer, because they are either gone or no longer have those possessions. And they can exploit no one. There could be, as an exception, someone adapted to the Revolution, able to understand the Revolution, and no one will deprive him of his vote. The point is, they are no longer a problem.

"That's why the elections have been of such a scope, and that is why in this process—which reflects the idea of unity and social and ideological progress of the Revolution—practically the whole people has been able to participate, hence the universal character of the suffrage, which the population has taken full advantage of.

"The recent elections in Matanzas have been the cleanest in the history of our country: elections without backroom dealing, without fraud, without demagogy, without politicking. No one had to hope for anything, because it wasn't personal aspirations that determined the nomination of the candidate, but collective aspirations. And without election campaigns, because the campaign here is the everyday life of the candidate nominated by the people: his campaign is his own life story, his conduct through the years, his record of service to the motherland.

Never have elections produced such enthusiasm! Never before in Cuba—not even in the years when even the dead voted*—was there a participation surpassing 90 percent in any election. The extraordinary thing is that this participation surpassing the 90 percent mark occurred not only in the first round of balloting, but in the second round as well!"

Compañero Coya, a judge in Cardenas, bears witness to the truth of Fidel's words when he explains to us the differences he perceived between elections under the pseudorepublic and those recently held for People's Power.

"In the years of the Republic the will of the people was not the deciding factor. There was a whole range of stratagems to make the minority's will come out on top. Now everything is radically changed.

"In the past, the citizen was forced to vote for a man who had turned political office into a profession, who utilized various agencies and systems organized by his kind to turn up forever on election ballots.

---

*A common type of election fraud practiced in the old regime by parties and politicians favoring the status quo.

"And do you know why voting was compulsory? Because they knew that if it wasn't no one would care to vote. Don't you think it absurd that when you are entitled to a right, you should be forced to avail yourself of it?

"But now, with the People's Power elections, without publicity, without posters filling every store, the percentage of voters was extremely high, and that speaks volumes for the people's consciousness.

"I was a bit amused when I saw the campaign method adopted, because the process was remarkable even in that respect."

Even though most candidates were known to the majority of voters, at least by sight, not everybody knew all the details of their revolutionary careers, so the revolutionary leadership decided that each candidate should be presented to the people through a political biography sheet accompanied by a photograph.

These biographical summaries with their respective photos were posted in the most conspicuous spots, while distribution was also undertaken by the CDRs and the peasants so that every voter could have enough time to study the candidate of his choice.

But let us see what made compañero Coya laugh: "There are two places where the people carry on most of their discussions—the grocer's and the barbershop. And it was in the grocery stores of the area that the candidates' photographs were displayed. There, if thoughtful criticism of a candidate was not forthcoming, you could always find some old woman muttering, 'Ah! So he's a candidate, too, uh . . .?' After some investigation of the reason for such a reaction, I found out that it was simply because the old lady knew the candidate had a girl friend." He laughs.

"The way the delegates were nominated was also quite interesting. It was the rank and file that proposed and discussed whether the person nominated should or should not be elected a candidate, his qualifications, etc."

Nothing in Common with Past Elections

After hearing the opinion of the Matanzas judge, a man of university background with a distinguished record in the field of justice, let us see now how a worker, already an old man, regards the process. He is with the "Frank País" fertilizer plant.

"As a veteran of many elections, what differences do you find between previous elections and those of People's Power?"

"The old elections were a farce. How do you think a candidate could afford to spend a hundred thousand pesos on mere propaganda during an election contest? What the candidate did was to plunder the nation, steal in order to recoup the money he invested and get much more on top of that. It was a sewer for adventurers, for thieves. After the election they set about recovering the money they laid out. Today things are entirely different. Consider the following: today the delegates have to go to work just like everyone else!"

"Can the present delegates get rich? Can they obtain special privileges?

"Not a thing! I know a delegate who lives in a place that would make you cry, in a tenement."

"And what might happen if you see a delegate moving to better quarters?"

"Well, we'd have to find out the particulars. Remember, a delegate is also a worker, and if he stands out as a worker he has a good chance of getting one of the new dwellings put up by the microbrigades.* So we'd have to study the matter first."

"And what meaning did the elections have for the people before the Revolution?"

"They were a joke!"

"A joke?"

"Yes, a joke. They were after the four or five pesos, which is what you got paid for your vote. It was a way to get some extra cash. What the people didn't know was that those five pesos would cost them a lifetime of toil."

"Did you know what socialism was before the Revolution?"

"Are you kidding? No one here knew what it was. The only ones who knew were part of a group that lived on the run. We were told from the cradle on up that socialism was bad, so what were we to do?"

At this point another worker, somewhat younger, who had stopped to listen in on the conversation, breaks in: "But it also happened that if a worker defended the right of workers to earn more money, he was called a communist. For me, that was the best argument the bosses could make for communism. If I'm in a capitalist society, and the bosses call such men communists, then it follows that communism can't be all that bad for me."

It is already late in the evening, and rain falls in torrents as we arrive at one of those small rural districts. It is located in the village of Concepcion, with scarcely 200 voters. Its delegate, Rubén Alvarado, was elected by 176 votes out of 200. But because of his excellent qualities as a

---

Microbrigades are small squads of community residents or workers who undertake the construction of housing and other urgent facilities under government supervision in their spare time.

revolutionary and his educational attainments, he was also elected the head of the "Máximo Gómez" municipality. This has forced him to give up teaching and devote all his energies to the job of being a "people's advocate."

We approach a compañero who attracts our attention because of the dynamism he displays despite his advanced age.

"Compañero, what kind of work do you do?"

"I am with the Red Cross, responsible here for public health. I run forty-eight rural medical posts here. In every little village, in every little farm, no matter how small, there's now a health brigade."

"And what did you do before the Revolution?"

"Well, I'm from this village. I was a cart-driver here, worked in restaurants, you name it, to make ends meet. Because in those days you had to do whatever you could. Not like now, when you can have pride in your work. No one here can say he has no work. Imagine, I work nine, ten, eleven hours a day. I went out at the crack of dawn and just got back. And everyone feels like this, the same way. We do our jobs with pleasure, because we don't look at the time, don't keep an eye on the clock, but concentrate on what needs to be done, because the Revolution needs it. I've liked this business of health care ever since I can recall. When the Revolution arrived, I joined the Red Cross, and to this day I try to do a good day's work."

"What does People's Power mean to you?"

"For me it's something great, yeah, great. You can see, everyone can see, that it's the whole people who rule. And when the people do things, anything can be done, things get done. Yes, it is that way . . .really! That's socialism. So different from the previous governments. I had the opportunity to see both. They used to depict socialism as something horrid, something terribly bad for us, but it was exactly the opposite. The facts will testify to that! Especially now!"

"Could you explain to us why you elected Ruben as a delegate?"

"Look, we met on this very spot, we, the people, to figure out which compañero could best represent us. Ruben is a young comrade, a compañero who really cares. His educational background is good. In short, a whole series of things recommended him as a delegate—his conduct, his principles, the people who love him. He was even my teacher. I studied the sixth grade with him, me, already an old man. . . .He had, he has, a whole lot of qualities we just didn't possess and—Well, as we say, the people have chosen the finest."

"Did you participate in elections before the Revolution?"

"Yes, and there's a great difference. These elections were truly democratic. The people went to vote for the candidate they liked, for whoever they felt was really the best. We knew the candidate was not going to make off with the people's money, as used to happen. For example, he was elected a delegate"—he points to the delegate—"and he knew quite well that he had nothing to gain as a delegate. This election was truly democratic. The old system was riddled with corruption, lies, you name it. They told the people they were going to do this or that tomorrow or the day after, and later they just laughed at us. Nothing was ever done. Look, this town produced senators, ministers, and so on, and the town was— I wish you'd seen it! Now things are moving the way they should, and it's the most beautiful town in the province.

"Look at me. I, too, was a candidate. Here I am, hugging Ruben affectionately upon his triumph and offering him my support. That simply would not be done in the old days. They [the candidates] were antagonists, foes, because of the money. However, here we are supporting him in everything, because his work is the work of the people."

Election Districts and Remote Areas

Delegates to the municipal assembly are elected on the basis of election districts. All municipalities are broken down into a number of districts, with each district entitled to elect one delegate. In this manner, each municipality has as many delegates as the number of districts it contains.

No municipalities are allowed to have fewer than thirty districts or more than two hundred, with assembly business expected to be handled better and more smoothly when this range is observed.

It is important to recall that not all districts contain the same number of voters. The largest represent as many as three thousand people, whereas the smallest barely comprise a hundred.

But why is it that the standards of equal political representation are exceeded in this case? Why doesn't Cuba have homogeneous districts with an equal number of voters in each?

Such a measure has been adopted with the deliberate goal of favoring the remote areas, where the population is more widely dispersed and larger numbers are consequently more difficult to assemble. On the other hand, owing to their remoteness from the centers of power, and the difficulties inherent in reaching them, these areas in the back country had long suffered from neglect.

Besides, the fact that they can now boast of their own delegate to the municipal assembly, someone who is simply one of the area's workers, allows for a better representation of the area's problems and more determined efforts to solve them.

Formerly, under capitalism, the people had to seek an audience with the mayor, to whom they had access only after a long and arduous journey, and only to be met with an inordinate amount of red tape, as such politicians had no particular interest in tackling the problems of remote and backward areas.

In addition to the regular election districts, Cuba now has special voting districts. These are chiefly composed of FAR military units, units of the Youth Labor Army, and boarding schools, where the members either in whole or in part reside permanently within those districts.

This particular measure was adopted in order to extend participation in People's Power to all those individuals who, because of the specific requirements of work or study, lived under a regimen barring normal participation in the everyday affairs of their native neighborhoods.

Nominating Candidates

Candidates for the municipal assembly are nominated by the people. In every election district, citizens of voting age meet to debate the possible nominees under the direction of a chairman democratically elected by all. For the meeting to be valid, more than half of the district's voters must attend. The candidates' names are not picked from a list submitted by the Party or similar organization; on the contrary, candidates names are proposed by anyone attending the nominating convention. If they wish, the people can make multiple nominations, provided that each is reasonably justified. Eventually the person who obtains the largest plurality at the meeting automatically becomes that particular district's chosen candidate to compete with similarly elected candidates from other districts for the post of district representative.

In the Matanzas elections of June, 1974, it was agreed that every CDR and rural district should constitute an election district entitled to nominate a candidate. As a result, each district had as many candidates as it had CDRs and peasant areas within its jurisdiction. The number of candidates was enormous.

For the elections of October, 1976, this standard was modified. Each district was divided instead into a certain number of election districts according to population figures. Those with fewer than 750 inhabitants were divided into two, nominating two candidates. Those exceeding 2,800 inhabitants were alloted eight districts and asked to name eight candidates.

Let us see how the "Ignacio Prieto" rural district, in the Cardenas region, went about this preliminary step during the Matanzas experiment. The credit for the account goes to Miguel Torres, a reporter associated with the news service of ICAIC.*

"The session was opened by the chairman, who explained in full the meaning of the election and the character of the various agencies of People's Power. He reminded the audience of the qualifications needed for participation. Then, after reading the election by-laws, he added: 'These agencies of People's Power, to be formed by our compañeros, will constitute the highest governmental authority at the municipal level, and will discharge great responsibilities. . . . This obliges us to think carefully before making a nomination, and to insure that the candidate is a compañero with the proper qualifications, a person of outstanding merit. The candidate must be capable of ably representing us, fully capable of tackling the problems that continually come up, a person you know well. He or she must have a bold, revolutionary temperament and be concerned with all the problems affecting the residents. All of you have the right to elect and be elected.'

"The participation by the comrades began at once:

" 'I nominate Juan Ortega,' said a mulatto woman who was holding an infant in her arms.

" 'Why do you nominate Ortega?' the assembly chairman asks.

" 'Well, I nominate him because I know him well. He's got good qualities. He's a good revolutionary, hard-working, gets along well with everybody, and besides, he was in the construction crews sent to Vietnam.'

"The chairman seeking to stimulate other contributions, requests the opinions of various residents.

" 'You, Compañero Sergio, what do you say?'

" 'That he's a fine person, a man fully qualified for the job, a good neighbor, so I'm in agreement with the nomination.'

" 'Let's have another compañero speak. Let's see. Juan?'

" 'We've known him since 1959. He has performed many tasks of the Revolution and done them well, and with integrity. Moreover, as another speaker already remarked, Compañero Ortega possesses the necessary qualities to represent us because anytime someone needed him, he was there. He's got the right qualities, yes sir.'

*Cuban Institute of Cinematic Arts and Industries.

"Will another compañero speak his mind about Ortega. Don't be afraid to speak up.'

" 'He's a compañero who has supported us in all the revolutionary tasks. During the worker call-ups he acted like a great comrade. He stands out because he's always sensitive to the problems of other people in the neighborhood and all that. And he's never said no to anything. So he has exemplary qualitites, and that is a fact,' said a voice.

" 'Yet another compañero. Speak up about his qualitites. Don't be shy. That's the reason we're here. This is democracy.'

"Despite his prodding the assembly remains silent. The chairman calls for new names, insisting upon the qualifications to fill the tasks ahead.

" 'I nominate Compañero Lalito, an elderly woman says.'

" 'Why do you nominate Compañero Lalito?'

" 'I regard him as a very active compañero; he works hard with the boys. Look, I think he's got the qualifications to be a fine representative from the area, for us.'

" 'Let's hear another compañero on Lalito. Don't be shy—'

"A tall, slender girl, standing to one side, decides to speak: 'The compañero belongs to our Party, is very revolutionary, very active, belongs to the CDRs. He's a person to reckon with in this area, because of his activites.'

" 'Let's have another opinion'

" 'I think Compañero Teodoro Riveros must be elected a delegate because he has revealed the qualities of a great revolutionary, discharges his duties well, with integrity, plus everything else Compañera Zoila mentioned,' another voice says.

" 'Let's keep this orderly. We want another compañero to speak about Lalito.'

"After several compañeros commented on Lalito's merits, all in agreement on his virtues, the chairman turned to a compañero who had remained silent in a corner: 'Let's see, Jorge. What can you say about Compañero Lalito?'

" 'About Compañero Lalito I can tell you that everything said here tonight is absolutely true. Because I know him well, right? And it's obvious. Because he's not the type to dodge any task. . . . And besides being a Party member he has always participated in the tasks of the Revolution, never requesting anything for himself. In addition, his wife works, cutting cane and all that, and he's always there pitching in, and always helping with the kids at home, etc. So I believe he has all the qualities to occupy the post, and to be responsible for all the problems we may introduce here.'

"At that, the audience broke into applause, enthusiastically confirming Jorge's evaluation.

" 'Would someone like to nominate someone else, for the post of delegate to People's Power?' the chairman asked.

" 'Compañero, I nominate Compañera Edelina,' said someone from the rear of the room.

" 'Why do you nominate her?'

" 'I nominate the compañera because she's very active in the area. She belongs to the brigades, the CDRs, everything.'

" 'Another person, please, on Compañera Edelfina.'

" 'About Compañera Edelfina the only thing I can say,' said an old woman, 'is that anytime you go fetch her for any task, anything at all, she drops whatever she's doing in order to meet the needs of the Revolution.'

"A chorus of approval was heard. And when the nomination of precandidates had run its course, a vote took place, and Compañero Ortega became the candidate for the area."

At another assembly which concluded with the election of a black compañero of about fifty years of age, a peasant of the area, we struck up a conversation with the voters.

"May we hear what you think of the candidate?"

"Look, compañero," a white-haired peasant replied, "Compañero Juan has been a fighter for a long time, and he had what it takes to fill the post. I've known him for twenty years and, as a revolutionary, he's just got to get the job. In terms of ability the people have found what they need. He is a compañero elected by the masses, not just one man, by one compañero alone or by whim, but by the will of the people."

"He's a man to be trusted in everything," a compañera exclaimed.

The candidate interrupted them. He was a bit uncomfortable with the compliments.

"I think they exaggerate a little. They talk like this because they know me. This fellow, like he said, has known me for almost twenty years. I was a labor leader before the Revolution, and after its triumph I've been in administrative jobs. That's why they say I have the ability to do the job, and the statements you have heard—"

"Well, frankly, because he's a man who has studied, because he's knowledgeable . . .and because he's a revolutionary above all else," another peasant asserts. "And we are sponsoring him because he's the man we need up there. He's the man who enjoys the sympathy of the people. He's going to win for sure!"

Next we stopped at the "Spanish Republic" sugar mill. There we encountered one of the few women named a candidate of People's Power.

For ten years she had handled the personnel section of the mill, a plant with approximately a thousand workers. She is highly respected by her neighbors.

We asked her to tell us how her election came about.

This is her version.

"Well, the first time, I was called upon to chair the nominating session. I was simply informed I had been elected. I said, 'But this can't be possible! I can't believe it!' And they said that yes, it was true. Anyhow, you know that a revolutionary can't turn down a legitimate task. So I accepted. Next I had to attend a seminar and then the other assembly, where the candidates for delegate were being selected. The assembly was held right here on my doorstep, and I was elected. Many people attended. I think about 82 people came, and 80 voted for me." A pause. Then she added: "In this district you have to work hard, because without hard work the tasks can't be carried out. Besides, it seems as though with People's Power things are going to improve around here. This is one of the best ideas ever to come down the pike! And, well, for some time we may not be able to improve things dramatically, but eventually we'll get them under control. Things will come with time, because the government doesn't yet have all the things it needs. . . ."

Eventually the names selected in these grass roots assemblies constituted the slate of candidates for each district.

Candidates with Police Records

The historical chain of events ushering in the nominating sessions was swift. The law promulgating the political and administrative structure took effect on July 5, 1976, and two days later the election law itself was enacted, with the national, provincial, and municipal electoral colleges constituting themselves between the tenth and the seventeenth. Then, between the sixteenth and the twenty-ninth of August, the whole country went to the assemblies to nominate candidates.

More than four milion people took part in the district meetings, putting forward more than 90,000 names, and from these, by a majority vote of those present, the final 29,169 candidates for delegate were chosen.

When the biographical profiles of these candidates were being prepared, however, it was found, that 1,276 (that is, 4.4 percent), had police records. Of these, 78 had been involved in documented counter-revolutionary activities and 60 in other suspicious matters; 80 had belonged to repressive agencies supporting the tyranny; and 231 had applied for passports to leave the country.

During ensuing talks with 633 of these candidates 156 decided to drop their candidacy, but 477 opted to remain in the contest, even though this meant that their biographies would note their past offenses. As for the other 643 cases, they involved matters of minor significance, and the charges were omitted from the biographical profiles.

These facts, which convincingly show the democratic character of the nominating process, also permit us to evaluate as insignificant the current threat posed to the country by the counterrevolution, especially if we recall that the right of suffrage is denied only to those legally insane and those whom the courts have declared juridically unfit on account of specific offenses.

The Election of Delegates

"The people will choose the best." This was the central theme of the posters that went up all over Cuba announcing the first national elections to establish the local agencies of People's Power.

On October 10, in a holiday atmosphere that typifies most popular outpourings in Cuba, and undaunted by local torrential rains, workers, peasants, housewives, soldiers, and students (over the age of sixteen) went to the polls to choose via direct and secret ballot those among their ranks who would henceforth act as their representatives.

Grade-school pupils were posted at the entrance to each polling place as well as on the inside as observers, thus offering a clear contrast with the display of armed police that normally accompanies elections in capitalist countries.

More than five million Cubans, or 95.2 percent of the registered voters, participated in the elections that day. This kind of participation underscored the interest of the Cuban population in the elections with candidates genuinely elected by ordinary citizens and directly responsible to them.

The province with the highest degree of participation was Guantanamo, with 97.9 percent. Those that trailed were Havana City and Cienfuegos, with a still impressive 93 percent turnout.

By 7 A.M., when the polls opened—there were 19,616 across the country—a significant number of voters were already waiting to cast their preferences. In all, 10,725, delegates had to be picked from a pool of 29,169 candidates. Since, in the more heavily populated districts, there could be as many as eight candidates, reaching the majority required by law—half of the ballots plus one—was sometimes difficult. Despite all this, during the first round of balloting 7,888 candidates were elected. In the districts where the first-round balloting didn't suffice to produce a clear winner—a total of 2,837—run-off contests had to be held on October 17.

In a way, the election's results served to underscore the very high percentage of Party members (PCC) and Party Youth (UJC) spontaneously nominated by the people. Thus 53.4 percent of the candidates came from the Party ranks, and 17.1 percent from the youth arm, making a total of 70.5 percent for the whole organiztaion. These percentages rose after the returns were tabulated to 75.2 percent, with 58.8 percent going to the Party, and 16.4 percent going to its youth.

Most delegates are young people: 31.1 percent are under thirty years of age, and 70.2 percent are under forty-one. On the other hand, only 8 percent are women. From an educational standpoint, 31 percent had finished grammar school; 26.9 percent had completed middle school, and only 5.3 percent boast college status.

By occupational background 26.2 percent are workers, 12 percent technicians, 13.1 percent managerial pesonnel, 6.7 percent service workers, 6.2 percent peasants, 4.9 percent members of the armed forces, 1.4 percent functionaries with the Ministry of the Interior, and 24.2 percent political leaders.

Direct and Indirect Elections

So far, we have only examined the election for delegates to the municipal assemblies, the grassroots organizations of People's Power. There are, however, agencies of People's Power at the provincial level.

As we know, all the organizations of People's Power—whether municipal, provincial, or national (the National Assembly is the supreme representative institution in the Cuban political system)—derive their power directly from the people, who nominate and elect their members. The assemblies are thus the principal agencies of state authority at their respective levels, and all other governmental institutes—administrative, judicial, and defense—accept their leadership.

When the Revolution came to power, there existed in Cuba a political and administrative structure dating fom the colonial period. The country was divided up into six provinces and 126 municipalities. During the revolutionary period this arrangement began to be changed. A regional level was introduced, for example, and new municipalities were added.

By 1973, when a commission was charged with developing a new political and adminsitrative structure, the country boasted 58 regions and 407 municipalities. There were provinces with an area six times larger than others, and with six times as many people. These disparities persisted all the way down to the municipal level.

The results of the study led the commisison to propose an entirely new governmental structure, in which, in addition to the usual considerations of population, geographical size, and economic complexity, new criteria would take into account the known developmental factors affecting specific areas—that is, all the decisions to be carried out in the next ten years affecting existing housing and road construction, ports and railroads, factories and schools, and so on.

The new arrangement recognizes only two links between the nation and the grassroots: the province and the municipality, with the provinces smaller and the municipalities larger than before.

The country was finally divided into 14 provinces and 169 municipalities. This is the basis on which the agencies of People's Power are now choosen.

But how are the elections for the provincial agencies of People's Power and the National Assembly conducted? Is the system of direct election utilized at the municipal level also utilized at higher levels?

No, in these cases the people do not choose their representatives directly. At the provincial and national levels they are picked by the delegates to the municipal assembly.

One delegate to the provincial assembly is elected for each 10,000 inhabitants or fraction larger than 5,000. Similarly, a deputy to the National Assembly is picked for each 20,000 inhabitants or fraction exceeding 10,000.

But wouldn't it be more democratic to have the deputies to the National Assembly elected directly? Why was this system chosen?

The answer is easy. It was thought that the delegates chosen by the people in the most democratic fashion, those with outstanding records in their regions, those who exhibited the highest levels of political consciousness and revolutionary virtues, would be the best equipped to choose the people's representatives to the highest state organs.

The Nominating Committee

The nomination of candidates to the provincial and national level is made not by delegates to the municipal assembly but by a special nominating committee.

What is a nominating committee?

It is made up of representatives of political and mass organizations at the level in question, under the chairmanship of the Party representative. For example, if the problem at hand is the election of members of the executive committee of the municipal assembly, the committee will be chaired by the Party representative to the municipality and will include representatives from the UJC, CTC, the CDRs, the ANAP, and FMC. Similarly, at the provincial level, provincial organizations will be represented on the committee.

But why is this mechanism favored? Isn't it better to let any delegate propose names? The rationale again is very simple: It is the Party and mass organizations at each level that are best qualified to judge the people best equipped to accomplish the tasks and responsibilities of People's Power. They know who has excelled in their respective organizations and the type of duties they handle best. It is difficult at the district level to have the clear vision needed to identify outstanding individuals to serve at the provincial or even municipal level.

Doesn't this curtail the voters' freedom?

Not at all. In the first place, the nominating committee must always propose 25 percent more candidates than the existing electoral vacancies. On the other hand, the assembly may reject, partially or completely, the list of candidates drawn up by the committee. The committee is empowered only to suggest names; the assembly retains the right to accept or reject them. In general, the committee's suggestions are accepted, for its members share the values and criteria of the delegates, and enjoy great prestige with the people because of the responsibilities entrusted to them in their respective organizations. Yet candidacies have been rejected by the assembly.

As mentioned above, unlike the delegates to the municipal assembly, delegates to the provincial assembly as well as deputies to the national legislature need not be elected directly by the people.

The nominating committee is not required, therefore, to limit itself to suggesting names from the pool of delegates elected to the municipal assembly: it may propose other names.

But how can we explain a committee empowered to nominate candidates not chosen by the people? Doesn't this imply a breach in the fundamental criterion of the People's Power experience, namely, the participation of the ordinary citizen in the election of his or her representatives? Don't we have here a case of tampering by the political organizations with the system of People's Power?

The proper answer can only be arrived at if we take into consideration the following factors: The elections for People's Power have as a basic unit the neighborhood, the place where people reside. They do not include as a basic unit the region's industries, where the outstanding Party members may be found. The fact is that many excellent workers, owing to the responsibilities they must discharge at the workplace, cannot afford the time for prominent participation in their neighborhoods, where they normally arrive very late in the evening after fulfilling their work and political duties. Indeed, the heavier their responsibilities as leaders, both toward the Party and the workplace, the more pronounced the contradictions between duties fulfilled away from home and the possibilities for collaboration at the neighborhood level. On the other hand, the population tends intuitively to favor those who have given a good account of themselves at the local level, while tending to disregard leaders with many responsibilities, considering them not particularly well positioned to handle the tasks of a People's Power delegate.

A second consideration worth bearing in mind is the great human and political quality of Party members and leaders, who are in general far better equipped than the delegates themselves to assume the tasks of leadership at the higher levels of People's Power.

Thus, by taking into account the revolutionary and leadership qualities of prospects, the nominating committee is able to suggest names overlooked by the masses in their search for qualified candidates. Furthermore, the reasons which prompted the committee to suggest the names are explained in full to the delegates to the municipal and provincial assemblies, bodies which may, if they so wish, reject in part or *in toto* tne candidacies proposed by their respective committees. Thus, as mentioned earlier, though it is true that the committee draws up the names, the delegates elected by the people still have the last word.

Moreover, the fact that Party members are recognized as "the best of the best," enjoying the greatest prestige among the people, without whose approval they could not have entered the Party, facilitates their election to leadership positions.

We believe that this is an excellent manner of determining the proletarian character of the leadership of People's Power, without resorting to quotas for participation according to social class.

How are the Candidates to the National Assembly Nominated?

Despite the fact that the revolutionary leaders have thought it appropriate, for reasons previously explained, to allow the nomination of delegates not elected to the provincial and National Assemblies by the rank and file, the same leadership has also established that there must be, at all times, a majority of deputies and delegates directly elected by the people. This is a way of respecting the popular will and of assuring that a continuing linkage remains between the top layers of People's Power and the most pressing problems of the population.

But how do we make sure that the municipal assembly will elect more than 50 percent of its delegates to the provincial assemblies and National Assembly from among those elected directly by the people?

With a single slate carrying both the candidates selected by the people and the candidates selected by the nominating committees, the probability of attaining the desired proportions would be low. It might happen, for example, that a municipal assembly picking five candidates from among six names, picked by the three rank and file and three by the committee, might wind up with three of the five victors not being elected by the grassroots. If this occurred all over the country, the final result would be a National Assembly with a majority of the delegates not being elected by people.

This consideration led the Political Bureau to direct that in those municipalities where more than one delegate or deputy was to be elected, nomination was to be made through two slates. The first, drawn up be the municipal nominating committee, completely independently, proposes as candidates members of the municipal assembly; that is, these candidates are directly elected by the people. The second list, suggested to the committee by the Party Politburo and the provincial executive committee, contains the names of individuals not previously elected. Without this arrangement at the national level the probability would be high that many municipalities would propose the same candidates. There is no doubt, for example, that Fidel would have been nominated by all the municipal assemblies.

6 PROLETARIAN CHARACTER OF THE LEADERSHIP

One of the most remarkable features of People's Power in Cuba is the proletarian origin of the immense majority of the delegates, and those who occupy positions of authority in the local organs at various levels.

Many are actually workers or peasants, others are younger Party members who were scarcely fifteeen years old when the Revolution triumphed, or students whose parents were workers. Still others, having been workers engaged in the struggle against Batista, soon became managers in the state or Party system upon the triumph of the Revolution.

To meet the new tasks of government, the Revolution, characterized in its infancy by an acute shortage of trained leaders, was forced to fall back on those who had stood out in the revolutionary struggle.

Very few among them, though, have shunned their class. Very few attempted to use their leadership positions to obtain privileges. In this regard, the revolutionary leadership has been extremely fastidious, and the example has been set by its top leader, Fidel Castro, who has always been willing to share with the people the greatest sacrifices: he was the first to spend days on end cutting sugarcane when the Cuban people were attempting to harvest ten million tons in 1970. He was the first to quit smoking when the people were asked to cut down on their own consumption in order to increase tobacco exports, a measure which secured the country extra foreign reserves at the height of the American embargo.

The Background of Some Leaders

We had an opportunity to meet four of the five members of the executive committee of the People's Power municipal assembly of Matanzas. Two of them, before being elected delegates, were workers. The president, José Failde, a mulatto of about thirty-two years of age, was a pressman with fifteen years of experience in that area of production. Feliz Isasi, a black of impressive height and physique, had been a waterfront worker, a stevedore, for years, though the Revolution had recently appointed him manager of a foundry in the region.

The youngest member of the executive committee, Rafael Fernández, the son of an industrial worker, was only eleven when the Revolution came to power. Thirteen years old when the Bay of Pigs invasion materialized, he joined the Rebel Army as part of an antiaircraft squad.

"We were all young kids," he says, "both in the struggle against the bandits and later against the pirates. That's why we have chosen sixteen as the minimum voting age. Because if the youth of thirteen, fourteen, and fifteen knew how to seize the gun in those difficult moments of the Revolution when the class struggle was at its height, if they had this vision of getting a gun and defending the homeland, then they can just as well have the right and the vision to elect those who will represent them in the state or to be elected to a representative governing body. Formerly, the other constitutions forbade minors (those under twenty-one) the right to vote. The same held for the military."

Lastly, the senior member of the group, a bank employee in 1959, devoted himself to the organization and regulation of work at the Ministry of Labor at the time of his election as a delegate.

Four days after they were elected delegates, on July 11, municipal assemblies were created all over Matanzas. These were presided over by what came to be called an "age board," that is, a board composed of the oldest delegate and the two youngest in that assembly. At the meeting those who were to chair future assemblies were elected: a president, a vice-president, a secretary, and two associates.

We would like to give some background details on three of the executive committee members of the Cardenas People's Power regional assembly, one of the principal regions in Matanzas, with a population of about 112,000 inhabitants, and similar information about two leaders with the Jovellanos regional assembly, a backwater region, far from the provincial center, with more of a peasant character.*

Alexis, the president of the Cardenas executive committtee, is a young man of about thirty-four, with light complexion and blue eyes. He was only nineteen when the Revolution succeeded. He was a student at a

---

*Regions were eliminated under the political and administrative structure adopted in 1976.

business school, even then, a member of the Socialist Youth. His father was an old Communist Party member. He was prominent in the regional battle against Batista. When the Revolution triumphed, this recommended his integration into the security apparatus. He remained in that capacity till 1962, afterward becoming a professional Party leader in the region. He got to be president of the Cardenas assembly without having been elected a delegate in any district.

Reinaldo, vice-president of the executive committee, is a young man, slightly older than Alexis, light-haired of rather short stature. He was studying typography and printing at a Havana school when the Revolution triumphed.

"I had to move then," he tells us, "because when I was a student here at the Institute, there was this student strike on the occasion of José Antonio Echeverría's death, and I started planting bombs. . . .My father was tipped off to get me out of there as soon as possible. That's how I wound up as a pressman's apprentice, at a school whose principal, a priest, was also my uncle."

In 1959, with the victory of the Revolution, he worked for a food concern, in the accounting department. Later, when business began to be nationalized in 1962, he became a clerk at the Cardenas central general store. After that, he was called up as a militiaman for seven months. Upon his return, he was promoted to the managerial section of the store. In 1968 he joined the Party. From 1967 to 1970 he was director of the Ministry of Domestic Trade (MINCIN), later joining the regional administration of the National Institute for Agrarian Reform (INRA) till 1972, the year he returned to Cardenas as director of MINCIN. He was not elected a delegate by the rank and file either.

Laureano, an associate member of the Cardenas executive committee, is thirty-five years of age, thin, tall, of light complexion and black hair, which he wears plastered down, combed straight back. He was a worker at the Las Villas paper mill when the Revolution came to power. There he remained till 1961, when he won a scholarship to go to Czechoslovakia for technical training. Upon his return, he began to manage factories. He joined the Communist Youth and then the Party, eventually becoming a member of the regional leadership. He was elected a delegate by the people and, according to Alexis, "is a particularly popular person around this town. When the elections were held, people stayed up till midnight to learn the results. When they heard the news of his victory, they carried him on their shoulders all over the neighborhood—all because of his work for the Revolution during these years, his humility, simplicity, his ties to the people. The compañero sometimes arrives late at meetings and

I ask him: 'Well, man, why the lateness this time?' He replies: 'Well, on my way here people stopped me every so often, raising this and that question, and I just couldn't leave without hearing them out.' Most of the voters knew him because he was a CDR area coordinator in 1963, and prior to his election as a delegate he was the region's cultural delegate."

Adolfo, a man of about forty, belongs to a well-known family of Chinese descent. He is the vice-president of Jovellanos People's Power. He used to be a worker in a retail business. When the Revolution triumphed, he was appointed government manager of nationalized properties in that field. Before his election to his present post, he was president of the local People's Power. He has been a Party member since 1970. He was not elected by any district.

Lastly, we have Luis, a mulatto, almost thirty years of age, a construction worker like the rest of his family before the Revolution, and a union official in that industry. He served in the militia till 1962, when retail business was nationalized. At that point he was assigned to nationalize several enterprises; after that he moved on to the Ministry of Labor. He was filling that post when he was elected secretary to the Jovellanos executive committee. He was not elected a delegate by his district either.

We were struck by the fact that most of the executive committee members of Cardenas and Jovellanos had not been elected delegates in their own districts. We asked them to give us the reason for this.

Laureano explained why Alexis, the chairman of the Cardenas executive committee, was not elected a delegate in his district.

"He lives in Varadero and works in Cardenas. He doesn't spend much of his time there. I'm confident that if Alexis had been there more often or longer, or in any district, he would have been elected at once. Besides, the population took it upon themselves not to nominate as candidates people already in positions or leadership at various levels, thinking that this would create problems. The people said: 'We have to look for someone really able to work, as these compañeros can't possibly do the job when they already have so much work to do.' "

Alexis interrupts: "Though you can't disregard the fact that I might not be too popular where I live."

The faces of the other compañeros show clear signs of disapproval of this "explanation."

"And in your case, Reinaldo, what happened?"

"Well, in my case things were pretty much the same. I used to work outside of Cardenas. But I should mention that in my district an old and very prestigious soldier of sixty-five years of age was being proposed. He knew everyone and simply overwhelmed the other candidates."

Something like that also happened to Luis, who explained to us: "At the time of the election I was working in Colon. I wasn't seen much in these parts. This might have had a bearing on the matter, in addition to other things. My life at the CDR wasn't anything to write home about, because I was always in Colon."

"And that has changed now?"

"Things have changed a great deal. Now I can make the CDR meetings more frequently, attend the delegates' meeting. I'm here in Jovellanos, and since they know I am with People's Power, they come by, drop in to ask questions. The situation has certainly changed."

The Delegates' Educational Background

A large proportion of the delegates to People's Power have barely finished grade school. And some 6.8 percent did not even reach that level.

In some cases, this low educational level affects the delegate's performance in a negative way, although this does not follow automatically. There are, in fact, superb People's Power leaders, as we will see when we meet Orestes Fundora, delegate for the Varadero district, who has a very low level of schooling.*

Concerning this problem, Alexis, president of the Cardenas assembly, pointed out the following: "You may attend an accountability session and see delegates who handle themselves very well, who are capable of furnishing objective answers to the questions raised, and you will also run into other delegates who do OK, too, but at a lower level of expertise, and still others who do poorly, because of their low educational achievements. You were asking us about college. Well. I've never set foot in a college, and the compañeros here haven't either. We used to be grade-school students. Now I am a student at the Workers' College, because, besides, being a People's Power leader, I am a Party member and am under an obligation to study. All three of us here attend Workers' College. There are many compañeros who do not have any education worth mentioning . . . . It is their political development through the fulfillment of revolutionary tasks that explains the preparation they have achieved. When foreign leaders and delegations come here, and see them in action, they say: 'It's hard to believe he only has a sixth-grade education. Look at the way he handles himself.' This is the result of all these years of revolutionary activity, which cannot be seen so readily in

*See Chapter 9, "The Accountability Session: An Exemplary Case."

other countries. During the early years of the Revolution, many of us had to quit our studies. Now things are different."

Indeed, all over Cuba today one can perceive a tremendous pressure to study, to raise the educational level of the workers, to the point it has become a requisite for model workers to be engaged in an effort to improve their education.

7 THE RECALL OF REPRESENTATIVES

In Trouble after Covering Up for a Grocer

"I think he was recalled because he tried to ignore something blatantly improper. Even when many residents were being affected and many complaints were being filed with him, he simply paid no attention to the problem and went right on dismissing the question till the residents themselves came to the realization that he was in cahoots with the grocer. The grocery store manager was hurting the neighborhood, but the delegate acted as if he didn't see what was going on. He listened to the complaints but took no action whatsoever. . . .It was better to remove him and substitute someone else willing to serve the interests of the people."

These are the words of María Julia Alvarez, a teacher at the Juan Aurelio Triana grade school, and a voter from the Twenty-fourth District of the Playa municipality. The delegate, we learned, resigned his post upon being informed that 1,105 of his constituents, or approximately 65 percent, had signed an eight-page accusatory document detailing charges against him because of his suspect attitude toward the manager of the grocery depot located at the intersection of Forty-first and Fifty-fourth Streets in Marianao. The document demanded his resignation. After a long debate, in a meeting especially convened on July 30, 1977, to hear the formal request for his recall, the People's Power assembly for the Playa municipality decided to grant it, considering, among other things, that the sheer number of signatures already amounted to a *de facto* recall, and that the delegate himself had insisted on presenting his irrevocable resignation.

It was emphasized, however, that the delegate had several opportunities to defend himself before the voters and that he declined to do so despite his being advised by the municipal authorities to do so. Nonetheless, there were some delegates who thought it would have been better to observe the complete recall procedure, according to which the delegate is summoned before the assembly to present his defense. (This was also the opinion of José Arañaburo, secretary to the National Assembly, who expressed this view to us during a private conversation.)

"At the end he opted to resign because he saw he was lost," María Julia says emphatically. "When charges were raised during the hearing, he never opened his mouth. He was well aware that what he had done was dishonest, and he didn't have the gall to defend himself in front of the people."

"You think the delegate should have faced the assembly?"

"Naturally. When we make a mistake—we are all human and we all make mistakes—we should face our errors and not just keep silent. Of course, that only happens if we can say something for our case. If not, it's better to shut up and keep quiet."

"And what happened to the manager?"

"He was transferred."

In order to learn more details about the case we talked to Alberto Horta, a current delegate from the district. Horta happens to work at the Municipal Food Plant No. 2 as a personnel specialist. He has, among his tasks, the duty of overseeing the performance of grocery store managers.

"We discussed the matter with the grocer and penalized him by transferring him," Horta says. "After that we realized—and so did the assembly—that he deserved a more severe punishment, so the plant decided to demote him to ordinary clerk. But the assembly then thought that in order to gather more information on the matter he was to be reported to the police. As a result, I—not as a delegate,, since I wasn't a delegate then—personally took the responsibility before the assembly and reported him. I talked to the district attorney and he advised me to file a formal complaint with the police. Judicial action is still pending."

"But can't the residents do something to be more vigilant?"

"Well, yeah. . . .If we assume a compañera buys a pound of meat and there are four ounces missing . . .and she had the weight of the package checked right then and there, before witnesses, then there's a case. But if she files her complaint after cooking the meat, the accusation is obviously worthless."

After this parenthesis we return to our conversation with María Julia. We want to find out want she thinks of People's Power after living through a recall.

"I see People's Power as extremely beneficial because any problems we may have can be taken up to the delegate and solved," she replies. "Before, we had to to down to city hall or to the regional or provincial capital in order to get some satisfaction, and solutions were rare. Many problems can be successfully handled in this manner."

"Has the new delegate been elected already?"

"Yes. He's a fine choice, very dedicated to the resolution of our problems. A determined person. When one has the will, the rest falls into place automatically! Yesterday I was talking to a compañera who has spent seven years living under very penurious circumstances. Half of her house caved in. We understand that housing is hard to come by and all that, but the new delegate took the matter in his hands and prevailed upon the compañera to accompany him to the Department of Housing, where he explained the situation. The upshot was that they were told there was no housing available, that other problems had to be tackled first, but in any case you can see that he just doesn't sit there when someone walks in with a problem. He tries to do something."

María Julia, whom we met on the street near the grocery store in question, takes us to the home of Guillermo Marrero and his wife Nancy, two of the seven people who filed complaints against the delegate in the brief requesting his recall. Guillermo is a technician with the experimental cattle cooperative "Valle del Peru"; he is former chairman of his CDR, union secretary at the plant, and a vanguard worker under scrutiny to become a Party member. Nancy is an office clerk with the Institute of Refrigeration and Air Conditioning, and the first to publicly accuse the delegate in the second assembly convened to hear the representative's accounting. Although there is a power blackout and her three children are playing in the dark in the next room, waiting for the dinner that Nancy is preparing as she talks with us, conversation goes on. The couple is very interested in giving us all kinds of details about this case which, if it does not fully deserve to be classifed as a recall, remains nonetheless, according to Guillermo, a "resignation under fire." Guillermo begins by giving us a sketch of the delegate and how he was elected. "We noticed him from the start because he was a CDR coordinator and I was chairman of my block. That is, we knew him the moment he set foot in the neighborhood. He was a retired person and earned some praise for his work. When the time to nominate candidates to People's Power came around, he began to intensify his activities, creating more of an atmosphere of support for his election.

"He possessed only one attribute, and that was the amount of time he had available, as he had no political background. The only post worth mentioning in his biography was that of area coordinator, but the people, ignorant of the realities of People's Power at that time, decided to support him, as he was one of the people they saw most often.

"So here and in other places in the district he had a few small rallies requesting support in the polling booth. On election day he visited all the polling places so the people could see him. No other candidate running for delegate did that. That disgusted us, since for us the delegate must be a humble person, not given to self-promotion.

"Then, during the first accountability session, I noticed he had serious flaws as a delegate. He made a presentation of how People's Power was organized, how we had to act if we wanted to solve a problem, and so on. At the end he asked whether the voters had anything to say. I stood up and said: 'There is a problem here that concerns the majority of the people. . .' I was going to raise the problem of the grocer, who was shortchanging the people, overcharging them, and generally abusing the consumers in a variety of ways; but I was not allowed to finish. It seems he saw what I was driving at and dodged the question by declaring that his office was open to the people on Wednesdays, and that all problems should be raised there. Immediately thereafter, he adjourned the meeting. The topic, however, hung in the air. Everybody agreed that the problem with the grocer should have been discussed. It wasn't just I, but two, three, many residents. A comrade then decided to put the charges against the grocer in writing, but the delegate did not process the complaint and merely sat on it. Besides, he never stood in line at the grocery store, and without being a worker, he took advantage of all kinds of benefits. Also, when the store was about to close he was still waited on, while others were turned away. It was clear the grocer was openly currying favor with the delegate. Because of these things the delegate began to lose face and authority before the people. Moreover, my wife was present when two MINCIN* inspectors stopped in."

Nancy tells us what happened on that occasion.

"Once, when I was buying some coffee and the grocer was waiting on me, two MINCIN inspectors walked in to carry out an investigation. The grocer became very upset. It even looked as if he were embarrassed to get paid. At that precise moment the delegate strolled by, and the grocer called him in to explain the matter to the inspectors. I though the whole situation was quite suspicious. I next heard the inspectors telling the grocery store manager that a number of complaints had been filed against the store and that they wanted to find out what was going on. He just laughed the matter off and told them: 'Look, how can they say such

---

*MINCIN: Ministry of Domestic Trade.

things about me? Here you have the delegate, he can tell you.' The delegate said: 'But no, my friend, these are just little intrigues dreamed up by some soreheads. They even say bad things about me.' He said this although he knew the residents had filed several complaints, including a letter in which the grocer was charged with cheating, plain thievery, price manipulation, etc. . . ."

Nancy continues the story. "The second accountability session came around. But just the day before, the outfit that ran the store dismissed the manager and all the employees at that outlet. Apparently, inquiries into the situation had shown that the people's complaints had a substantive basis. Everybody was very happy. They had been taking us for a ride! Yet when he was making his report, the delegate suddenly sang a different tune. He wanted to make it sound as if he had taken a very active part in nailing the grocer all along. So when he asked whether everybody was satisfied with his report, I asked for the floor. I had overheard the good word he'd put in for the grocer before the inspectors, and I said: 'Just a moment, Mr. Delegate. I'd like you to clarify something for me. What was it you really did? Because I have my doubts about you. . . .I happened to be there when you went to bat for the grocer. . . .'

Nancy adds: "He was very much taken aback. He said that all I was saying was pure slander, that he was a man of repute who wouldn't tolerate my saying such a thing. He wanted to intimidate me, but as I was sure of what I was saying I told him that it was I who couldn't accept his calling me a slanderer, and that he was welcome to summon the two inspectors before the assembly. He became angrier and kept insisting it was all a calumny of mine. But, spontaneously, other constituents began to stand up and press the case. Another compañero, after explaining that she had sent a letter of complaint, told him: 'Look, I don't doubt your word, but could you tell me how it came to pass that I sent you a letter about the grocer and the next day, when he looked at my ration book, he blurted out, "Hey! Here's one of those accusing me"? How did the grocer learn that I was one of his accusers when you were the only person who knew about the letter?' Several other persons said similar things. Well, as you can imagine, that meeting got really hot. . . .It didn't even adjourn as usual.

"A few days later another assembly was convened. A great number of constituents attended it. News of the charges against the delegate had spread like wildfire. The climate of the discussion soon got pretty volatile, and the people requested the intervention of the municipality. At that point, the secretary to the municipal People's Power requested the floor and explained to the people that the situation had to resolved by them and not by the municipality. He outlined the procedure for us. A new meeting was then scheduled in order to deal exclusively with the matter of delegate recall."

"It wasn't that simple," says Jorge Vivo, secretary to the municipal executive committee. "The election law specifies that recall procedures can be initiated if 20 percent of the voters demand it, but the law—naturally—doesn't spell out how the signatures are to be collected. A show of hands does not suffice. How do you decide who is and who isn't a qualified voter in a crowded meeting? Even the kids raise their hands."

"Given these procedural wrinkles, Compañero Vivo adds, "the executive committee decided to send a three-man committee to the next assembly. There they proposed the formation of a committee in which each CDR in the district would be represented by a member. The same committee to which the plaintiffs were attached, and which grew to comprise thirty-two members, was instructed to formulate the charges in writing and then collect in each CDR the signatures of those who wanted the delegate's removal. Naturally, both Guillermo and Nancy were members of the committee—one as a CDR reprsentative, the other as a witness for the prosecution. Through this committee's work, new incriminating details came to light."

"Through the recall committee we learned that a neighbor of ours, a MINCIN inspector, had been assigned to conduct an inquiry into the matter," Guillermo remarks. "When he stopped by the delegate's house to get his answers to a questionnaire, the delegate asked him to leave the questionnaire with him because his wife would answer it, as she was the one who did the shopping. He's the one who always does the shopping, who's always skipping the queues, and he had the gall to come up with that! After collecting the nineteen questionnaires the inspector noted that only three had favorable comments on the grocer, and one of them happened to be the delegate's wife. The committee drew up a document in which the chief witnesses for the prosecution detailed the irregularities committed by the delegate in connection with the grocer. The document closed with an analysis of the reasons for the recall. A total of twenty copies were made, one for each CDR. The committee called the voters for a particular day, and after reading the document, those who wished to press the recall charge affixed their signatures to it after showing their IDs. The CDR head, who had possession of the registration rolls, swore under oath that the signatures were authentic. Sixty-five percent of the constituents signed the request."

"It's interesting to note," Nancy says, "that on the delegate's block only four or five people signed, three of them Party members. On that block the delegate's daughter was the CDR chairman. It's quite obvious the neighbors felt under pressure. If the vote had been secret, there's no doubt that he would have gotten even more votes against."

We ask now whether our respondents think the case was a resignation or a proper recall.

"Even though he stepped down," Guillermo replies, "it is clear he was rejected by the majority. His resignation came only after he'd learned of the number of signatures against him."

"So you feel this was accomplished as a result of the people's actions?"

"By all means," Nancy replies at once. Sixty-five percent of the people signed the recall, and the great majority were fully aware of the delegate's shenanigans. Not only did we boot out the delegate, but we also got rid of the grocer and his minions. Selected compañeros took their places. The new store manager is extremely cooperative, always tying to help with the customers' problems, and doesn't play favorites."

"The new crew is totally different from the old one," Guillermo adds. "The people used to call the old team 'the bandits.' "

"After this experience, what, in your opinion, are the most important qualities a person must have in order to qualify as a delegate?"

"The main trait should be the person's commitment to revolutionary principles," Guillermo says emphatically.

"But is it enough just to be a good revolutionary?"

"No, but the criterion should never be just the amount of free time the person has. For if that were true, we'd have to elect bums, even though a modicum of free time is required to carry out the delegate's functions."

"He should not show any tendencies toward favoritism. He must have integrity," Nancy adds. "On the other hand, the delegate must take the complaints of the people up with the appropriate agencies."

"For example," Guillermo says, "faced with the problem of the grocer, he must take the initiative and conduct an inquiry of his own. He should not remain passive while complaints accumulate."

Although the case just described does not strictly involve a question of recall, since the accused delegate resigned before the process was completed, we have thought it instructive nonetheless, for it illustrates clearly how the people themselves, through the mechanisms of People's Power, can combat favoritism, and other unsatisfactory behavior displayed by their representatives.

Recalled Because of Poor Performance

"If the delegate doesn't fulfill his assigned duties, the people themselves request his recall," Emerio Valles declares. He is a sixty-six-year-old former mechanic and a voter from another district, Sancti Spíritus, where a recall procedure has recently taken place. "The people themselves initiate the process," he repeats. "Because here anyone can make a mistake and there may be persons who appear at first eminently qualified for the post and who later show they can't adequately represent their constituents. Previously, under capitalism, the people had to put up with such people till they finished their terms. They kept their jobs for the prescribed time. Not any longer."

"We are the ones who must exercise caution in the selection of the delegate, because we are the ones who have to bear the consequences of our errors later on, and we won't even have someone to represent us. We're gonna be hamstrung, as it were, and no one will pay any attention to our problems."

These words by Celio García, an old-timer with a tobacco mill in the Thirty-fifth District of the Taguasco municipality, are based on the experience his district went through. His delegate was recalled by the voters on account of "poor performance in the fulfillment of his duties." As other districts forged ahead, solving the problems raised by the people, this one in contrast, dropped behind in complete paralysis. We discussed this recall case with both the mill's employees and a group of local peasants gathered at the gate. A few minutes earlier we had also been apprised of the views on this matter of the municipal leaders of People's Power.

"What happened to the delegate you had in this district?"

"The delegate resigned because he had a lot of work to do and couldn't meet the post's demands," says Celio. "Imagine! He had too much work and we were left without a delegate."

"Did he resign or was he recalled?"

"The compañero resigned because he was overloaded with work and couldn't discharge the job properly," Irma Hernández, the office's statistician, says.

"That delegate didn't resign," Leonor Hernández, an office clerk puts in. "He was recalled by the residents. Some people are still confused about the matter, but the compañero was recalled."

"And why was he recalled?"

"Because he didn't do the job. We'd brought a number of problems to his attention, but he did nothing. The compañeros would stop by his office, and he wouldn't be in. We also learned that he didn't attend the meetings at the municipality. That's why he was recalled. We all signed the document requesting his removal."

"It's true," Celio says. "We recalled him, but he said repeatedly that he couldn't do the job because he was much too busy, and we were left without a delegate. He didn't do a thing, anyway. We asked him to look into a number of things, for example, the need to fix up the Social Club, the problem with electric power, which we still don't have, and a lot of similar things—"

At that point Irma springs to the defense of the delegate: "He was a good person," she declares, and continues in a warning tone, "Sometimes we should be careful about the way we talk because it's easy to do someone an injustice. This person was elected because he was good, right? . . .Look, at first we spent quite a lot of time with him waiting for constituents to show up, but they didn't. . . . .The accountability sessions were poorly attended, and the delegate began to lose heart. I agree that he failed, but if we had shown him more interest and support, he'd have made a superb delegate, because he had fine human traits. He was a fine compañero."

"I think that's right," Leonor says approvingly. "We let the compañero down. It was a failure on both sides—his and ours. Because it's not right to bury the delegate under a mountain of problems. We can also come up with solutions to a few things."

The peasants gathered at the factory gate offered similar arguments in connection with the delegate's dismissal. We probe to determine whether their faith in People's Power has been damaged by such an experience.

"The fact a recall takes place for this or that reason has nothing to do with the performance of People's Power. I see People's Power doing a fine job, with an excellent record, and that surely benefits the people," Estangilao Valdés replies.

"But while your delegate was out of commission, didn't you hear that in other places People's Power was working out well in the solution of problems?"

"Of course! Look, right nearby, in La Majagua, People's Power operates quite smoothly. Everything they needed has been procured. Despite the shortages and the problems, quite a few things have been ironed out."

"And now, do you have a new delegate?"

"Yes, and he's already held an accountability session. This young chap is working out fine. He's passing the test with flying colors. And just as the possibilities for this or that open up, he seizes them."

"After the experience you had, what would you say a delegate's chief qualification should be?"

"To begin with, he should be a good revolutionary sort, because this is a job which requires a lot of sympathy for the workers' lot and for the people in general. The delegate has to try to obtain anything from a sack of cement to bricks to roof tiles, if he can get his hands on them. He's got to be a fellow really sensitive to the problems of the people, with a real sense of urgency about them, as if they were his own."

"And what about if the fellow is shy? Do you think he'll do a good job?"

"No. If he's shy, it just won't work out. He's got to be aggressive. He's got to collar the problems, wrestle with them, and call on anybody or anything required. . . .He's got to be self-starter."

"Yes," Adriano Martínez says, "the comrade is right. The delegate must have plenty of pep and show lots of energy on many fronts. He can't afford to be timid about presenting the people's problems. He's got to go to bat for them."

"And what do you think, Irán?"

"Well, the delegate's got to be very sharp if he's to lick the workers' problems!"

"Is the delegate only supposed to take the problems you raise up to the municipal level and bring back a reply, or is he in charge of other things?"

"Many things can be resolved without calling on the municipality," Félix Sánchez replies. "For example, the delegate can organize the work force to tackle a particular thing, if the materials have arrived."

"Well, what happens when materials are scarce and there are many houses to fix?"

"We have a commission here, directly elected by the residents, that is in charge of distributing the materials according to demonstrated need."

"That means that no one can get in ahead of others, that there are no cronies getting the lion's share?"

"I think that's being gradually stamped out," Estangilao says. "Besides, if we see something like that taking place, we simply stand up and block it. On the other hand, the commission's members are very good."

"Have any of you here been affected by the commission's ruling on housing priorities?"

"I have," Félix Sánches replies. "But as we didn't have all the materials I was asking for, that is, cement and tiles—I mean, we had the cement but there were no tiles—they moved me on to the next round of allocations. And I already have the ticket to pick up the materials."

"Has anyone here put in a request for materials from the commission and been denied them?"

"I have," another peasant answers.

"How did you feel when you learned that your request had been turned down?"

"I didn't have any hard feelings. I knew the materials had gone to needier comrades. My turn will come."

This reminds us of the words of Celio García, the old office clerk and a member of a housing materials distribution commission, when we asked him whether he had ever been approached by friends requesting "preferential treatment." He replied without hestitation: "Favoritism? Forget it! At my age and with this much gray hair, it's hard to have one's integrity second-guessed by people."

On the way to this remote rural district we had talked at length about the recall case and other experiences with the president, Ramón Piloto, and the secretary, Felipe Vareda, of the Tahuasco municipal executive committee, in the province of Sancti Spíritus. It was Vareda who explained to us the procedure for recall.

"What happened to the delegate of that district?"

"He started out with a few mistakes. For example, he wouldn't show up on the days set to hear his constituents' problems. Then he was also rather weak in representing their problems. His constituents became disillusioned. Eventually, one voter, Wilfredo Camacho, came to see the Tahuasco executive committee to discuss the situation. We told him that the municipal assembly could not recall the delegate; that it was up to them to take the necessary steps. We advised him on the procedure to follow. The people then just took it from there.

"In the first place, they gathered more signatures than the 20 percent initially needed to start a recall. They eventually gathered 63 percent of the signatures and drew up a petition to the municipality detailing the reasons for which they were demanding a recall. As soon as we received the document, we summoned the delegate and advised him of the situation, giving him ten days to file his objections, if he so wished, to the arguments raised by his constituents. In that period the delegate took no action in his own defense. Apparently he accepted the recall."

"But what did he say when you informed him of the charges filed against him by his constituents."

"Naturally, he made a few points concerning his job as a school principal, but we know that this didn't prevent him from discharging his duties, because every delegate sets aside one day a week to see his constituents; moreover, delegates may be away from their jobs a certain amount of time every week or fortnight, so they may discuss, push for, and, in general, advance the cause of the voters. This situation was verified by the Municipal Department of Education, which told us he was perfectly able to fulfill his functions both as a delegate and as a teacher.

"Neither the voters nor the municipality could brook such a shoddy performance, especially since he'd already lost the respect of most of the people. When the ten days went by without our receiving anything from him, the problem was taken up before the municipal assembly where a committee was appointed to go ahead with the process of recall."

"Did the delegate attend that municipal assembly?"

"No, he was the only one who didn't attend. We had a 99 percent attendance."

"So what was the next step?"

"The committee called a meeting to allow the people to cast secret ballots."

"Did you explain the reasons for the recall at that meeting?"

"No, because the voters had already had a meeting for that purpose, when the gathering of signatures was taking place."

"But when you collect the signatures, how do you establish who is really a legitimate voter?"

"Well, since this is a small district, with only 280 voters, everybody knows everybody else. Besides, in all these electoral processes close collaboration with the CDRs is standard procedure. They control the registration rolls, and it was precisely the three CDRs in the district—which is divided into two zones—who set up the meetings to debate the problem and collect the signatures necessary for recall. And 62 percent of the people signed for recall. This percentage rose later to 72 percent when the secret ballot was taken."

"How do you explain this increase?"

"Constituents who failed to attend the meeting debating the recall may have been present for the vote," says the assembly president. "It's also likely that relatives of the delegate may have avoided casting a public vote against him but joined in on a secret recall."

"Once the delegate is recalled, what's next?

"Well, you follow the steps prescribed by the law, which allows ninety days for choosing another delegate," the municipal secretary replies. "First, the voting register is brought up to date. Next come the meetings to select the president of the nominations assembly, then those meetings take place, and, after that, the vote itself."

"And who was chosen as a replacement?"

"His name is Humberto Reinas, and he works as a chauffeur. The election took place last January 8, with 235 voters participating, or 85 percent of the district's voters. Humberto got 167 votes, a large majority. That was the final count. The compañero is doing very well."

"Do you thing the experience weakened or strengthened People's Power?"

"We believe the system was strengthened, because from a political standpoint the delegate's attitude was making People's Power look unresponsive to the people's needs. But from the moment the people joined the recall process, it became clear what kind of role they play in the government, that they may revoke, decide the leadership's direction in that area. All this confirms that it is the people who wield power."

"The new delegate," the municipal president breaks in, "has given People's Power more prestige. He works hard at it." A pause, then he adds, "I'd like to make clear that we, before going for a recall, gave the delegate plenty of opportunities to shape up. We called him up innumerable times, show him where he was failing, talked to him face to face. I personally saw him on two occasions. I spoke to him from the delegate's standpoint, and from the Party member's standpoint. What we'd like you to understand is that if a delegate has problems we usually try to help him. When he shows specific deficiencies, the first thing we try to do is to try to work with him. We seek him out, ask him to bring the problems out in the open. Only when we see that he is failing to respond do we contemplate the possibility of a recall. We have plenty of regular contacts with the delegates. Monthly contacts. We keep abreast of their progress. They are welcome to see us any day to discuss their difficulties, and there's also contact through the assembly; that is, there are ties that allow us to keep close watch on his performance. In the case of this delegate, we worked with him, we tried to alert him . . . ."

"How many delegates do you have in the municipality?"

"We have 76."

"If the recalled delegate was elected by the people—how do you account for such a surprise? Was it an actual lack of qualifications?" We put the question to the secretary.

"I've formed an opinion about these things. To begin with, the delegate had the requisite talent. He was the vice-principal of a school. I think the compañeros badly miscalculated the amount of work involved in People's Power. Maybe he thought this was just one more institution and that whatever he did it would be all right. He didn't take into account the work with the people and the assemblies that was required; and when he came to that realization, he was taken aback, because he saw that his studies at the univesity might be hampered."

"Why do you say, 'was vice-principal'? Doesn't he hold that post any longer?"

"No, he's no longer the vice-principal. He's now a plain teacher. We felt that with his shortcomings, with his loss of status as a delegate, he was no longer entitled to hold a position of such responsibility, implying a level of distinction, a certain amount of public recognition. For if I lack the prestige to act as a delegate before the people who elected me, I don't think I can have the authority to discharge another job requiring a leadership ability."

We press the subject a bit further. We want to know very clearly what happened to a person who was first considered suited for the post of delegate and later found wanting.

"In our opinion, he just gave up. I think he thought things would be a lot easier, and when he met resistance, he just decided not to make the effort. He didn't display the best attitude, an attitude of sacrifice. Being a vice-principal involves lots of work, but that doen't excuse a poor performance as a delegate."

The president of the municipality breaks in: "He wasn't doing that well at the school either. He had problems of temperament, and that's the reason the Department of Education decided to transfer him. I believe that he took advantage of his situation as a student and just decided to coast."

"And you, comrades, you are both delegates and members of the municipal executive committee, did you have any idea of the amount of work involved in being a delegate?"

"No, not precisely, but we knew it was a demanding job."

"It wasn't easy to imagine it. We have been learning many things about this along the way, but no one could have fully anticipated what being a delegate really required?"

"Could you mention some of the things you have learned through experience?"

"Something we have come to regard as extremely important is the role played by the delegate in the solution of problems," Ramon says. "Not infrequently, snags that can be resolved by the delegate with the people's participation, at the grassroots level, extend up into other levels. The delegate has to have 'presence' and initiative; he has to act as the engine propelling the people who chose him; he has to go to the people involved in the solutions of the problems."

"You mean, then, the delegate must be far more than a mere conduit."

"Well, some things must be brought to the attention of higher authorities by the delegate, but we believe the delegate must start off with a wide-ranging analysis of his district's problems, giving the people a say about the way these problems are to be handled. So we believe that any problem admitting of resolution by the people themselves should be left to them. Besides, in our view, this revitalizes the participatory instinct. It may be said that when the people are given a chance to define and resolve their problems as they see fit, when they see themselves as directly in charge, as the real doers, all this engenders a new climate, a different atmosphere, a new sense of keen involvement in public affairs. We pay far more attention to things because we're controlling the processes affecting us. In general," the municipal president concludes, "our work has conformed to this philosophy and given us excellent results."

An Essential Aspect of Proletarian Democracy

Delegates to People's Power or executive committee members can be recalled at any time by the voters in the same democractic manner in which they were chosen if their constituents conclude they are remiss in fulfilling their assigned duties, or if their conduct falls short of the standards expected from a People's Power official.

A delegate can be recalled only by those who elected him. Delegates to the provincial assembly and deputies to the National Assembly can only be recalled by the municipal assemblies that elected them. Similarly, the executive committee of the provincial assembly can only be recalled by the provincial assembly.

As seen earlier, the recall process cannot be put in motion unless 20 percent of the voters demand it. The recall can also be initiated by the assembly to which the delegate belongs.

The recall proposal must be filed in writing with the president of the municipal assembly where the delegate serves. The president next advises the delegate of such a motion. The delegate is then given ten days to file a defense in writing. After these formalities are met and the ten days have expired, the president convokes a meeting of the municipal assembly to advise the members of the recall proposal and to introduce the arguments presented by the defendant. After the case has been debated, a date is set to call the district's voters for a vote on the matter. To be valid, more than half of the voters must register their support of recall. After the delegate is recalled, a new election is scheduled.

It is important, however, to distinguish between a recall and a substitution. In the latter, the delegate is found to have objective impediments to the fulfillment of his duties, international assignments, sickness, relocation to another area, studies abroad, and so on. Up to June, 1978, 666 delegates had been substituted for at the national level, whereas 77 were recalled.

The right to recall representatives elected by the people highlights one of the fundamental differences between bourgeois and proletarian states. Even in the most ostensibly democratic bourgeois representative systems, delegates chosen by popular vote, the vast majority of whom are presented as candidates by parties beholden to the interests of the ruling classes, lose all real contact with the voters soon after the election is over. The voters are unable to control the delegates' actual performance after that, or to interrupt their terms, which last, irregardless of position, for the period stipulated by law. This helps to explain, after a fashion, the great electoral apathy one finds in the United States of America, a country that insists on billing itself before the world as the foremost example of representative democracy. In the 1976 presidential election 46 percent of the American people preferred to stay home. For how interested can the American people be in the elections if they know very well that the campaigns are chockful of demagogic promises made to attract votes but never honored? In Cuba, in contrast, delegates must stay in touch with their constituents, advising them, keeping them informed of their activites, and they are subject to recall at a moment's notice.

8 ASSEMBLIES AND DELEGATES

The Delegate: A People's Advocate

We now proceed to explore in more detail the question of a delegate's background.

"I think," says Reinaldo, "that this experiment has been useful to the revolutionary leadership and shown many things to the people. The latter have realized that a delegate must possess, in addition to his personal traits, the ability to be of service, to debate any problem in the assembly, and to offer suggestions. It's not enough for him to be a good, genial sort who goes there just to listen quietly and to raise his hand occasionally. He has to be persistent, dogged, in the defense of his constituents' demands before the assembly. He has to be able to explain to the voters why certain things can't be solved right away. In Matanzas, many compañeros with indisputable revolutionary records were elected, only to show that they lacked the temperament to stand up for an idea. This explains why fewer than half of the former delegates gained renomination as candidates in the recent 1976 elections."

"Was the low educational level of the delegate a major factor in this area?"

"We have to distinguish betweeen the level of formal scholarship, which may be low, and the person's cultural development, which is another matter," Alexis says. "For the latter has been accumulated over the years of struggle and contact with the people. We find comrades with a sixth-grade education who can sit down with you and discourse on botany, medicine, and history. These are comrades who had to educate themselves. Any of our leaders, coming from union struggles, or Party ranks, and not even with a sixth-grade education, as is the case of Fundora, but who is an old working-class soldier, one who has fought the battles alongside his fellow workers, may wind up with a very impressive cultural level. Life itself has been his teacher. On the other hand, we have comrades with college degrees who have given extremely lackluster performances as delegates. They are good revolutionaries, but they are also unimpressive as members of the assembly. That's why this experience has been so important to the people. Now they are better equipped to elect superior advocates for their particular concerns."

"This topic," says Laureano," brings to my mind Che Guevara's thoughts on the Party member's chief characteristics. Naturally, formal education has a certain importance in a delegate; but personal experience is fundamental because, as Alexis just pointed out, although this Revolution has suffered from material limitations, it has never been poor in political work. That has never been rationed in this country. So the Revolution has been like an open book. And the people have drunk from this revolutionary experience, the confrontation with imperialism, and from the everyday political struggle taking place at all levels of society. This process has made the Cuban people a highly politicized people, with ample resources to face, at any moment, the different challenges that have come up in the political, social, and economic spheres. That is why individuals with poor scholastic records may also possess a high level of political sophistication. Through the Party's schools, through individual study, and through the roles they have been called upon to play, they have acquired a political education."

"What other characteristics must a delegate possess?" .

"We have to consider a number of factors. Besides the intrinsic professional capacity, the delegate must show true sensitivity to the problems raised. Another very important point," Alexis continues, "is that the delegate must pay serious attention to the solutions favored by his constituents. He's not supposed to give his undivided attention to the analyses presented by the bureaucrats. Also, weekly meetings at his office with the voters are indispensable because many citizens are incapable of speaking up in an open assembly. . . . The person may be embarrassed or inhibited, and may even think that he's going to be upbraided for saying something he's not supposed to. In private consultation with the delegate, however, the person has an opportunity to speak up, no matter how inarticulately, and to vent his feelings. The delegate must also be willing to listen to his constituents anywhere, even on the street, and to offer some sort of satisfaction right then and there. Sometimes, because of the amount of work, it's more cumbersome to set up an appointment

...to have the person come up to the office...it's more complicated. We have learned that it makes sense to try to help our fellows as soon as we are advised of their problems. One must have sincere empathy with other people's problems."

Laureano interrupts: "I think what Alexis has said is very important. One must learn to listen to the people, be receptive to the questions they ask. Because we have already had the experience of finding that it was the least likely citizen who solved the problem. On the other hand, we often hear of problems that hurt deeply, and we must spring into action at once."

"Yes, that's crucial," Reinaldo exclaims. "I was an administrative leader and know a bit about the population's problems. Many times, in the past, the people were given the runaround. They were asked to come back the next day, or the day after, for we didn't really understand the nature of their problems. Now we can feel them as our own, and this has improved the situation.

"Just now, on my way here, I was delayed because a compañera dropped in to tell me about a problem she has at home, and I was glad to accommodate her. This is a source of a lot of satisfaction, that people should see me as a person they can trust in the clarification of any problem. That's one of the greatest experiences we've had. That's why we should like to advise future delegates to draw close to the people and get to feel their problems."

The Functions of the Delegate

What is the role played by the delegates? Are they in charge of directing the production and service units located in their districts? Are they the ones who mobilize the people for different tasks?

The first thing we must explain is that the delegates do not *direct* but *represent* their constituents before the People's Power agency in which they carry out their duties.

Neither do the delegates direct the production and service units located within their jurisdiction, for this is the task of the respective administrative bureaus, so that anarchy can be avoided. This does not mean that the delegate may not approach the director of a given unit to advise him of some growing dissatisfaction or of the concerns and suggestions advanced by his constituents. What he cannot do is order him about or dismiss him.

Nor are the delegates personally responsible for the mobilization of the people in connection with production matters, or of any other kind. It would be impossible for any one person who is also a worker to mobilize seven-hundred or more people residing in his district. For this task he can rely on the mass organizations existing in Cuba. The unions, the CDRs, the Women's Federation, the ANAP, the student federations, and, in particular, the Union of Communist Youth and the Party.

One of the delegate's functions is to convey to the municipal assembly and its executive committee, the needs, criteria, and concerns found among his constituents, and to defend their interests in that forum. Similarly, toward his constituents he must serve as a conduit for the policies followed by the municipal assembly of People's Power, explaining the difficulties encountered by this body while seeking solutions to the problems raised by the community.

Raúl Castro clarified this particular function of the delegate in his speech of August 22, 1974, at the closing session of the seminar for People's Power delegates, in preparation for their new tasks: "In each collective contact with his constituents the delegate will have to report on the activites of the municipal People's Power and its various responsibilities, on his own personal performance as a delegate, on the manner People's Power has tackled the problems raised by his constituents. He will note the problems that have a solution as well as those which do not, and those that require a longer term; he will clarify the whys of each solution and measure. Nothing must be left unexplained with regards to the massses.

"The delegates must learn all the reasons that compel the adoption of a measure taken by the state organs, whether municipal, regional, or provincial People's Power agencies, or the central agencies of the State. If a price goes up, the reasons behind it must be explained; if a distribution quota is modified, the reason must be made clear to the masses; if a product takes longer than expected to reach the people, the causes [for the delay] must be explained; if the schedule on which a particular service is rendered is changed, the people must know the reasons; and in each and every case the explanation must be convincing. The delegates must never be bearers to the masses of absurd explanations of convoluted reasonings designed to extricate them from a tight spot; such things convince no one. The delegates must demand on the floor of the assemblies they belong to, and of the corresponding executive committees, all the explanations they need so they can satisfactorily convey these to the masses.

"On the other hand, the delegates must collect all the complaints and suggestions transmitted by their constituents and represent these before the respective asemblies. Any complaint, suggestion, or opinion raised or supported by the majority of the voters must be transmitted by the delegate to the People's Power agencies, even when the delegate happens to disagree with the people. The delegate is not representing himself, but a mass of voters who have selected him, it is their problems and opinions that he must represent and not his personal problems and criteria.

"It is necessary to recall, as Fidel mentioned on July 26, that 'what cannot be denied is an explanation to each citizen requesting something, explaining with honesty and sincerity if things are possible or not: no one must ever be deceived.' "

The delegates are not simply the transmission belts for the people's cares, they must also work in the People's Power agencies to find solutions. In reality, this is their principal function, and in order to fulfill it, they must make use of all their creative initiative.

This does not imply, however, that in order to solve a series of problems, the delegates must assume tasks that belong to other agencies. It is not the delegate who must carry out administrative functions such as distribution of construction materials among the residents of his district. This task is met by the appropriate bureau of People's Power. The role of the delegate in these matters, which are vitally important to the population, will be to participate, as a member of the People's Power assemblies, in the adoption of decisions insuring a fairer distribution of those items, and to see to it that the bureau charged with the implementation of such resolutions acts in accordance with them, without violating them or establishing practices of privilege, favoritism, etc.

To fulfill his mission the delegate meets every four months with his constituents and reports on his activities. These assemblies, whose success is so directly a reflection of the delegate's ability to satisfy his constituents, must be well organized if district residents are to have an incentive to attend and not to be bored. So the delegate cannot just confine himself to reading the report to the municipal assembly and then the letters he has received in reply to the problems raised by his constituents during the previous accountability session. His report must be vigorous, in tune with the heartfelt concerns of the people. The answers must be convincing. And he must promote maximum participation from the audience. It must be a lively meeting.

Direct Attention to the People

But the delegates do not limit themselves to this collective contact with their constituents. They also have a "grievance day," every week, devoted to any grievance, proposal, and suggestion, the people may care to make. The procedure is well established in the community.

We ask Laureano, a popular delegate and member of the Cardenas executive committee, how he handles this routine.

"Where do you confer with the people?"

"It's up to the delegate. In my case, I see people at home."

"Approximately how many people come to see you, and what kind of questions do they raise?"

"About four or six people come to each session. I receive the people on Fridays, from 8 P.M. on, until all matters have been discussed. The topics vary, from problems of my jurisdiction to problems concerning other places, since everyone knows I'm also a member of the regional management. All visitors have one characteristic in common: No one comes demanding a solution to his problem. What they are seeking basically is guidance. They raise problems of education, of children's gardens, housing . . .since we have a huge demand for this item."

"Do you see them in private or in public?"

"While I confer with one, others wait in the same room. Now the truth is that this specific day for consultation is something they don't pay much attention to. Wherever they see me they stop me, or they drop by the house at any hour!"

"What are their main concerns?"

"Housing, as I said earlier . . .the problems of repair and maintenance of things . . .school questions."

"Does it ever happen that they ask you to fix something for them, on the 'buddy system?' "

Alexis intervenes at this point. He cannot hold back any longer. He has accumulated a great deal of personal experience in this matter.

"Well, it so happens that some delegates believe that giving better service entails doing everything, even taking a broken stove to the repair shop. . . .We are trying to explain to the delegates that this isn't done, that normal channels exist for that sort of thing. Now your question. What you bring up doubtlessly occurs. At times, someone may come up and say: 'We know you can't help with this matter . . .but we've known each other for so long and I never asked for anything before, in all these years. Look, now I'd like you to give me a hand with this.' I usually reply: 'We are here to struggle against this. When I begin to play favorites I begin to go astray.' They say: 'Well, I thought you'd say that, but I gave it a try anyway.' Acting in this manner cements the respect of the people, their belief in our honesty and integrity, that we are telling them the truth. We don't recall any cases of favoritism. Keep in mind that the compañeros have been elected and can be replaced."

Laureano interjects "The people have elected the best within the boundaries of our cultural underdevelopment. We have men who have given their level best during these fifteen years of revolution, but who lack formal education, a secondary license, are people of humble origin, from the working class. When we held the elections and the photos were attached to the political biographies, people could be heard to say: 'Well! Look at this fellow's career! He sure has come a long way, and I didn't know it!' "

A more laconic answer, but in the same mould, is given to us by José Failde, the president of the Matanzas executive committee:

"We feel the pressure, but we can't pay any attention to it. Someone may come up to us as an old friend, but he is precisely the fellow we have to give a no-nonsense answer."

Nonprofessional Officials

The delegates elected by the rank and file follow their usual work routines and devote the rest of their time to the jurisdiction's problems and to attending municipal meetings whenever they take place. It is the best method to keep them close to the people and free from becoming bureaucrats.

"The delegate is constantly in touch with the people," Alexis says, "and is under an obligation to account to them. But at the same time he must be a good worker, and if he is a Party member, besides his Party duties, he must engage in a program of study. It is one more obligation. It isn't easy. The people understand this. In fact, the people have great affection for their delegates. Moreover, they are at the disposal of their constituents any time they are needed. It is true that a certain day has been set aside to hear complaints, but mostly to make sure that on at least one day they can reach their representative. In practice, they are free to contact him anytime they wish. And the delegate doesn't listen only to the problems of his district; because the compañero is also a worker, just like the others, problems at work are also raised. Like: 'Look, compañero, here they are serving the croquettes cold!' Or: 'Look, in such and such a place there's a hole that needs to be filled.' That kind of thing."

How Women Delegates Operate

Despite heavy competition from the final match of the national boxing championships and one of the closing episodes of the television docudrama "Doña Bárbara," the assembly of delegate Raquel Mediavilla had a record 82 percent attendance. It was the highest attendance rate ever registered by an accountability session in any of the districts comprising District 77 of the "10th of October" municipality.

The impressive turnout, the excellent report presented by the delegate, and the inspired participation of members of the audience prompted us to investigate why People's Power had done so remarkably well in that corner of Havana.

We met with five of the most active persons in the district: Isabel Fonseca, CDR coordinator for District 77; Rosa María Castedo, head of CDR No. 1 and a worker at the "Monaco" supermarket; Antonia García, a retired housewife, member of CDR No. 25, and also secretary general for the neighborhood FMC; Paula Ramos, housewife and education secretary for the area CDR; and René Corvo, a plumber with the Communications Brigade of the Department of Communications.

"Look," Rosa says, "at the INIT dinner there were complaints that the hot dogs were much too small . . . that the croquettes were being served alone, that the ice cream was so warm it melted. So there goes Raquel. Without warning, she just drops by and orders an ice cream and a hot dog, so she can see everything for herself, and later asks to see the manager, with whom she irons out the wrinkles. This is what happens with all establishments we have here. The same happened with the pizza parlor. The manager once asked her to sample a pizza. Raquel told him: 'No, I'll just stop in one day and will see if there are any deficiencies." And the day she did drop by was simply a bummer. They took forever to wait on her, and the same thing happened when she wanted to pay. She's like a ghost. I don't know when she finds the time to get some sleep.

"Another thing that was finally licked," she adds, "was the problem of the long lines waiting to pay for milk at the supermarket. It wasn't in the guidelines, nor did the state contemplate having one out of three checkout counters devoted entirely to checking out milk, but it was done and the results were excellent. Anyone buying milk could pay at a special checkout counter."

"Just for the record, it was my idea," Nica says.

"Well, but the idea was dropped when the higher echelons heard about it, because it wasn't taken into account in the guidelines. So she [Raquel] went up to the regional level and brought Compañero Vasquez one Tuesday evening, so he could see for himself, explaining to him why it was necessary to assign a special cashier to the milk. And he saw her point. So that goes to show you that when she doesn't get what she wants at a particular level she just goes on to the next, and so on, and she drags the leaders down to the grassroots."

"One Sunday morning," Paula interrupts, "when we were making the rounds of the district, a compañero approached us at the Minimax market to inform Raquel that he'd gone to the fish market and despite the fact there was a line of people waiting to buy fish, the compañera behind the counter would not sell any because her calculator was broken. 'That can't be!' Raquel said. 'The people can't be left without fish! Let's go over to the fish market.' There she found that one of the women was claiming she couldn't handle the numbers without the machine because she lacked the education, while the other was arguing that she had to be in the back doing something else. The fact is, they didn't want to work; what they wanted to do was to close up and go home. Raquel told them that a broken calculator was not sufficient reason to let the people go without fish. She explained the situation to them, and the women saw that they were wrong and started waiting on people.

"In this zone we have rallied around the slogan: 'One Sunday with Raquel to inspect the district.' A CDR leader alway does the rounds with her," Paula adds.

"On the other hand, Raquel does not confine her duties to deficiencies within the district. She had also worked on programs or activities for kids on vacation. She also rapidly implemented a proposal from the assembly to have a district playground for children between the ages of seven and twelve. All of us CDR members cleaned and cleared that spot, and on the next Sunday we had play shifts operating according to CDR areas, with a comrade in charge of each."

How to Prepare an Accountability Session

"I think it's important for you to hear about our experience with the accountability sessions," Paula says. "The particulars might be instructive to other districts. When Raquel learns the date set for the assembly, she meets with the area's leaders while we handle other tasks. For example, we divide the areas, that is, we organize the twenty-six district CDRs into four areas. Next we ask the leaders of these areas to get together with the CDR coordinators in order to form a support committee capable of organizing the mobilization required. They act, therefore, as publicists for that assembly."

"And where do you post the publicity?"

"At the most frequented spots: the store, the Minimax, the fish market, the cinema, the pizza parlor, on each corner," Paula replies. "After that, the area leaders meet to form a committee of two people for each area. These compañeras work hand in hand with the CDR heads, refine the details about the mobilization, the schedule to be observed, the kind of discipline suited to the event, and so on. Those two compañeras from the committee in charge of each area must be present the day of the assembly to make sure that everything goes well, according to plan."

"I'd like to say something on this subject," Rosa interjects. "The first assembly in this area was something to remember. Let me tell you the way Raquel operates. You are supposed to stand up and say your name aloud, specifying the CDR you belong to. Now, when she answers you, she's likely to say: 'Marta, what you mean is this and that or that.' She doesn't say 'Comrade,' or 'Citizen,' or anything like that. Just your name and 'Marta, what's on your mind?' And if you haven't been too sharp in expressing yourself, she rounds it out for you because she's awfully witty. She catches everything at once, everything right away, and responds to each person on a first-name basis."

At this point Raquel herself joins our group. The people give her a warm welcome, and the conversation continues enthusiastically.

"From what you have told me, I gather the CDRs play an important role in this scheme, but what happens if a CDR isn't working out too well?"

"In our district we don't have many problems with our CDRs when it comes to this question. Nevertheless, we do have a few CDRs we have to reinforce because there are some deficiencies in them . . . not in the leadership, but at the consciousness level. . . . If you'll let me digress a bit," Isabel says, "thanks to the triumph of the Revolution, thanks to our commander in chief, and our Party, the political awareness is high among the people, even when some throwbacks to the past still persist. Because of this, not all CDRs have the background needed to digest quickly the implications of People's Power and what our delegate represents. In our area the majority understands, but we have some problems with some CDRs, and these are closely watched by the leadership. We specifically had difficulties in two CDRs. So we converged there, met with the secretary, carried the publicity load, door to door, getting out the vote by personal effort. We paid them a visit a week before election day, then three days before, and twenty four hours prior to the event. We also saw them after the assembly was over. I'd like to mention here that one of these 'problem' CDRs wound up second in attendance, right behind the leading CDR, that is, No. 10."

Raquel intervenes at that point, addressing me: "You see, Marta, this is the group that keeps going. These people! They are like an irrepressible engine! If I don't go forward, they'll kill me! The problem here is that I'm supposed to prepare the way for them. But it's not I, but they who drive me. With the contagious enthusiasm of these people, with their élan, their spirit of sacrifice, you've got to keep moving forward—because if you don't, they'll just bulldoze you, yes, sir. You have seen the spirit of these folks. These are people I can truly depend on, anytime."

Delegates and Administrative Officials

"Going back to what you told me at the beginning, I understand the delegate can do many things without having to rely on the municipality, isn't that right?"

"Exactly," Rosa says, and adds: "Look, let me tell you something. The day they burned the paper trash at the supermarket, and the whole place was strewn with papers, a compañero walked by and said to Raquel: 'Look, Raquel, this is an offense you have to report.' But Raquel didn't pay any attention to that. Instead, she came down here to investigate what had happened. She went down to the supermarket and talked to the people in charge, and the papers were picked up immediately, without a report being filed. Now, that's initiative."

"I thought it wasn't fair," Raquel expalains, "since I am on very good terms with the compañeros in the Commerce Department, and we keep in close touch on any problems. I think a more severe attitude might be justified when you have discussed the matter with them and they still fail to act on the recommendation."

Still, the delegate wants no misunderstanding with regard to her policy vis-à-vis the bureaucrats: "The delegate has no authority whatever over the Commerce Department. Here our understanding with them is something of a fraternal coordination. What we have to watch out for is poor service, poor workmanship, and so on. The delegate's role is important because if she has maintained a close relationship with the administrator, problems are more easily licked when they arise. But it should be pointed out that the delegate doesn't have to become a "cure-all." The manager must take care of that angle; that's his responsibility. So what is it that we delegates contribute? If we spot a problem in a particular enterprise, we have to see the manager so corrective measures can be taken. If, despite our insistence, the problem remains unsolved, if the answers are not convincing, if there's a bottleneck, we are forced to fall back on the relevant bureau, and if this, too, proves unable to solve the problem, then we have to apply to the member of the municipal executive committeeman in charge of that department. This person has set aside one day a week to hear the delegates and the problems of their respective districts."

At this point another compañero joins our group, asking himself, apparently, what the gathering is all about. Rosa introduces him.

"It's Compañero Fernando, our supermarket manager."

We take advantage of this opportunity to put a question to him: "What does it mean for managerial personnel to have to deal with People's Power? Do you feel under pressure because of it?"

"Yes, of course! It's terrible! The compañera visits us two or three times a week. But it's not just a question of watchfulness; many problems have been eliminated after talking with her, such as the question of the paint, for example."

"Do you attend the accountability sessions?"

"Yes."

Rose breaks in: "Our assemblies are attended by any managers. During the last assembly, for instance, we applauded our grocery store because those people are really on their toes. You never find a line there, not even on days when rationed goods are going onto the market, because that is the day they get up earlier than ever, and by the time the first customers arrive they have everything under control."

"We take extra pains with them," Paula adds. "They are invited, and as the posters announcing the assemblies are hung in their stores, many attend. I think it's important that they attend because that way they learn better about what the people are thinking."

"Do you think that a delegate can confine himself to collecting the people's complaints, only to read in the next assembly the replies he got from each bureau?"

"No way. That can't possibly be. There are many things the delegate can tackle himself. We also have to admit that, in our case, very few problems really elude Raquel."

"About this question," Raquel adds, "I'd like to say that we are instructed by our executive committee that we are under no obligation to accept unconvincing answers. For example, yesterday I rejected four answers given to me by various deparments. I just didn't buy them. Why not? Because I couldn't understand them, and if I can't understand them, then I can't possibly make them clear to my constituents. Yesterday I turned down one explanation on the phone, and another one which was delivered to me personally, telling me we couldn't make some repairs. I told them that after three months they just couldn't give me such a vague answer, especially one so lacking in precision. For it's not enough to tell me that the matter was being included in some repair schedule. They had to specifiy a date, a year—2000 or 1979 or 1980—a precise year, a precise date. I just couldn't take that and then have my neighbors rise in disgust in the face of such sloppiness. The delegate must know the problem inside out so she can discuss the matter properly with the pertinent department. For instance, if this can't be done, why not? What are the measures you're going to take? So I can explain everything to my people. The delegate must show the people that their problems were handled properly in the appropriate bureaus. She must be able to face up to an administrator and ask: 'Well, what's this? How many times do I have to hear the same thing?' Now, if the delegate accepts a poor answer, that's not the department's fault, but the delegate's. I am responsible for the problems before the people. Because if I'm told that a particular repair job is contemplated in the plan of a given ministry, I have to ask: "Yes, in the plan, but in what year, when, how, in what manner, etc.'

It is useful at this point to recall an interesting initiative adopted by the Tahuasco municipal executive committee, in the province of Sancti Spíritus, to combat the problem of bureaucratic answers.

"We on the executive committee pay a tremendous amount of attention to the problem of red tape," the secretary says. "We watch very closely the work done by the department heads vis-à-vis the demands of the population. Each member of the executive committee oversees a group of departments, and when the people have raised a problem, we are interested in knowing what answers they're going to get. Besides, they can't provide an answer without discussing the matter with us, without our approving it first. Why? Because there are people who, to save themselves the effort, will give unsatisfactory answers to the questions raised by the electorate. We control the work of the administration. This insures that when the people get an answer, it answers the question raised. The executive committee keeps close tabs on the issues raised by the population, both those that have been resolved and those that are still pending."

The Local Agencies and Their Prerogatives

Alexis relates the following incident: "We reached an accord here that was very popular. The street where you find this building [the building assigned to People's Power] is also Cardenas's main street. Here you find the cinemas, the retail shops, where people go walking with their families. A few years back, because of traffic, the traffic bureau decided that bicycles were to be banned from the street. I don't know whether or not you are aware of the fact that Cardenas is the Cuban city having the most bikes: there are about sixty thousand residents and thirty thousand bikes. Naturally, this step was badly received by the people. In Cardenas a bike is like the clothing on your back—you've got to have it. The people protested vehemently.

"When People's Power took over, this was one of the first issues it had to confront. The municipal assembly decided to drop the measure. Now this is a typical problem that can be easily resolved at the municipal level.

When the traffic of bikes was allowed to resume, on December 21, there was an outburst of popular jubilation. People just went around greeting everybody. The measure had its significance. Before People's Power no regional bureau had the competence to decide the question." Let us now see in more detail how the local agencies of People's Power are organized and what specific functions they fill.

The municipal assembly is the basic agency of People's Power. It is made up of delegates elected by the people in each district. This assembly is empowered to elect delegates to the provincial assembly and deputies to the National Assembly.

Once in operation, the municipal assembly's first job is to choose from among its members those who will carry on the work of People's Power at the municipal level between assemblies and implement its resolutions. This body, called the executive committee, has a president, a vice-president, a secretary, and a number of committee members varying from two to twelve, depending on the size and importance of the municipality. The executive committee elects its own president, vice-president, and secretary, but these choices are subject to ratification by the assembly as a committee of the whole. These posts are filled by persons working full time on the tasks of People's Power. Among the committee members there are professionals, that is, those who head the various departments, bureaus, offices, and nonprofessionals, that is, those who devote time to People's Power only after their regular working hours.

The provincial assembly is made up of statutory delegates (the heads of municipal assemblies) and of other delegates elected by the municipal assembly. (There is one delegate for every ten thousand municipal residents, or fraction thereof larger than five thousand.)

The municipal nominating committee is in charge of nominating candidates to the provincial assembly.

It is important to bear in mind that these candidates need not be elected directly by the people. The committee may recommend people who, while not directly elected, amply fill the qualifications for People's Power at the provincial level.

The provincial executive committee is picked from the delegates to the provincial assembly, employing the same mechanism utilized by the municipal assembly. The number of members varies from seven to twenty-one.

Assembly resolutions are adopted by simple plurality of those present, save for exceptional cases, such as a delegate's recall, which require a prior endorsement vote and then a plurality exceeding more than half of the assembly membership.

Summing up, the local organs of People's Power are empowered to do the following:

1. Debate and decide upon all aspects of economic planning for province and municipality;
2. Supervise the administrative departments and their performance in carrying out assigned duties. Transfer units from one department to another, when such a step is deemed advisable to improve performance. Appoint administrators and managers and other leading personnel in People's Power;
3. Set up permanent and ad hoc commissions to inspect and supervise production and service units under jurisdiction. These commissions can assist the assembly in policy-making, in order to optimize the use of material and human resources;
4. Organize delegates' accountability procedures to their constituents, and the mechanism to effect recalls;
5. Elect and recall judges according to the jurisdictional authority, municipal or provincial.

The Executive Committees: Learning from Experience

Reinaldo, a member of the executive committee in Cardenas, says: "The executive committee had a good deal of trouble at first disentangling the matters it was supposed to handle as the assembly's executive arm from those intended for the attention of the assembly itself. As a result, during the early months of the Matanzas experiment the assembly sessions were inordinately long, covering almost any topic. The first provincial assembly lasted a full day and a half. Now they take two or three hours, since the agenda has been refined to include only topics germane to the assembly, thereby raising the quality of the debate. I'd like to give you an example: During the first provincial assembly, more than an hour was spent discussing, of all things, the quality of croquettes found in the 'Amarillas' municipality, in Colon. It's obvious that the quality of a municipality's croquettes doesn't belong on the agenda of a provincial assembly. It's something that has to be tackled by the comrades who live in Amarillas, by their administrative authority. Yes, mapping out the topical perimeter consumed considerable time."

Laureano and Alexis confirm Reinaldo's assessment: "We started to run the government without knowing exactly how we were going to do it," Laureano says. "We attended a seminar for a month; then we were given books to study. Next thing, everyone chose an office and the meetings started. We began to receive some orientation from the National Commission. 'This should be done this way; that should be done that way,' etc. The early People's Power assemblies were hard to believe. There was one delegate who introduced as many as nineteen points—"

"The assemblies used to begin at nine A.M. and end at eleven before midnight," Alexis interjects.

"That was an interminable business," Reinaldo says, smiling. "Some had to be resumed the next day. The debate just ebbed and flowed. Many topics shouldn't have been discussed at such length. But, in the long run, we gained a lot, especially in political savvy. Many resolutions, for example, had to be stricken later as unfeasible. Because we inherited exactly the same resources that Local Power had (CDRs), the same Department of Education had, the same Department of Interior Commerce had, etc. And, besides, we were forewarned: 'You're not going to get shiploads of cement; you're not going to get anything in any special way. You must learn to make do with the resources at hand.' Despite all this, many a resolution was passed which was clearly contrary to existing possibilities.

"If we now went down to Sancti Spíritus, full of optimism, and began to operate in that town as a regular government, we'd set about creating work commissions at once, and we'd pay a lot of attention to what these commissions should handle. We'd advice delegates that all the problems they wished to present before the assembly should first be cleared with the executive committee, and checked further perhaps by a special commission capable of advising us whether or not the bureau affected by the proposal would be able to meet its demands, whether or not the resources existed to entertain such a beautiful proposal. Only then would we take the proposal before the assembly for final approval. If we had a technical advisory board that could tell us, for example: 'Look, this resolution is not feasible at the present time, but try again in six months' time,' we might be able to give the delegate a more complete reply, and the delegate, in turn, could inform his constituents at the accountability session that that particular motion could not be enacted at the time for this or that reason. . . . Dreaming up solutions is easy, if realities are not taken into account."

"Yes," Alexis says. "Sometimes we get carried away adopting resolutions. . . . We're likely to look at things superficially in their complexity."

"It's true we often looked at things superficially," Laureano says. "We were simple-minded, no doubt. But it was the beginning of a stage in which everyone had to pay his dues. It so happens that the new is resisted by the old. Anything which threatens something only makes this something more stubborn in its determination to hang on; but the new, if powerful, will carry the day. This is an inevitable law of history. People's Power emerges in Cuba as a new thing, and so it is immediately resisted by everything old; but it is strong, so it goes forward. Yes, the first year was that kind of stage, with those kinds of assembly resolutions, with delegates walking onto the floor to unfurl twenty-one points. . . .It was hard to make a go of it."

"How does this executive committee operate? And what has been your most valuable experience to date?

"The first thing that should be pointed out," Laureano says, "is that this hasn't been an executive committee directed primarily by Alexis. This has been, throughout its life, an executive committee organized around collective decision-making.* There is no doubt that the president, because of his position, has many more responsibilities, has more chances to accumulate information. But that doesn't mean he may say: 'We're doing this,' and that's what's going to be done. Here we conduct exhaustive discussions on the problems at hand, submitting them to a vote to reach a final position. That's the way of People's Power. It wasn't done that way before. Discussions could go on forever, but at the end the head of the organization could say: 'This is what we'll do,' and that was that. That doesn't happen here anymore. We do debate matters at length, but at the end Alexis must ask: 'Those in favor of this resolution? . . .Four against one,' or whatever. And if he happens to be the 'one,' he has to yield to the majority. How we change our outlook! In this manner no one feels inhibited by the talent or rank of the person who is the leader at the moment, but feels, rather, that he is a partner in the ideas examined and responsible for their disposition."

"Laureano has said it," Reinaldo says. "The most valuable experience we've had during this period is that of conducting a collective leadership. Sometimes we've had to abandon a decision, to backtrack, because it's been questioned by the assembly, and that's a positive experience. It forces us to consider matters more carefully, and if we are wrong, the comrades can always set us right. That way things inevitably improve."

*Laureano had to resign his leadership functions on account of illness, retaining only his work as a district delegate.

9 THE ACCOUNTABILITY SESSION—AN EXEMPLARY CASE

On the night of July 18, for the fourth time since being elected a delegate OrestesFundora must offer his constituents a progress report on the problems affecting them. On the wide veranda of an old colonial house festooned with flags of Cuba and the 26th of July Movement, more than a hundred people have congregated to hear the report. The women and some children are sitting on school benches and chairs brought out by residents. Most of the men are standing, some leaning against the pillars of the balustrade, others sitting on the railing. Behind a household table covered with a red table cloth and decorated with a vase of flowers, the delegate is already sitting, a white-haired old man, with deep furrows on his face. He was one of the few candidates elected on the first round, getting 260 votes out of a possible 443.

The Delegate

We strike up a conversation with the delegate while we are waiting for the latecomers to show up.

"How old are you, compañero."

"I'm sixty-four."

"Do you still work?"

"Yes, I work for a power plant. I've spent forty-three years working at that place, but now I'm in the process of retiring. I'm grooming my replacement in all pertinent aspects of the job."

"When did you join the company?"

"I joined when I was twenty-one. Before that I was a peasant. I used to live in Pedro Betancourt, in the Jovellanos region, which belongs to this same province. By the age of fourteen I was already out in the fields, working the sugar cane. In those days that was something to behold! I began to work for the utility in 1931, as a lineman. I used to climb the electric poles in the streets, things of that nature. Two years later I joined the Communist Youth."

"Have you lived in Varadero for a long time?"

"I've been here since 1940."

"Was life very hard then?"

"Life here was extremely tough. We struggled a great deal, but it was difficult because factionalism infected the workers' movement. But some of us struggled and fought on till we got what we have to day.

"Although Varadero was a tourist resort for people from the United States, townspeople were banned from the beaches. They had guards so the people wouldn't get through. Du Pont had a big spread around here. Another tycoon had another slice. The place was full of fences. In other words, there was always a 'No Trespassing' sign for the people. We couldn't attend the nightclubs, nothing. The hotels, all that, were off limits. The blacks? Need I say it? It was even worse for them. Blacks were supposed to be household servants, nothing else. They couldn't take part in any amusement unless they were attending it as beasts of burden. Let me tell you a little story. At one time Compañero Lázaro was in bad health, and they sent him up here. They told me: 'Get a hotel room for him.' I went out and couldn't get any. So I finally put him up with a black compañero who had a decent room above his bar. He said to me: 'Man, I'm gonna get chewed out for this, but I just can't turn my back on Lázaro Peña!' So he gave him a room. And he gave it to him because he was black himself; otherwise, nothing doing."

Lázaro Peña was an active Communist Party member and outstanding union leader during the Batista dictatorship. After the triumph of the Revolution, he occupied the post of secretary general for the Confederation of Cuban Workers, till his death in 1974.

"When the Revolution arrived, everything changed, even though at the beginning, since they were still among us, the counterrevolution was busy weaving conspiracies here. They, the capitalists, the Yankees, used to get together and plot these things. I was in the militia at the time, but after a while the thing began to die down. About two years after the Revolution the hotels began to be nationalized and placed at the disposal of the people. That put an end to discrimination. Blacks could now stay at any of these posh hotels. And the workers, especially those who were looked down upon because they cut sugar cane, they, too, could go in. After that the workers' recreation plans were introduced, and the working people began to visit these places in great numbers, on vacation. Now the number of workers who have passed through Varadero and enjoyed the place is enormous. They have even come from the remotest corners of the island to enjoy these luxury resorts where they were formerly regarded as undesirable. . . .I tell you, it rejoices my heart to see all this!"

"You said you became a member of the Communist Youth in 1933. Did you join the Party afterwards?"

"Yes, of course. Twice, in keeping with the Party strategy at that time, I was nominated for city hall. I never made it. There was always fraud. Even the candidates were not allowed to go near the polls when the ballots were counted. It was outrageous!"

"It seems those election were a far cry from those you just had in Matanzas—"

"You bet! In those days the whole thing was a hoax. Money ran the show. Everything revolved around patronage and bribes. The candidate with the fattest purse made it. Well, you know about these things because you have it, too, in your own country, right? The two things can't be compared. It's like day and night. In these recent elections everything was done openly and freely. One could nominate as a candidate anyone who was a member of the assembly, provided he met the political and revolutionary qualifications. The people always choose those who have fought the hardest. And the candidates here didn't go around soliciting votes, pumping hands, or anything hypocritical like that! And when we cast our ballots . . .everything was different again. Every school serving as a polling station was decked with flowers. There was a tremendous joy, a magnificent joy in the air."

"And were the people hostile to the Revolution allowed to vote?"

"Yes. Here everyone could vote. Look, here we only blacklisted those who were candidates of the bourgeoisie in 1958; they couldn't vote; they're banned from the electoral process for thirty years. But everyone else can vote. Everyone voted here."

"And all the voters knew you?"

"Well, I've been here for thirty years. So you can figure it out. They had to know me. But in any case the election surprised me, because I thought I was burned out, washed up politically. I'm very old, but it seems I'm not that spent after all."

"And who were the other candidates?"

"Well, young people. Very good people, of tremendous value. They deserved to be elected?"

"How come you were elected?"

"My record, I guess. The fight all the way from the bottom, with the people. A good attitude. One has to have honesty, steadfastness, to accomplish things. Well, that's my view, anyway. A lot of contact with the people. I always advise the young people to stay down below, with the masses, to be part of it, to sense what it is thinking at different times. I don't know, I think that's the key to everything."

"What do you think of the defeated candidates, five, I believe?"

"They're fine people, really good people. But this longer struggle, of thirty years, it really leaves marks. Even if you are just average, the people are not liable to forget you. Not because I was the best. In my view the other candidates are much better, they even have better education and can serve People's Power much better, in cultural aspects, everything. I always say that we have to study more, that the people have to be better prepared. And the other candidates had this. And for socialism, which is scientific, we must demand capable compañeros."

"And did you have a chance to study?"

"Never. I never had the opportunity. I only made it to the fifth grade. My children were able to study, and so will my grandchildren."

"As a government official, as a delegate, do you have to make a lot of promises?"

"No. We don't make any. We only promise the future, which we are certain is good. But we don't promise what we can't deliver; you can't deceive the masses. And when we don't have something, we say it up front: we don't have this, because of this or that. And when we have it, well, all the better. What bothers us most now is the housing problem, construction. That's one of the people's most pressing needs. Yet when we explain in assembly why it can't go to this or that person, because the materials have to go to a farm facility, a children's center, a school, or a hospital, then, everyone is satisfied and happy. The people understand and accept this."

"And what does the electorate complain about when they go to your office?"

"Well, diffrent things. Sometimes it's troubles with a grocery store: the distribution was fouled up: a particular plan is affecting the people: too many lines, etc. Well, things like that. Then we ask for suggestions from the very people who raise the issues, and we take these to the other assembly delegates. We thus find out the people's opinion and what they want."

"What would happen, compañero, if you didn't fulfill your mandate?"

"Well, they can recall me, because I'm just an intermediary, that's all. The people can take away my mandate because they are sovereign. They just remove me and call for new elections. Of course, they'd give me a chance to clear my name, defend myself, but if my arguments aren't convincing, they just drop me and call a new election. That's the good thing about being a delegate. There's but one duty: to measure up to the people's expectations."

"The Varadero tourist complex does not depend directly on People's Power for its administration. What do you do if you find something amiss there?"

"In case of a deficiency in an INIT* or recreation center, we can point out the defect. Any anomaly, anything out of line, the people can point it out to their delegate and he can bring it up to the appropriate bureau, so they can straigthen the thing out. When the managers are critized, they react as revolutionaries and try to fix things up, if that is in their power. They appreciate it, because everything is for our own benefit."

"And what do you think of the Party?"

"It's the greatest thing there is. I was nominated to be a Party member, but I'm too old now. You have to take up studying, and I just can't hack it. It might 'wasre me,' 'burn me out,' as we say around here, and I might not be any good. I think that here I can go on pitching in, and contributing to the Revolution. I can't abandon the struggle. My election was very touching...and I have to measure up. The Party officers, in fact, are the best. I can see them, the efforts they make. And those I see I certainly tell they have to study hard. And I raise the example of the USSR, where many people were peasants, sons of peasants, and they are now engineers, great military strategists, doctors, everything. Why? Because they studied. Fidel—there you have it. He's the greatest there is. Thanks to his extraordinary effort we made it to the Revolution which, if it hadn't been armed, might have been crushed. That's the truth. The day the people win an election and are allowed to stay in office, well...that'll happen when the world is already three quarters socialist. Any other way and capitalism is ready to pull some dirty tricks. They are simply criminals. They don't care whether ten or eighty die. We care. Right here we could have done a lot to them, but we didn't. Fidel had a great political vision in that regard. The criminals were brought to justice, and the rest were permitted to leave. And then you get the Bay of Pigs, that's an example."

"Compañero, you're already advanced in years. What would you do if the Revolution was suddenly threatened?"

---

*INIT: National Institute of Tourism, or Cuba's Tourist Board, is in charge of hotels, restaurants, and other facilities devoted to tourism and recreation.

"They'd have to kill me defending the Revolution, and I think the whole Cuban people would do the same. They'd go into the trenches to defend the motherland. All this has yielded its fruit. The people have now seen the fruits, they are convinced that there is no turning back."

"What is the greatest thing about this Revolution?"

"There you have the agrarian reform, public health, education. Hospitals and schools free for everyone. You can't imagine how hard it was to become an engineer under capitalism. Today anyone can become one. Before, if they had some money in a family, they could educate one kid and leave the others without schooling. That usually meant the family's ruin because the one who was studying soaked up all its resources. Without the Revolution the worker's son could not have studied, because capitalism didn't leave a crumb for the workers. Besides, we have total democracy here. The worker has experienced democracy; the worker has spoken. The counterrevolution, of course, has been suppressed. But everyone else enjoys democracy. And I have always stood by this. I am a rebel. And within the process I've always pointed to what is not right. That's my kind of democracy. Everything is open to discussion. If the compañero is not in agreement with something, he analyzes it, he talks about it, he says what he thinks. Look, at the beginning of the Revolution I used to argue with a Spaniard who was not overly impressed with developments. I was a militia commander in those days. I used to discuss matters with him because we were neighbors, coming from the same part of town. Eventually, he became one of the best sugarcane cutters in the region. He was a servant to one of the local rich families, and it pained him to see the bourgeoisie dispossessed. But there you have it. He still goes out to cut cane voluntarily. He once said to me: 'You didn't convince me that day, but events have!' In those days I spoke to him of what the Revolution was all about, what it would mean to the people, him included, and why the rich had to go through this. But later this man was a *machetero*,* so what do you think? We don't have docile workers here, and I don't like those who are. The worker expresses what he feels and says it. In the old days it wasn't like that. I know. I was part of the working-class movement under capitalism; we were just four communists in a power company which had four thousand workers. You see, the facts have shown and will show the justice of the Revolution. A better democracy? Try and find one!"

*Machete-wielding cane cutter.

The Constituents

As this conversation was taking place with the delegate, elsewhere in the room the following exchange was taking place among some residents, early arrivals at the accountability session.

"Compañero, how many candidates did you have in this district?"

"Six."

"And you voted for Orestes?"

"Yes."

The reply comes as a small chorus from people who, moved by curiosity, have gradually surrounded the only person they did not know among those present.

The group is composed of Isabel, a young woman; Rosalia, a heavy-set compañera of about forty years of age; Carlos, a young Party member; a rather elderly compañera everyone calls "Grandma"; Maglio, a black compañero, an old worker from the area; and Alberto, a compañero with the appearance of a teacher.

"Did you have a runoff election here?"

"No, no way!"

"Orestes just swept into office! He got thirty-eight votes, more than half of the total."

"Why do you think Orestes was elected by a landslide?"

"Because he had the qualities required for the job. He is a revolutionary compañero, a compañero well regarded by the people—"

"But the compañero is quite old, he's more than sixty years old, according to what I heard. Didn't that go against him?"

"Absolutely not! He's younger than the lot of us the way he acts. He's still full of energy." says Isabel, smiling.

"What has People's Power meant to you?"

"A success," Maglio says with conviction. "Now we shoulder the people's needs more directly. The people participate directly in all of the population's problems."

"But before, with the CDRs, you also raised the problems—"

"Yes, but the solutions were not so good."

"But why do you have better solutions now?"

"Because People's Power gathers together more resources than Local Power, more means. . . . Then too, every three months they have to make a report; that wasn't so before. . . ."

"And every first Saturday, every month," Grandma interjects, "there's a meeting of delegates at the municipal level and the people can participate, not with the right to speak, though, but to listen to what's been done, and to learn about the new proposals."

"Have any of you ever attended the municipal assembly?"

"I have," says Maglio, "and have done so because I like to watch. Many compañeros come."

"I never miss one!" Grandma exclaims enthusiastically. "I've attended them all."

"And what's you impression?"

"Well , things are handled well. The grievances are publicized there, and we hear the suggestions the people have made to the delegates. The delegates inform the assembly. Problems are discussed, things that have to be resolved, the course that will be adopted. I really enjoy going."

"Listen," Maglio says, "the grievances we present to him"—he points to Orestes—"we go and see whether he introduced them and fought for them, because we have to fight if we want things to improve."

"About what you were asking . . .now we know the needs of the people much better. We used to have types who asked for sacks of cement to fix their homes and then turned around and sold them. Not now, because there's a CDR commission that studies the needs."

"If I tell Fundora that I need cement to fix my house, he tells the commission to go and check. If they decide I need ten sackfuls, that's what I get," Isabel adds.

"We also have complaints about transportation, what kind of a job are they doing . . .the problem with the stores . . .everything is more direct now," the teacher says.

"But surely there are problems that People's Power cannot solve—"

"Well, they try hard to get things done," Maglio snaps, somewhat irritated. "For example, we have a microbrigade here that put up five buildings—some six hundred apartments—and they still weren't enough because—compañera, I'd like you to know something. When we first began to build houses for workers in this town, we found that seven families were living in each house. . . .Do you understand?"

"Yes, but what I'd really like to know is what you do with problems you can't find an easy solution to."

"Well, they're being solved according to the country's means," Alberto explains.

"And the people—do they understand?"

"When the problems can't be solved, the delegate explains why."

"Doesn't it happen that those who know the delegate better try to get preferential treatment from him?"

"He who's elected is elected because he's good, and not bad. It's because he's revolutionary."

"The delegate who doesn't work out is removed."

"Has anyone been removed here?"

"No. One person resigned here, but because of illness. He was very good. He was three quarters into a mental breakdown when he resigned," Alberto explains. "He was a good fighter."

"Tell me, what collective problems have you resolved here through People's Power?"

"The milk problem. Before, they just left it on the sidewalks, in front of the stores. The dogs would come by, and you can imagine. Now they put it in boxes stacked up on a shelf."

"And the polyclinic. We have more doctors."

"And the transportation problem. Now we have more buses to go to work."

"What difference did you notice between the elections of People's Power and the others, before the Revolution?"

"Dear girl! That can't even be measured!" Maglio exclaims.

"But, tell me, what were the candidates like before?"

"Before, they bought votes, they made up false identification cards—"

"They just made promises, promises . . .and after the election they just vanished. You didn't see them anymore."

"And Orestes, is he a Party member?"

"No, but he's being screened," says Carlos, the young Party officer. "He was a founder of the Communist Party in 1938, a member of ORI. . . ."

"How do you explain the fact he isn't a member now?"

"Well, it seems he was ill for a while, and it apparently delayed his admission—"

"But he's an unofficial member!" Grandma says enthusiastically.

"Anyone here a Party member?"

"She's being screened for the Youth"—they point to a young girl standing by the door—"and this one"—pointing at the young member.

"I'd like someone who isn't a Party member to tell me what it means to be inside the Party."

"Well, now! A Party member must show the best qualities, with the family, with the block, on the job. . . ."

"He's got to be a model because the process of scrutiny is very severe."

"Have you attended assemblies where model workers are elected?"

"Yes, of course," several voices reply.

"And has anyone been rejected?"

"Yes."

"Why?"

"Well, the candidate may have a number of qualifications, but somewhere along the line, he may be weak in some. . . ."

"And if a Party officer makes a mistake, can the people criticize him?"

"They can go to another Party comrade to present their grievances," explains Carlos. "The case is then discussed among the leadership and there they may decide to take his card away or adopt some other sanctions. No one is above criticism here. The Party must be in the vanguard. A compañero may fail, it may not be a conscious thing. There are different measures."

"And wouldn't it be better, simpler, if you, who have as prime minister, as commander in chief, Fidel Castro, who is known all over the world for his extraordinary talents, if instead of discussing the economic plans, instead of setting up People's Power, instead of utilizing the device of criticism, you let Fidel run the whole thing?"

"Let me answer that," Maglio says, leaping in ahead of others who appear equally eager to tackle the question. "No, I don't think so. I think Fidel is the way you describe him because he encourages this, handles the situation this way. If Fidel didn't act this way, he wouldn't be Fidel. What you conjure up is a Fidel I don't know. The one you invoke I don't recognize; I only know the one who does the things you see all around Cuba, in the correct way. Because, in the last analysis, Fidel is unique, and unfortunately, one day he may not be there, but what we'll always have is the people, the workers, and its vanguard, which is the Communist Party. We, the workers, follow the Communist Party, its line, its slogans . . . because that's our example, and that's our vanguard. They are the best. We cannot follow the worst, we have to follow the best. And these are not the best in the bourgeois sense, but in the intellectual and moral sense, meaning they don't use their relative superiority to oppress and manipulate the people, but to help others. What I was saying is that if Fidel is famous for what you say he is, it is because he has accomplished this, a people thinking about Revolution. It's better if many think, and not one alone, because better results are obtained in that way. Fidel is well known around the world because of this, because he has gotten his people to think this way. . . ."

The Assembly

It is nine P.M. Although a heavy rain appears imminent, compañeros continue to arrive, a few judiciously carrying their own chairs. The veranda has become too small to accommodate the assembly, and latecomers huddling around it outside elbow their way toward the inner circle. Some children play in a festive mood, as the occasion has permitted them to stay up late.

Orestes Fundora is now seated, ready to preside over the meeting. The secretary sits besides him. Even though the post does not exist formally, Orestes has summoned the schoolmaster to help him with the records of the meetings, since he "lacks the schooling."

Someone in the rear puts on a recording of the Cuban National Anthem, and the audience rises to its feet.

When the song ends, as the people sit down, Orestes, now standing, opens the assembly:

"Look, compañeros, we are going to present a report, covering the past three months, prepared by the municipal People's Power. We've also prepared an agenda, and if you wish to add any item or items, you're free to do so."

In a solemn manner, the secretary reads: "First, the reading of the report of the municipal assembly. Second, transportation. Third, commerce and foodstuffs. Fourth, education. Fifth, miscellaneous. . . ."

"This is the day's agenda," the delegate says. "Do you wish to add anything to it? Those of you who approve the agenda as it is raise your hands."

The agenda is approved, and the secretary rises again to read the resolutions of the People's Power municipal assembly. But before doing so he advises the audience, "Only the more important points will be read." Then he continues: "In the first quarter, the assembly held three meetings, in which forty-eight resolutions were passed. Among these the following deserve special mention: First, in order to effect repairs, all the broken television sets serving the municipality's social services have been collected, and they will later be redistributed in a more rational fashion. Second, to eliminate the experimental sales system operating in the industrial products stores, as the system was not well received by the population and to return to the old system. Third, the Las Borlas bus route was modified in accordance with the wishes of the people of that neighborhood. Fourth, is was decided that an in-home television repair service should be inaugurated."

A woman interejcts: "This has been approved already?"

"Yes, from now on you don't have to take your television sets to the repair shop if they can be repaired at home," Orestes asserts.

"Man! that's really good news!"

A wave of jubilation can be felt among the audience. A compañera whispers: "Look, mine was already repaired under that system."

The secretary resumes his reading: "Fifth, to set up a camp for Pioneers* at 'El Frances,' during vacation week."

---

*Pioneers, the Party's organization for children.

Orestes clarifies: "This has already been done."

The secretary continues: "Sixth, that the Commerce Department see to it that more appropriate clothing be made available to butchers and grocers to improve their hygiene.

"Up to this point these are the resolutions of the municipal assembly. Now we shall review the resolution passed at the regional level. Seventh, that the Department of Health must draw up the necessary plans with a view to improving conditions at the regional hospital, making the patient's stay more pleasant, offering more comfort, recreation, internal communications means, and information, factors which may raise the over-all quality of the services being provided.

"Eight, it is recommended that an agreement be made with the other regions of the province in order to discontinue the distribution of products on Saturdays. This creates a host of difficulties since shops are closed on Sundays, and the products cannot be distributed till Monday. As a result, merchandise accumulates, with the attendant problems of transportation. Moreover, many of these products are perishables. A fact that contributes in no small measure to the monthly losses. . . ."

"This concerns agricultural products," the delegate explains. "They arrive on Saturday, and sometimes they spoil quickly, peppers and fruit, for example."

The secretary reads on: "Ninth, an increase in the school enrollment for the 1975-76 period is noted, at both the primary and the secondary levels, and this requires the construction of new facilities and the restoration of others. It is recommended that the municipality and the region evaluate and analyze their respective needs and that they initiate the restoration and construction of the necessary facilities at once. Tenth, in order to insure the development of the areas under construction, it is advised that all levels of People's Power study the most efficient ways of utilizing skilled labor. And that the labor of the masses be coordinated through their organizations. The provincial assembly finds, categorically, that the limiting factors in the construction process is not the work force. . . ."

At this point a murmur of incomprehension sweeps over the audience. The secretary pauses for an explanation; "Well, what this means is that we, ourselves, should resolve the construction problems with our own people. Is that clear?"

The audience nods affirmatively and he continues.

"Eleventh, that while supporting the proposal to turn our province into a garden province, relying resolutely on the action of the CDRs, the provincial assembly recommends that the norms and decrees relating to public ornamentation be observed, so that our province may maintain the clean and orderly aspect it desires. We wish to bring to your attention an incident that underscores the importance of the people's contributions to the revolutionary process. It concerns the municipality of Martí, which, with the help of the masses, has successfully completed the reclamation of Menéndez Beach, closed to the public for fifteen years, and which through the work of five-hundred comrades was recently put at the service of the people. Examples like this confirm our motto that 'People's Power is True Power.' "

The delegate interrupts him at this point: "Look, compañeros, we have received a memo from the People's Power office in which we are advised that we don't have to wait for the next assembly to solve a series of questions amenable to direct solution within our district. Previously we had to await the response of the executive committee; now things will be a lot faster. So now you are on notice: Those with problems should come and see the delegate, who will try to solve them as quickly as possible.

"And we still have the water problem. It has not been dealt with even though we already have the materials to cover the line. We need the authorization of DAP [Department of Public Water Supply]. The compañeros should not attempt to cover it on their own, because we don't know what kind of pipelines exist there.

"Now, if there's something that was raised during the last meeting and which still awaits resolution, do speak now and let me see what it is.

"There are no pending problems from the last meeting?"

Several people in the audience say no.

When all the resolutions are read and approved, the meeting turns to the specific problems of the district.

"Look, here's the compañero in charge of commerce. He'll answer questions relating to this area."

The manager in charge of commerce for the area speaks up to explain that, acting on complaints, the weight scales of local businesses will be checked to insure merchants are not shortweighting the people.

"With regard to the problem relating to the rice allocations, we have found the problem may lie with the weights used to measure, which are too old. This was discussed with the administration so that they would correct the situation and the people should get the quantity of rice they are entitled to. Another matter concerns cartons. Since several soft-drink cartons have been broken, the municipality will replace them, so each family can have its own. In addition, it's important that you should know about the fish deal. Until now Varadero had consumed only its per capita allocation; but now, with People's Power, the availability of fish has increased, because we have entered an agreement with the municipality of Cantel-Camarioca. There, as a matter of habit, people do not consume a lot of fish. Accordingly, the surplus from that area has come to augment the Varadero per capita. So instead of being wasted there, we get it."

The audience shows its approval of this.

"If there's nothing further to say on this question, let's discuss the transportation problem," Orestes proposes.

A man in the rear stands up to speak: "When one has to catch a bus during the lunch hours, everybody seems to be out to lunch. The same at breakfast time. There are no buses in circulation."

"So what's the big problem?" Orestes asks jestingly.

A compañero with a waiter's jacket in his arms rises to his feet. "Look, when I work serving lunches to the people, I don't just go out and have my lunch. I do it when everybody has finished having his."

"But what is the exact complaint, so we can record it here?"

The compañero who spoke first takes the floor again: "What I mean is that at lunchtime there are no buses, and then they all come in packs."

A young girl, without rising from her chair, explains: "They chew the fat, smoke a cigaret, relax, and then leave."

A black comrade sticking his head out from behind one of the pillars on the veranda. "That kind of situation doesn't occur just at lunch time and breakfast. Today, for instance, there was a big crowd standing in front of the Cahuaco Hotel, waiting for a bus, and all the vehicles coming down were 'Santa Marta,' 'Santa Marta,' 'Santa Marta.' The first was packed, the second had a few passengers, and the third was empty. One right behind the other. What is gained by that? Just think of all the fuel spent by these buses on that route."

In the face of such an avalanche of complaints, Orestes proposes a solution: "Look, when this happens we will advise the compañeros to jot down the number of the bus, the day and the time these things take place. Only in this manner can we go with concrete facts to the Transportation Department to file a complaint. We can't argue with them without some evidence. And we must know that when the seven vehicles are in operation, we have one every fourteen minutes here in Varadero. But this doesn't happen when they are not all in operation, because they're very old and need constant repairs. . . . We've had days when only two buses were running. Because when we can't do a thing about something, we have to accept it, but not if we can do something and improve the situation. Anybody want to say something else about this?"

"Well," a voice says, "during the last assembly we were told about a bus that ran out of gas. But no one knew how. This week, that bus, which is always on time, ran out of fuel on its first trip, in front of the park, at 6:30 A.M. I don't see how a bus can run out of fuel on its first round."

"He didn't check it before going out," someone exclaims.

"It's been the same bus and the same driver both times."

"The other day the driver stopped on the road . . . about twenty-five minutes, and we just sat and waited there. . . ."

The secretary makes careful note of the complaint.

"Anything else about transportation?" the delegate asks.

Silence. Everyone understands the subject is exhausted. They have said what had to be said.

"Then we go on to the third point, concerning commerce and food. Do you have anything on this? . . . There are some deficiencies in the restaurants . . . here and there . . . low quality and that sort of problem. You haven't run across this?" Orestes smiles maliciously.

The young girl in the front row: "Of course! The case of those stands—"

"Aren't they okay?"

"No way! It's sheer garbage!"

There is a burst of laughter. Rosalía offers her interpretation: "I think it depends on the kiosk and the person who cooks."

"Yes. It depends on who cooks," her neighbor says.

"Look, at home my kids really love that fried stuff, and they buy it all the time. Some days it's exquisite, but other days it's only fit for the trash can. It can't be eaten. Just imagine! The kiosk in the park, when that man cooks, you just can't swallow the stuff!"

A murmur of approval reverberates through the audience. The waiter who spoke earlier offers his expert opinion: "Yes, because the dough is the same for all. It is the way you cook it."

"Although I agree wih you," Orestes says, "I don't think it's only that. Don't you think that when the stalls were first opened they used to offer better quality?"

Various opinions are heard:

"They don't carry mustard or tomatoes now."

"At first they used to give you bigger portions."

"Quality has dropped."

"Especially if we consider that mustard is decontrolled. . . ."

"Even if they don't give you the other ingredients, they charge you the same."

"We pay sixty centavos to get the whole thing, but now they leave everything off and still charge the same. It just can't be!"

"Well, I want to emphasize that it is the people who run things here. It is the people who must exercise vigilance in everything," the delegate emphasizes. "If you read Raúl Castro's speech, you may recall he was not happy with this sort of thing. And neither am I. If you go to buy bread and croquettes, that's OK: it has a price. But if there isn't any bread and they sell the croquette by itself, they can't charge the same price. If it doesn't come with bread, the croquette should cost less. This is a problem pointed out by Raúl, and it's happening here. When something is not available, well, then, it isn't available, but if it exists, then it's negligence in serving the people. Surely, if this were a private business-man, he'd be on top of it to satisfy the customers and increase his profits. We should not allow a drop in quality if the ingredients are available."

A compañero who looks like a bank employee adds:

"I've noticed that all the restaurants opened by INIT begin wonder-fully, but quality soon starts to deteriorate. They begin with a lot of products and end up with a few, and I know that all those products are available."

"We offer all these criticisms," the delegate says, "in order to improve services to the people. Anything else on restaurants?"

A man at the rear of the group, who had spoken before, takes the floor again: "Let's talk about this a bit more. The managers of Tagua Canto, when one of these commissions comes around—what do you call it?"

"Of Control and Assistance,"* some voices reply.

"Well, when one of these commissions shows up, the managers try to put their best foot forward, but after that things return to normal."

"Let me say that you can tell when you go to one of the restaurants and the commission is there," a young mulatto woman with a turban on her head says emphatically. "The patrons can tell, well, at once."

"Orlando, the little plane that belongs to INIT?" a voice from the front row inquires, setting off an explosion of laughter. He is referring to the plane that sprays against mosquitoes. "It hasn't fumigated since last Saturday."

"Let me tell you something about that little plane," Orestes says. "I have a proposal for the next municipal assembly. Scientific problems have to be respected, but we have practical problems, here, such as the mosquito plague. There have been years when we've held our own with plenty of oil and sawdust dumped on various puddles. I'm going to propose that the CDRs receive oil and sawdust so that they can cover the puddles in their blocks. That's a practical, feasible step. Do you agree?"

The entire audience agrees.

An elderly woman has a complaint about the quality of the bread.

"There's a problem with the ovens. They don't work too well," Orestes explains. "They're being repaired, so, for the time being, the bread can't come out too well."

---

*The Commission of Control and Assistance is designed to oversee the centers within its jurisdiction. It visits the units every so often to verify compliance with INIT regulations.

"I'd like to know what's happening with the milk bottles. They get dirtier by the day," a feminine voice complains. "On Tuesday a compañera who lives with me, who couldn't attend because she has two small kids, showed me a bottle with a green, slimy stuff at the bottom, totally green! She asked me to mention this here. The truth is the bottle was a real horror!"

"I saw it. I'm going to file the complaint," the delegate says, with determination in his voice.

Amid whispers in the audience, the commerce official, who is responsible for this kind of problem, rises to explain the action he has taken on the matter: "Every month we have a distribution conference with all the managers. There you hear about the difficulties the agencies may be having. During the last meeting a series of problems was mentioned relating to milk: open containers, dirty bottles, half-filled containers, and the like. This was passed on to the next regional council, which is on the twenty-seventh. You know that the dairy here in Cardenas is an old plant, and even though we installed a new cleaning device, the brush doesn't always reach the bottom. But you know that we are supposed to deliver clean bottles. So if this happened, it means that some compañera returned her bottle dirty. Maybe the one she was using was broken and she sent back another she had at home, dirty. Maybe she didn't think that very dirty bottle was going to go right back to her. . . ."

"But when they bottle the milk, don't they check things as they go?"

"Yes, there's an inspector, but milk is not transparent. Whatever is stuck to the bottom can't be seen, and so he thinks the container is clean. But we must admit that in comparison to what it used to be years ago, things have improved a lot."

"Yes, they have."

"And while we're talking about containers," the commerce official says, "we need every family to return four bottles each. The bottles are being bought at twenty centavos each. We need them to bottle beverages. So it's necessary to pick up as many as possible. It's a job for the masses. Every bottle lying about, vinegar, beverages, should be returned to the store."

"Milk, too?

"Those are also being bought, at twenty-five centavos."

The news creates a ripple of excitement among the audience. It seems that many people have unused bottles at home.

"I'm sure we have ten or twelve bottles at home," says a compañero, about thirty years old, who is wearing a taxi-driver's cap.

"At home there's a sackful," an old man adds.

Above the din of the audience, several voices can be heard: "Tell me, do we have to return the bottles at the grocery store?"

"Tomorrow the store will be chockful."

"Four bottles, one peso, and from there straight to the Copelia."*

The commotion subsides. Orestes smiles, amused by the reaction, and turns to another page in his notebook: "Let us now discuss the question of public health. . . .Do you have anything to say about the polyclinic? . . . You all seem to be in pretty good shape."

The compañeros laugh. A woman who has been busily discussing each item, now rises to speak. She does it with resolve in her voice: "I'd like to ask something. Do you know when the garbage truck is supposed to come by? Because, as far as my house in concerned, I haven't seen one in three months. They get down as far as Tito's corner, then turn around and leave."

Someone shouts to her: "And they don't even say hello!" There is a burst of laughter.

"We left the trash in front of Pastrana's house," the woman continues, unflappable, "and sometimes three days go by, and it's still there. They just look at the cans and take off. I ask you: don't they like our cans?"

"We'll talk to them to find out where the cans should be placed so that garbage can be picked up," Orestes says gravely.

The secretary takes everything down.

"Hey," says another compañera, getting up. "Why don't they just put one big can on each corner so the people who come to the beaches can drop their beer cans in there, their ice cream containers. . . .Mondays, the whole place can make you puke."

"Measures are being taken," the delegate explains. "All the buses arriving on weekends are going to be routed through a specific area. It'll be an area for picnics, with facilities to change, eat, etc."

"That's a good idea because, you know, one walks through these woods when taking the children to school and one can see almost anything . . . you understand? Anything." Laughter.

"Is there anything else on this point?" Orestes asks. "Well, then, let's go on to education."

"There's a big problem with mothers who work on Saturdays," Isabel declares. "The children's centers and the day schools close at noon and the children are left stranded on the street. Couldn't we find a way to stop this, for example, by keeping the centers and day schools open all day Saturday?"

---

*Unit that sells ice cream.

"We had a program like that before, but very few children showed up on Saturdays," the compañera in charge of education asserts.

"But I've heard many complaints about this situation now," Isabel insists.

"But they don't send them," the officer for education reiterates.

"What happens is that those who don't care to send their kids are actually injuring those who do," someone says.

"But it's only a few kids," the education officer says stubbornly.

"A few make a big difference," Isabel retorts.

Seeing that the discussion is leading nowhere, the delegate decides to intervene: "Look, I've got a suggestion. As we have a parent-teachers association, let's leave it up to them to reach an agreement, to define the situation. If there is nothing else about education, let's move on to general matters. Do you have anything to say, anything to state here? Well, compañeros, I think we're closing this meeting on a combative footing, with no one keeping anything inside, because this is the key to the Revolution's success: whatever is good or bad is said openly. So we are adjourning this assembly."

For a while the participants hang around discussing with the delegate some of the matters raised in the meeting. Then, a few at a time, they leave the place where they have exercised their authority.

10 IN THE RURAL AREAS

"The basic problem there was the influence of the Perico Sánchez gang, which operated nearby. There was a lot of ignorance, and the area was far away from the urban centers. For starters, I went to live with one of the local revolutionary families. There was so much fear that some people even avoided contact with us. Others counseled us that we should leave the zone because the bandits might kill us. Despite all these difficulties, we began to visit the residents. Some doors were shut in our faces, but we would return the next day. We took stock of the forces in the area and did a study of the causes facilitating such a situation. We worked with everyone, the revolutionary and the indifferent; with the enemies we debated.

"On one occasion, the situation was so difficult that the Party's municipal committee suggested that we sleep in the city. We did not agree. What we did was change houses every night, so they would not discover out location. Of course, this was possible because we had awakened confidence in us among many compañeros; that is, we had brought them into the revolutionary camp.

"So we strengthened the grassroots of the mass organizations; we started study groups; in sum, the area began to live a revolutionary life. The presence of the Revolution began to be felt.

"In that area, despite the problem with the bandits, we were able to change the balance of forces in favor of the Revolution, while winning most families over to revolutionary work.

"In 1963 we were transferred to the area of Quemado Grande, where some peasants were collaborating with the bandits. Our mission was to draw them into the revolutionary camp, while teaching them how they had been duped. In fact, this assignment was beautiful. In that place we set up a school for worker-peasant improvement and had to teach, even though we did not have the requisite background. I think I got good results. When the job was done two years later, mass organizations were in operation, and there was revolutionary activity.

"I think the critical quality of a rural [political] orientation cadre is perseverance. After that, it is a question of finding the way to best relate to the peasants, and of discussing with them, of speaking to them, to persuade them of the truth of the Revolution.

"The fundamental aspect of our activity is ideological work. The solution of material problems is very important, but no one should believe that by resolving the material problems of a given region one has solved the ideological ones as well. The consciousness of a human being does not change overnight. It is a long-term proposition."

The speaker is Gilberto Caballero, one of the first rural orientation officers. He worked in Matanzas Province when the counterrevolutionary bands were still active in the area.

Favoring the Remotest Areas

It was precisely in the remotest areas, the hinterland least favored in earlier periods, where the counterrevolution sought refuge after Batista's defeat.

In those days middling proprietors still existed—latifundia owners expropriated by the First Agrarian Reform—with farms of up to four hundred acres. Their policy was to sabotage the agricultural target plans, while lending their support to the counterrevolutionary bands.

The revolutionary leadership, however, soon took the situation under advisement and proceeded to send a great number of orientation workers into these areas. They did an excellent job among the peasants, especially in the ideological area, explaining to them the revolutionary process and how they were the true beneficiaries of the revolutionary measures already adopted and of those in the process of enactment. The Revolution always respected the lands of small farmers.

These sectors, together with the renters and sharecroppers to whom the First Agrarian Reform handed over land, threw their support behind the Second Law of October 3, 1963, which reduced to sixty acres the maximum holdings controlled by each farmer.

As early as 1961, the political leadership of the Revolution had organized the small peasants into what is called the National Association of Small Farmers (ANAP), which in 1974 boasted 136,448 members.

Nevertheless, despite the Revolution's progress, there are still remote regions in Cuba which present very specific problems, and whose very remoteness has made them into highly neglected areas.

This situation was taken into consideration when regulations were being drawn up for elections under People's Power. Instead of allotting to all districts the same number of voters—which at first glance, seems more equitable—a way was sought to favor the out-of-the-way areas, where the population is more dispersed and far more difficult to call together. So that People's Power would have a presence among these constituents, the minimum requirement for a district was set at 100 voters, with adjacent peasant locales being grouped so they could choose one delegate.

Whereas in the more densely populated areas a thousand voters are needed to elect one delegate, the remote countryside areas require only a tenth of that figure.*

According to Alexis, it is in these small districts set up in the remote areas where "one can best observe the effects of People's Power and the people's participation. It's logical, as these were the areas most neglected by the old regime. Previously, they had no one to go to with their grievances, except the local mayor, whom they could reach only after a long journey. Now they have got a represenative right in their midst."

An accountability session in a small peasant district may be the best way to see in practice what People's Power has meant to the residents.

Progress under People's Power

"Now the problem with the well has been solved here. Oil and other things routinely wound up there. No more. We got the materials, and all the compañeros here, the CDR, the Federation, pitched in. Another problem, the bus stop across the street, we also tackled successfully. We already have the materials, we are only waiting for them [the engineers] to come around and make the survey. The electricity problem is already largely under control. Also, in La Guaira, there was a grocery store that didn't open on Saturdays; now it does. In the other peasant locale we also

---

*In municipalities having more than eight thousand inhabitants, districts are created for approximately every thousand residents. As the population drops, the number of districts increase proportionally. Between eight and five thousand inhabitants, nine districts are created; beween three and five thousand people, seven districts are set up; in those under three thousand, five are set up. In the villages, there is one district for every five hundred inhabitants, and in remote peasant areas the minimum per district has been set at a hundred people.

inaugurated a new grocery store, and licked the plumbing problem, because they didn't have running water. Now we're going to merge the La Guaira school with that of Peñas to raise the quality of the instruction, while freeing some time for the teachers. The kids are also getting lunch."

"And who is requesting all this?"

"The people, that's who. I take the matter up to the executive committee, and we discuss the question with the appropriate government office. If it can be done, it's done. And if it isn't feasible, then we explain to the people why it isn't. That's the policy we've followed. And what the people see is the effort the People's Power government is making for their sake. And they are kept informed about everything—the yeses, the nos, and the why-nots."

This is the explanation given by Jesús Díaz, delegate from the Cantel-Camarioca rural district, when he is asked about progress made in the area since the arrival of People's Power. He is a young man, about twenty-five years old, presently responsible for a workforce at the textile complex "Juan Agramonte," which makes fibers out of henequen, a plant abundant in the province. Jesús was the director of the school shop in factory.

We strike up a conversation as we await the arrival of some more residents in order to begin the accountability session, the third since the coming of People's Power.

Outdoors, on the grounds adjacent to the Peñas school, sitting on benches in the shadow of framboyan trees, about eighty people, peasants and workers from the area who got to the place on foot, on horseback, or by bicycle, are waiting for the delegate's report.

Quite a few women attend with their children, although a similar number has been forced to stay at home because of household duties. Distances are much too great to bring the children, as they might have to make their way back very late in the evening.

Although these residents belong to the small District 20 attached to the Cantel-Camarioca municipality, with scarcely 210 inhabitants, the delegate has decided to divide the accountabiltiy report into two parts. Today he is reporting to the Peñas residents; in a few days he will render a report on matters affecting the peasants.

"What are the main problems raised in your district?"

"The first thing they came up with is the problem of electricity. Several areas have no electric power, no light. The problem was raised during the first accountability session, in December, 1974, so it is already filed, assigned a priority, and we are waiting our turn."

"Tell us, what difference is there today with People's Power?"

"Everything is easier now. Each area has a delegate. One day a week I come down to this little school, and for three hours the compañeros come to see me, to present their complaints. And every three months I have to meet with all of them to give an account of the work performed, in terms of both private and public problems. One of the toughest issues here is housing, construction. Here in this country there are many construction plans, but it's difficult to execute them because of the cement shortage. Why? Well, it's well known. . . .There are so many things to build, all kinds of social facilities—schools, children's centers, etc. So we have to wait."

"Is the participation better now than it was under the CDRs?"

"Yes. There's more participation. Here the people speak up and receive an answer. They see the development process, the good offices of People's Power. They see that it really goes to bat for their problems."

"You, compañero, are you married."

"Yes. And you can imagine—I spend the whole day away from home. I leave home at six A.M. I work as a leader with the vegetable fibers utilization project. I go on foot. I get home around four P.M., or five. After that I'm supposed to go back to the executive committee to see whether the problems are being resolved. I get home very late at night."

"And you wife doesn't mind?"

"No. She realizes the nature of my work. Before our wedding she knew full well who I was, and what my work for the Revolution entailed."

"Your father, what does he do?"

"He's an agricultural worker at the fibers plant. He's always worked there, ever since it was a U.S.-owned enterprise before the Revolution. He's spent twenty-eight years at that place."

"Where did you study?"

"I studied here till the sixth grade. Afterwards, I went to high school at Varadero. Next I did my military service and from the service I went into teaching. I was a sergeant. I spent three years as a regular enlisted man. From teaching I switched to INRA [National Institute for Agrarian Reform]."

Overhearing our quetsion about the CDR, the local CDR chairman joins our group.

"I understand the CDR has participated in the tasks undertaken by People's Power. Could you give us an example?"

"They participate in all duties. I'll try to make this clear for you. For example, there may be a peasant who requests cement to cover his dirt floor. But such a floor requires sand as well as cement. When the moment arrives, we call out three or four compañeros from the CDR, and we go and load up the sand on a truck. And the day we lay the new floor, it's us, again, making the mixture and acting as masons."

"So the establishment of People's Power had meant even more work than before?"

"More work. Because practically all our leisure time has been devoted to organizing People's Power, and this is an innovation with us. Just imagine: when we have an assembly, since we are in the countryside and the houses are not huddled together as in the city, where can you mobilize a whole block in half an hour, in order to get an assembly off the ground, we have to make the rounds from one house to the next. And they are far apart. So its takes more than just a while. A day is more like it."

"Compañero, where do you work?"

"Transport. I'm a taxi driver in Varadero."

"What did you do before the Revolution?"

"In the old days I used to be a jack-of-all trades. For example, I repaired engines. In general, if someone brought something to me and I could handle it, then I did it. Like laying tiles. Upholstering, fixing a chair's leg, whatever. Because we didn't have work like now, when we are masters of our lives, with work guaranteeing our livelihood every month, the year round. With the cabs, I just get into one and work it for eight or nine hours a day, depending on the situation, and the economic question takes care of itself. Then, of course, the remaining hours I devote to other things."

"Where are you from?"

"I was born in Ranchuelos, Las Villas. From there I came here, to Camarioca."

"And what will be the most important problem to be discussed in today's meeting?"

"Well, I think the most important thing will be the delegate's telling the people about what has been done and the way things are going. And, if someone has a problem, he may bring it up during the meeting."

"And what about the women's participation?"

"As this is a rural areas their participation is difficult. Because, you know, we men can actually make it on foot or on horseback. I'm not saying women can't do that. But what happens? We have many elderly women here, many women with children, and it's not easy for them to attend. Because it grows dark and they're caught at nightfall with their young, who have to have their meals at a certain hour. Well, it's just not simple. They do take part, though. During the elections, they all came and voted. But more women here can't do this so easily. The meeting is held too far from where they live."

"Compañero, as a leader of the CDR, can you tell us how many members you have?"

"There are 78 CDR members, and about 71 nonmembers. Because here we have lots of small kids and older folks who, well, let's be realistic, couldn't care less. And as we force no one. . . ."

"Did the people who do not participate in the CDR vote in the People's Power elections?"

"For People's Power elections, well, just about everyone came. Here we had a solid turnout, with only 8 people, I think, unable to vote. Ninety-two percent voted."

Other residents have joined the conversation with the delegate. We take the opportunity to draw them into the discussion.

"Compañeros, how were you represented before the Revolution?"

"Well, at that time everyone went his separate way," one of the compañeros exclaims. "Everybody was concerned just for his own business. In those days it was every man for himself."

"You voted before the Revolution. What was it like?"

"Come now! . . . We sometimes had to hide in order to avoid being dragged out to vote. Because if the guards caught you they said: 'Hey, man, you've got to vote whether you like it or not.' ".

"Why did you come to vote now?"

"Now . . . well, I even secured transportation for those who told me they weren't going to make it on account of this. . . ."

"No one was forced to vote?"

"No! That was before!"

"Compañeros, what do you think of the delegate? Does he deliver?"

"We couldn't have found a better guy!"—a compañera exclaims. "He is truly concerned about our needs, everything."

"Have you brought any problems up yet?"

"Yes," several voices reply.

"What kind?"

"Well, there have been problems relating to housing repairs. He has gone to see the executive committee, and the problems have been taken care of."

"Look," says another. "This fellow's house had a dirt floor, and now we've poured a concrete floor, and a new doorstep, too."

"But who, precisely, did that?"

"Not just me. It was the peasants here," the owner of the house says.

"And the cement, who got it?"

"People's Power."

"I'd like to clarify one point about the cement problems," the delegate says interrupting. "There's a construction commission. We meet with the commission and set priorities. What does that mean? Well, we may have twenty requests for cement. So we give top priority to the neediest cases, according to an established procedure, like, if there are any children, dangers of slide, older folks. If we have twenty cases such as these, we allot the cement according to the deliveries we get in descending order of urgency. Our policy, the People's Power policy, is always to allocate the materials according to the quantities we get, because this municipality contains twenty-six districts . . . twenty seven if we take into account a military compound. So in proportion to what we get, we distribute it around each district. And the materials go to the neediest people. This commission was elected by the people, just like me. The people elected its own leaders."

"Compañero Jesús, since you were born here, you must have a lot of friends. What happens if a fellow comes up to you at a given moment and says: 'Look, now that you are a delegate, and we are such good buddies, why can't you take care of this little matter for me?' Does that kind of thing happen?' "

"No, it doesn't. Because where duty begins, friendship must end. That can't happen with a revolutionary. If someone is in more accute need than the friend, then he gets it. That's what the commission is for; that's what I am for. We can't let this thing happen. Where duty begins, friendship ends. I'm perfectly clear about this, because I'm fulfilling my duty."

"I understand you are a Party member. . . ."

"I'm a member of the Communist Youth."

"How did you become a member?"

"Well, I was elected a model youth, and then went through the process of personal scrutiny. After that they elected me."

"How many young people were elected model youths?"

"The educational workers presented a slate of twenty-three youths. After the inquiries, the reports, and so on, only three of us survived."

"What does this investigation entail?"

"The first thing is to present the name of the candidate, his attitude toward work, toward study, his attitude toward the defense of the Revolution. The inquiry goes then to the place where he has worked, and every conceivable detail is unearthed—the social, political, and cultural life. How he behaves in society. Then he is assigned some tasks and they watch to see how he discharges them, the way he carries himself in the street, how he meets the challenges."

We address another youth who is listening intently.

"Compañero, are you a Party member, too?"

"Yes."

"And how did you get elected?"

"Well, at my place of work. I'm a teacher. At work I was elected a model youth. At that time they elected fifteen or twenty compañeros."

"And how many of them became UJC [Communist Youth] members?"

"About ten. The others will be considered in the future. Because there are compañeros who may be lacking in some qualification, or they are too new, with little experience at work, little political maturity. . . .After being elected a model youth, I passed a [scrutiny] process."

"Who elected you a model youth?"

"The people. My work center. . . .After that you go through a series of inquiries, investigations, interviews. If you give a good account of yourself in all this, it is understood you are fit to become a member of UJC."

We turn again to Jesús: "And if there's a problem with your performance as a delegate, what happens to your standing as a UJC member?"

"Well, if they recall me, we have to see what kind of recall it is. If it is on account of illness, poor work, it is a problem analyzed by the UJC itself."

"If it's negligence in the performance of revolutionary tasks, he can lose his Party card," another Party members explains. "But if it's caused by infirmity, or if the people themselves have decided that this or that problem is affecting him and he should be removed, well, that isn't held against him. That's a different matter."

"And you, compañero, as CDR chairman, are you a Party member?"

"No."

'And what do you think of the Party?"

"The Party is the crankshaft of the revolutionary engine."

The conversation has been so lively that time has gone by swiftly, and the delegate has yet to begin the meeting. A resident reminds him that it is already after five P.M. and that there are women and children who cannot stay too late.

The Assembly

The accountability session commences with the electricity problem. As the delegate had said earlier, it is the area's principal problem. Despite the efforts made, a solution is not yet in sight, and this fact must be conveyed to the people.

"The electricity problem is still pending," the delegate says. "You know this question has been filed at every level. I filed it with the municipal executive committee; the committee filed it with the region; and the region took it up at the provincial level. Because this [power] line requires some construction, since it is being laid brand new, and the lines already in operation are being expanded besides. . . .As I advised you at the previous meetings, the provincial Department of Investments has already decided what needs to be done. We're waiting for the order to go ahead with the work. But, remember, this is going to be carried out with the help of the people. The management of the power company delivers the materials; we do the actual work. That means we have to dig the trenches, under their technical supervision. It means they lay the cable and all the rest, but we must actually put it into place, well, with the help of the people, right? And if we run into rocky subsoil when tackling the job, well, it means we'll just have to use a jackhammer. . . .

"We must understand that this is not an overnight job. We would all want to see electric light here tomorrow, because this is such a useful item for everyday use and the other needs of the area. We are attending this very meeting with oil lamps, right? Unfortunately, things must happen in their own time, as the country is still undergoing development, and there is an immense number of production plans calling for electric power—livestock stables, microbrigades, factories, hospitals, polyclinics—all that consumes electric energy. The Revolution will give us light, but only when our turn comes."

After this explanation, a series of problems are mentioned as solved in accordance with proposals adopted in the last assembly. The discussion then turns to the question of whether or not it was advisable to close down the small school at Peñas, merging it with one in La Guira, so the students could secure better services.

The debate is opened by a teacher at the Camarioca Technical School: "The question I'd like to raise concerns the consolidation of the La Guira school with the Francisco Vicente Aguilera facility. I can see that the transfer—the closing, rather—of this school is a problem for all the parents and people who live nearby. If it is difficult for the children to go to school in cold and rainy weather, it is doubly difficult when they have to walk two and a half miles. That school has been in operation for twenty-eight years, since the days of the pseudorepublic. The policy of the Revolution is to open new schools, not to close them. I think this school should be expanded, enlarged. Enlarge all schools. . . .New schools should be built. But under no circumstances should we close any.

"I know that they want to consolidate them to improve scholastic achievement. Now I'd like to mention that the scholastic record of this school has always been good. For what promotional level* are we seeking? At present it is low, owing to a series of circumstances I'd rather not go into.

"So I ask the assembly, the parents here, to study the problem of closing this school."

"With regard to the promotion question . . .you know what it's all about. You're a teacher," the delegate says. "There have been three or four grades that have complained of not being given sufficient time, with one teacher handling all of them, and as the teacher has little time to devote to each subject, the quality of teaching drops and thereby lowers the scholastic quality."

"I'm sorry to say this," the teacher insists, "but you were a teacher, just as I am, and you know that in the short time assigned us we taught four subjects. And a teacher with four hours to handle a class. . . .Well, that's an absurd argument. Look, I'm perfectly willing to come to this school and . . .help to fix it, anytime. But now, as a parent and as a resident, I oppose the transfer or closing down of the Peñas school. That' my opinion and specific proposal."

"I put this on the agenda because I knew this problem was going to crop up today," the delegate says. "Now I've been informed that consolidation is advisable because of the short time spent on the subjects and the quality problem with the classes. Nevertheless, those who disagree may make their proposals after the meeting. I'll just take it up with the leadership and bring back to you the reply they give me or, if you prefer, let them come down and explain the situation . . . ."

A compañero of peasant mien, who has followed the teacher's argument attentively, requests the floor: "I'd like to explain why I agree with the closing of the school. I have my daughter there and quite a few children show a low promotional ability, not just this year, but going back several years. We have pupils approaching fourteen who are still in the fourth grade. And you know what the reason for that is? It is because the teachers haven't got enough time to teach their subjects adequately. With regard to the question of promotion, Compañero Vicente takes his cue from his own children, who, of course, have no problems; but we should remember that his children, if they don't understand something, just say: 'Dad, what is this?' And their father can teach them. But that can't happen with me. My daughter very often asks me questions, and

*The rate at which students pass from one grade to the next because they have met all the curriculum requirements at that scholastic level. Normally, the rate is considered a reflection of the school's facilities and the teaching staff's qualifications.

now, with the modern math, she's in the third grade and knows much more than I—because I don't know a thing. And the other parents face the same problem. We've had cases where a child has been demoted, sent down to a lower level, from second to first, because the kid lacked the ability and couldn't get by in the grade where he was placed.

"There in La Guira they are going to set up a double shift of classes, so they'll be doing doubly well. I think that way the teacher will have more time to teach the courses, to the children and better use will be made of the instruction.

"Of course, it will be harder to take the children there, but they'll be getting a better education."

Eventually, the assembly approved the consolidation of the two small schools.

Obviously, it is not an easy matter to place a school still farther way from the already distant student homes. In a meeting of the Peñas' school PTA, a collective solution had been sought to the transportation problem affecting the children, and plans had been drawn up to offer luncheon to those students from the outlying areas.

The best solution, of course, would have been to have enough teachers available to insure good scholastic accomplishments at both institutions. But the educational demands existing in Cuba today make this impossible.

The policy of the Revolution in the rural areas, with dispersed populations, has been to try to group the population because adequate services —schools, stores, grocery shops, assistance centers, transport, etc.— cannot possibly be furnished to each remote settlement. The upshot of this policy has been the building of new towns in many rural areas, but the problems of underdevelopment, and, chiefly, the scarcity of cement, have prevented the extension of these measures to every corner of Cuba.

11 ADMINISTRATIVE DECENTRALIZATION

The Ministry of Education, Before and After

The inauguration of People's Power introduced a great wave of administrative decentralization. Most of the production and service units previously managed from the top now passed to the local agencies of People's Power.

We discuss the subject with José Ramón Fernández, minister of education since December, 1972, a tenure that has allowed him to experience both the old regime, when all educational activity was centralized in the Ministry, and the present, when an important part of the duties has passed to the local units of People's Power.

"The Ministry of Education, just like other centralized state agencies, shed a number of its duties. I think this is not only a positive step, but an indispensable one if we wish to improve our work and become more efficient. It was practically impossible to administer the units scattered all over the country efficiently. The Ministry of Education, just like Health, Internal Commerce, and others, was supposed to direct and manage diverse facilities that could be found in Baracoa, Guane, or Cienfuegos, supervising from the top not only their competence, but their performance as well. It was supposed to handle repairs, maintenance, and the everyday operational needs of these educational centers. At a practical level, it was difficult to satisfy the actual beneficiaries since facts were hard to come by. Today, with People's Power embracing these administrative areas, except for the questions dealing with teaching methods and norms—these remain under the jurisdiction of the Ministry

—service to these people has improved considerably. Under the new structure the people affected can participate much more directly. When the school performs poorly because of the teacher, because of supplies, because of problems with physical maintenance, because parents neglect to demand school attendance from their children—the people can, through their delegates, through work commissions, which also play a role, affect and influence the course of action to be taken by the authorities charged with correcting the problem. On the other hand, through the activities of the Ministry of Education certain goals are achieved. First, the unity of the system is maintained, and optimal allocations of available resources are secured throughout the country. Second, research is conducted in various areas and general standards developed for the whole nation, while efforts are made to utilize all pertinent information from other countries and from the municipalities and provinces of Cuba to improve the quality of our services.

"Now, the authority in charge of implementing the central authority's guidelines, insuring school attendance, seeing that the school is properly maintained, securing adequate supplies, imposing discipline, hearing complaints, opinions and recommendations from the whole community —who's that? It's the local agency of People's Power.

"Of course, we also play a part; we carry out spot checks to make sure that norms and methodology are being observed, like study plans, bibliography, etc."

"Does this mean that the People's Power educational authority receives orders from two sides—from the local People's Power and from the Ministry?"

"No, not at all. The orders are issued by the local unit. Our inspectors only check to see whether plans, programs, schedules, disciplinary approaches, and many other aspects are being observed. Anything good or bad is discussed with the school's authorities at once. Then, after several schools have been inspected in the municipality, a "summary meeting" is scheduled with the municipal leadership, perhaps the president or a member of the executive committee, the educational authority, and any other government officials the situation may call for. And it is the local agency of People's Power which must take the necessary corrective steps. We give no direct orders to any school."

"What is the role played by the people in this process"

"The people's participation is crucial to the whole process. Without the people, there's no sense of cooperation and determination to see that everything is done according to the highest standards, taking into full consideration all the possibilities and resources. This approach is already beginning to pay off. It's obvious that all of us must first familiarize ourselves with the new functions, oil up the mechanism of social interaction, and keep a sharp and critical eye on the actual accomplishments of our plans. But this concern shown by the people, their direct participation in governmental matters, is not only a factor of profound democractic meaning, but also a method of great effectiveness in the search for a better use of material and human resources in each case."

"Could you illustrate for us some of the things you had to deal with before and which now no longer turn up in your daily routine?"

"Well, there are many instances. The Ministry of Eductaion, which has more than twenty-thousand schools, would get letters from small villages complaining about a lack of electric light, a roof that needed repairs because the school was flooded whenever it rained, the need for a new paint job, a scarcity of school benches, and so on. Can you imagine? Can you see how difficult it was for us at the Ministry, eager to solve the problem but four or five hundred miles from that isolated spot, and unable to determine either the size of the problem or the justice of the request? It was a situation that made good administration extremely difficult. We even heard of cases of quarrels between parents and teachers. Now all this has become a bit easier. All these cases can be handled by People's Power. Another problem was that from here we had to appoint the principals to all the most important schools in Cuba, more than fifteen hundred institutions. This doesn't mean that we now don't participate at all in the nomination of educational personnel assigned to the most critical schools in the nation, but in each high school our involvement is rather formal, as it is impossible for us here to really know the candidates. The whole procedure is much more efficient now, because it is People's Power who appoints them, and they really know who these people are. There are numerous examples of this type. . . ."

"And now, with the time you have saved, can you devote yourselves much more to study projects, to the tasks of general guidance?"

"Yes, of course. Our tasks are spelled out in Law 1323, Article 71, which deals specifically with the Ministry of Education."

He reads from the text: "Design the national plans for the development of general industrial and polytechnical education, special education, adult education, technical and professional education, and the preparation of pedagogic personnel;

"Determine the different types of schools corresponding to the different educational subsystems under its jurisdiction and norms;

"Plan and supervise the application of educational norms binding upon different types and levels of instruction under the Ministry, including those implemented by other state and social institutions and by the mass political organizations. Approve study plans utilized by other educational centers subordinated to other state agencies charged with the development of professional qualifications, and orient and direct the unified state policy binding upon the technical training of the work force;

"Provide technical assistance for the application of normative principles connected with educational and methodological practice;

"Develop and refine a system of education for future teachers; direct, normatively and methodologically, all experimental research in the field of pedagogy;

"Conduct inspections, both general and specialized, of schools and departmental facilities."

"Moreover," he tells us, "teachers' colleges are directly subordinated to the Ministry of Education, which supervises the application of all educational policy under the methodological guidelines of the Bureau of Higher Education."

"About student promotions, is the local agency of People's Power responsible for setting policy in this area?"

"Well, we bear the load jointly. I'd say People's Power is the executive arm for all departmental guidelines in the pedagogic area, while also seeing to it that the whole educational enterprise is maintained by paying the teachers, fixing the schools, etc. About this problem of student promotions, I'd like to make clear that one often hears opinions on the matter that are not entirely correct. A promotion must be seen as the culmination of something. A good level of promotions is gained as a result of good work, where there's good scholastic organization, when teachers prepare their lectures well, the calendar of classes is observed, habits of study and self-teaching are instilled in the pupils, the material resources are properly utilized, there's a good state of discipline and morale, and models for emulation function appropriately. If this all exists, then we have a good promotion rate. But just to say that a school is good because it shows a high rate of promotion may be misleading. We must see the promotion rate as the outcome of work; it is the crop, as it were, of a particular labor. But it may also happen that subterfuges are used and that a good promotion rate is shown when, in fact, the pupils' level of attainment, the disciplinary level, the educational and formative work with the students, is not as good as it should. So we have to alert the compañeros. They should not just obtain a good promotion rate; they must obtain a good promotion rate because they've done their jobs well."

"You may be better informed than I about the fact that in order to secure a better promotion rate some teachers are not above lending a hand to their pupils during exams. . . ."

"Yes, Fidel touched upon precisely this subject in his speech at the Federico Engels School in Pinar del Río. Even though it's not a common practice, it's something we have to watch. To make promotions alone the lodestar, and not the quality of work, may lead some people into self-deception or into efforts to justify poor performance with good appearance. This is a very important concept in terms of individual integrity, and one we should strive to instill in the young."

The Philosophy of Bureaucratic Decentralization

The inauguration of People's Power throughout the country implies, as we have seen, a great measure of decentralization. Many factories and service shops ceased to be controlled at the national level and passed thereafter to the control of provincial or municipal agencies.

But what is the criterion used to determine the level each unit must be assigned to?

The essential criterion is that all units and enterprises which are budgeted by and work for the community, that is, the locality, should pass to the control of the locality. Those working for the municipality pass to the municipal assembly; those working for the province pass on to the provincial assembly, and those which operate on behalf of the entire nation remain under the tutelage of the central government.

From the moment People's Power was introduced, all centrally managed cinemas disappeared. Retail shops and schools are no longer administered centrally either, although the sugar mills, operated for the benefit of the whole country, remain under central management. Similarly, the merchant fleet, the basic industries, the railroads, and the great interprovincial transport fleets, all of which work for the national economy, remain under central control.

Fidel focused on this topic in his speech of July 26, 1974; "I hope you will understand clearly the criterion I have outlined. The State is one. The revolutionary state must administer everything, because private proprietors have vanished. The people are the owners, so the People's State must manage everything now.

"But is it impossible to manage all this from the center. It is impossible.

"Therefore, this criterion implies a profound decentralization of administrative duties.

"As we said earlier: The State is one, but it organizes itself at various levels and administers at various levels.

"This doesn't mean, of course, that in each locality the community can do whatever it pleases with the schools, the hospital, the stores; that it can raise and lower the prices, raise and lower the salaries, modify the curricula, use any textbook it pleases. No. Because, we repeat, the State is one and indivisible, and all these activities have to be regulated and must be similar in all localities, and similar across the country.

"It doesn't mean that in one hospital you may begin to do things differently than in other localities, or in one province, in a different fashion from another. No. They will be run uniformly: they will accomplish their function of caring for the health of the people, through established techniques, in accordance with totally regulated routines, because the relationship between the central bodies and People's Power is already clearly worked out.

"No one need worry that the hospital may suffer a drop in the quality of its services. On the contrary, it may improve, because sometimes there is a shortage of service personnel, the staff is short, for example, or there is some other deficiency, a maintenance job to do, get a few things out of the way, and the locality can't do much about these because the locality doesn't run the place. From here on out, People's Power will be in charge of everything relating to this hospital, how it functions, the manner in which it is maintained. All that. The community will no longer be alien to the management of the hospital."

People's Power Administrative Apparatus at the Local Level

Among the significant local production and service units subject to the agencies of People's Power one may find the following: (1) *local industries*, such as bakery shops, pastry shops, candy shops, ice factories, etc.; (2) *small businesses*, such as pharmacies, grocery stores, butcher shops, etc.; (3) *services*, such as dry-cleaning establishments, auto repair shops, service centers, barbershops, artisan shops; (4) *gastronomic services*, such as restaurants, coffee shops, bars, etc.; (5) *community services*, such as the maintenance of social buildings and facilities, i.e., clubs, theaters, cinemas, parks, polyclinics, hospitals; (6) *health facilities*, such as hospitals, polyclinics; and (7) *educational services*, which include schools, kindergartens, etc.

In order to manage the units under their jurisdiction, the agencies of People's Power rely on an administrative system composed of specialized departments.

Each department is organized to handle a number of related units at each level of People's Power. Its number declines sharply from the provincial to the municipal level.

For example, during the Matanzas experiment the provincial level boasted fourteen administrative departments, but the municipality had only half as many.

In Cuba one can distinguish two types of departments: one"functional," the other "sectorial."

Functional departments are those entrusted with such activities as planning, finance, and work specifications. Their decisions are binding upon the rest of the apparatus under People's Power.

Sectorial departments are entrusted with the direct management of a specific branch or sector of production and services, such as retail commerce, transportation, education, public health, etc.

The number of departments established under a municipal or provincial plan depends on the number of enterprises and units found in each particular branch or sector existing in that province or municipality. Thus, in a given municipality there could be a department in charge of retail commerce and another handling restaurants and recreation facilities, owing to the number of enterprises present in that economic sector, whereas in another municipality, where the number of enterprises is far less impressive, these could be directly subordinated to the executive committee without creating a special administrative bureau.

The Principle of Double Subordination

People's Power administers these units in conjunction with the state's central agencies of administration: ministries, commissions, and institutes. The criterion, as expressed earlier, is simple. The local activities are subordinated to the central bureaus in those areas pertaining to their normative or methodological aspects, such as the observance of production and service plans, applications of economic controls, application of existing national plants, guidelines for the use of human and material resources, and so on. On the other hand, the repair of buildings is left to the local authority.

This double subordination insures uniformity throughout the country for activities having similar characteristics, while also guaranteeing the consideration of local peculiarities and a better utilization of available resources.

Some examples may help to clarify this arrangement.

In all municipalities there is only one educational authority. This authority operates, as explained above, under a system of double subordination. One the one hand, it is subject to the Ministry of Education, which concentrates on teaching methodology, programs, bibliography, texts, evaluation systems for pupils and teachers, etc. On the other hand, it is subordinated to the People's Power agency, which is mainly concerned with the enforcement and implementation of tasks and guidelines issuing from either MINED (Ministry of Education) or the municipality itself. Thus, it is the job of People's Power to insure that the local Department of Education implements the methodological instruction issued by the Ministry, that teachers and students fulfill their roles according to plan, and that the physical plant of schools and other facilities is kept in good operating condition.   .

Grocery stores, butcher shops, and other centers for the distribution of goods, as well as the departments they fall under, are subordinated, on the one hand, to the corresponding central agency (i.e., Interior Commerce Ministry, MINCIN, or similar bureau) and, on the other hand, to the local agency of People's Power. Thus grocery stores, superettes, butcher shops, etc., together with the local Department of Commerce overseeing them, are subordinated to MINCIN insofar as distribution regulations and patterns are concerned, but they remain subject to People's Power for repairs, general maintenance of plant and equipment, and so on.

Similarly, cinemas are subordinated to ICAIC with regard to equipment repairs, types of film fare, and so on, but subject to People's Power as far as it concerns building upkeep, projectionists' performance, and other matters.

It should be borne in mind that the principle of double subordination does not mean that two institutions—the central agency and the local agency of People's Power—can issue conflicting orders to the same person on similar or different matters. The central agencies, as a rule, issue *methodological guidelines and instructions*, while People's Power (provincial or municipal) executes the same within their respective jurisdictions.

In addition, the municipal or provincial agency of People's Power is expected to watch over the performance of all enterprises and institutions within its jurisdiction, even excluding those not expressly assigned to it.

Functions of the Administrative Departments

The administrative departments and their directors and officials are held responsible for the management of all resources and activities falling within the purview of each level of People's Power.

In these functions the departments exercise complete autonomy over a whole series of operational questions, with the managers of production and service units subordinated to the department also free to make all kinds of decisions in matters of relatively lesser import.

This means that it is not the delegates, the assembly, or its executive committee, president, vice-president or secretary (to the executive committee) who directly manages the activites entrusted to that level of People's Power, but the appropriate administrative department or office through the managerial teams in charge of specific operations. The assembly and the executive committee appoint these officials to perform these functions; they pass the resolutions and lay down the guidelines regulating the activity of the functionaries; they orient, supervise, and inspect their performances; and when the need arises, and poor performance so indicates, they have the power to remove them.

At each governmental level the administrative departments are subordinated to the assembly and its executive committee. They present separate periodical progress reports to both. The heads of departments at each level must hold frequent and systematic executive conferences with the members of the executive committees.

Lastly, it should be noted that while the delegates are not directly responsible for the management of production and service units within their jurisdiction, they still remain active with respect to negligence or shoddy performance detected in any unit by personal observation or through the advice of their constituents. Under such circumstances it is the duty of the delegate to contact the officials affected, and, through brotherly conversation, make them see the necessity of correcting their faults, inefficiencies, or poor service to the community. Only in the event that such a direct approach should fail are the delegates at liberty to contact the appropriate agency of People's Power. If this agency also fails to make corrections satisfactory to the citizens, the delegate must take the people's case to the special executive committee member assigned to oversee the administrative department in question and to the municipal assembly itself.

Progress in the Struggle against Bureaucratism

One of the most significant consequences of direct popular participation in the affairs of government has been the creation of systems of control and supervision over state officials. These systems have effectively curbed bureaucratic abuses.

Thus it was soon perceived that all services and activities entrusted to People's Power were registering a dramatic increase in their operating efficiency, even when, as a result of the changes, some initial difficulties had to be ironed out.

"Look, let me tell you about my own experience in this area," Reinaldo says. "I used to be a MINCIN functionary in this region, where the department had fifty-four officials. Now the whole field of commerce is serviced by five comrades. And the problems are getting better attention. What's more, they are receiving *better solutions*."

He then recalls: "Every time the party would call on me to solve a particular problem, I'd come out with these forty statutes, seventeen normative guidelines, or what have you, and tell them: 'Look, this can't be resolved.' Thus the transfer of a simple administrative staff member, a janitor, for example, had to be approved at the national level! It just couldn't be done till we got the okay from the Minister himself or the national office. And that often took three or four months."

"And we have to keep in mind that those who say no, that this or that can't be done, are also revolutionaries," Alexis adds. "But they're just acting 'square.' "

"What was the role played by People's Power with regard to bureaucratic practices?"

"Previously, the bureaucrats were not subject to pressure from the people. They'd often say, 'Yes, we'll take care of it,' and they just wouldn't. They'd sit on it. And they always had a nifty excuse ready. But with the pressure brought to bear by People's Power, like, for instance, the obligation to file progress and performance reports with assemblies and executive committees, the managers suddenly found themselves in a tight spot, on their toes, because the delegates could bring up almost any problem. And the executive committee also leans on them in such a way as to force them to really seek solutions. Of course, this doesn't mean that all problems have a solution, because, in truth, there are some problems that elude solution at this point at any level—municipal, provincial, and even national. But there are many that can be solved. Before, it was just a lot of red tape. There were managers who didn't solve the problems because they just didn't feel sufficiently motivated, and there was no pressure. Now, from the bottom up, they are really compelled to look alive and find solutions. The new setup has changed many a manager's outlook."

Alexis elaborates: "The managers and officials running the show before the advent of People's Power operated on a series of ministerial directives and prerogatives that effectively insulated them from actual accountability. This situation often turned these individuals into nothing but deadwood sitting behind their desks.

"What's the situation today? They can't hide behind their bureaus and directives when some question is thrown at them. It's the executive committee and the assembly itself, with anything from 30 to 200 delegates, that's going to tell them what's expected of them. And the whole people are watching and listening. Some administrators feared that this would soon degenerate into something like a Roman circus, that they were going to fall into the hands of an assembly and a people prepared to draw blood. Because their regional hierarchic order, evolved during their tenure—two years, three years, ten years or whatever—their ability to act in a high-handed and almighty fashion—just vanished into thin air. That arrangement had to go up in smoke because, from that moment on, they didn't have the last word. From that moment on, the assembly had the last word. And between assemblies, the executive committee. They therefore became managers subordinated to a local assembly. They were no longer subordinate only to the head of the ministry. There were cases in which some managers were specifically called to task, because they still thought of themselves in some fashion as running transportation, foreign commerce, public health, and so on. They still didn't feel they were at the direct service of the people. So it became necessary to meet with them several times to review their functions with them. That was an initial battle that had to be waged. For example, it was necessary to make them understand that they didn't have to turn to the provincial government for facts anymore, that they could just get them from us. Things would crop up, like: 'The air conditioning units can't be relocated here because this is a matter to be decided by the Minister . . .' But what on earth does the Minister have to do with the moving of air conditioning units? But the official would insist that if the Minister didn't agree, the units couldn't be moved."

"I was commenting on that with the compañeros," Laureano says, "about the struggle we've had with some of the managers. Because practically overnight they've been told: 'Now you work for People's Power.' And their job complexion and routines have changed accordingly, but what isn't so easily changed is what lies in here." He points to his head. "In other words, we've encountered some resistance. But now we have genuinely reached a point where managers are beginning to talk like true members of People's Power. Before, they related to the system as something remote; they didn't see themselves as a part of it. Now things are different. They are likely to say: 'We, of People's Power. . . .' "

"One of the fellows who underwent a profound metamorphosis was the head of the Department of Education" Alexis says. "Whenever someone went to see him about a particular question he would dust off some resolution proving it was unfeasible. Directive such and such. And now, in spite of this history, he's become one of the directors who have responded best to the executive committee, and who have resolved most problems in this region. I believe we have seen many more compañeros whose work performance has improved as a consequence of the new system than people who've had to be replaced. And replacement has occurred, not because of errors or deficiencies, but because of recalcitrant attachment to old ways."

We ask Laureano about the measures taken against officials who resisted the new arrangments.

"We've had to remove compañeros from some specific activities," he says, "but they've continued in positions of leadership. Where? Well, in another activity better suited to their character. Others have been transferred to other lines of work as simple workers. We've tried hard to be fair, but recently we were compelled to replace some people in the restaurant and food sector in the Cardenas municipality. And not because they failed to understand what People's Power meant and all that, but because they started to take personal advantage by coasting. Yet they aren't representative of the majority. Even though we've been quite demanding, we've tried to destroy no one, to give everyone a chance to prove himself, not to be implacable, to make everyone understand that we're now supposed to give a bit more of ourselves than we were used to doing. Sometimes certain things are not resolved and we say: 'We've done everything in our power.' And we leave it at that. For example, we're in a meeting and a compañero is asked: 'Say, why wasn't the candy distributed to the schools this morning?' 'Well, there was a lack of vehicles.' 'So what did you do?' 'I did everything I was supposed to do.' 'I'd like to hear, compañero, two or three steps that you took to solve the situation.' 'Well, I advised such and such principal.' 'That's fine, but did you try to borrow some equipment from these people over here?' Or: 'Did you try to put your own transport equipment on the job and call the school's principal to arrange an early drop, before eight, for example?' 'Well, no, I didn't do that.' 'Then you didn't exhaust the possible solutions.' "

"According to my information you replaced a lot of officials. Don't you think you may have overdone it?"

"Yes," Reinaldo affirms. "I think in some cases we were rather unjust, rash, and even let many comrades go to other agencies outside People's Power when they could have contributed a lot to this experiment. In Matanzas, at least, we'll try to keep that from happening again."

"These hurried changes of personnel—were they made because the people's impatience was focused on the bureaucracy and it was easier for you to quickly remove those ostensibly responsible than make an effort at reeducating them?"

"I don't think that was the problem," Reinaldo declares. "The problem is that we always think new things require new faces. I said earlier that I was a bureaucrat myself, and there were many occasions when people had to tell me that I was thinking like a *minincero* [from MINCIN]. . . . Why? Because our outlook was shaped by the bureau. That was true of many of us."

"Something new came up, so let's go replace the people," Alexis says. "I think that, all told, the changes were salutary. To recall poor delegates is salutary. But we must also respect the value of specialization. We must allow people to gain deeper expertise in their assigned areas; we shouldn't go about transferring them every three months because of some mistake. If they're helped to grow—and there's no doubt there was room to grow—it's much better. To let someone alone for ten years is better than to transfer him every year. Ah! But if he doesn't perform, doesn't work out, doesn't seem to be gaining expertise in his subject, and fails to adopt new attitudes when they are necessary, if he is becoming routinized, if he's always the same, then we have to remove him."

"And didn't you have cases of bureaucratism within People's Power itself? For example, a delegate asking questions he might have handled to the executive committee or the assembly, or the regional and municipal assemblies dumping problems in the provincial assembly's lap when they could have handled them perfectly well?"

"Yes, of course. It's important to talk about this, lest the public get the impression we've always done things flawlessly. We've been guilty of debating problems forever, *ad nauseam*. This happened. And there have been delegates who didn't grasp a problem correctly and got off the hook by saying: 'I took this matter to the executive committee and they haven't given me any answer.' So many things are discussed, and answers are hard to come by; things are not easily and properly defined. For example, there's the delegate who should ask a department why a particular problem is not being handled, but goes to the executive committee instead. So we have to tell him: 'Look, pal, didn't you go to such and such a place to inquire there?' To avoid headaches, they come dump them in the executive committee's lap. And as we said before, sometimes we take matters up to a higher level when they could have been perfectly solved at our own, or we could have suggested a solution.

There's some of this, too. Sometimes we give inadequate replies to the people and fall into superficialities. We are not exempt from these perils.

"Sometimes we don't really seek a solution and make an excuse instead. That has happened to us. Sometimes we are too gullible, accepting an answer given to us by some department. The name and the individual may be different but the reply may be the same. We have to be more intransigent . . . We are sometimes so convinced that something can't be done that we don't even try to find out whether or not this is really so."

12 PEOPLE'S POWER VS. BUREAUCRATISM

During one February accountability assembly in the Twelfth District of the Playa municipality serious problems were discovered in the management of the Department of Buildings, Housing & Water Supply. Two voters—Josefina Sánchez and Jesús Fernández—leveled grave and harsh criticisms against the personnel involved. In an adjacent district Compañero Iraido Cartaya was raising similar issues. And while we were interviewing them in an effort to learn the details of their complaints, a review board of the municipal assembly, specially appointed in April, was conducting an in-depth investigation of the Department's administration and of the performance of its subordinate units. The upshot of the final report of the work review board was that the municipal executive committee decided to transfer several of the department's top managers, a measure that was announced to the public at the scheduled municipal accountability session.

We decided to follow as closely as possible this process involving the administrators. Accordingly, we did not limit ourselves to random interviews with the people, but endeavored to learn in detail the workings of the Buildings Review Board and the opinions held by the executive committeeman charged with overseeing the department, and the channels utilized to keep the people informed.

The Delegate Advises His Constituents of the Removal of Administrative Officers

We watched Fernando Pérez, a hydraulic engineer, as he conveyed the news to his constituents in one of the districts of Playa municipality:

"During the last session of the municipal assembly, one of the most heatedly debated subjects was that relating to the performance of the Department of Buildings & Housing. In the report prepared for the executive committee, marked deficiencies in that department were underscored, among which poor general organization and a sloppy assessment of problem priorities clearly stood out.

"There was a firm consensus among the delegates that the faults were real. We therefore felt that it was irresponsible to let the situation continue without taking concrete action against the managerial echelons involved. Some voices asked for immediate measures against these comrades, while others requested that a fact-finding board be set up first to conduct an inquiry and assign responsibility. Eventually a resolution was passed requesting the Buildings & Housing Review Board to investigate the matter. This meant a tremendous work load for these six comrades, as the board sat for thirty-one days. Important results were obtained, however. To sum up, the analysis revealed that the Buildings Department was characterized by an inordinate degree of disorganization and lack of responsibility. It was obvious that the leaders of this department didn't think it necessary to give an adequate response to the problems raised by the people, so they simply disregarded most problems or left them hanging. And the conclusion was reached that such behavior was totally unrelated to the real problems of scarcity afflicting the nation. Indeed, much more could have been accomplished if available resources had been marshaled in a more appropriate way. This whole episode serves to illustrate, however, how the people can exert their power through their delegates.

"You have directly achieved the removal of the Buldings Department head, of his deputy, of the director in charge of Water Supply and Sewers, and of the director of the multiple dwellings unit. This was achieved because power remains in the hands of the people. This is not just a mere slogan but a very real thing. In our district meetings we saw, in session after session, that problems pertaining to construction appeared systematically hard to crack. This forced the assembly to insist on several occasions that proper priorities be worked out for the problems at hand in order to try to solve them once and for all. And we, as your representatives, brought the matter up with the compañeros in question many times, finally taking the question to the municipal assembly. There we stated that such a situation had become totally indefensible and that it had to be resolved by compelling the compañeros to be responsible. Indeed, several delegates raised the issue in that assembly. And the overwhelming opinion was that an inquiry was in order. Examples of sloppy performance abound in our district. One single case may suffice to illustrate the Department's performance. I can tell you, for instance, that Compañero Evangelisto Toral first contacted me on May 31 of last year with the problem of a cesspool that was undermining his building. At that point I made several inquiries and nothing happened. Many compañeros from that building also went to the water supply unit to present the problem, but to no avail. They were given the runaround. They were told that the workers would drop by the next day, and they didn't. The callousness and impudence were such that I was advised in writing that the problem had been resolved on February 22, and that was a lie."

Next the delegate offers the floor to the constituents so they may express their feelings on the subject. After hearing them out, he reminds them again of the power they now have to control their destinies.

"The people would drop by the office, give their names, take a number—which would usually get misplaced—and nothing would ever happen. A bunch of comrades was earning a salary for doing this and nothing was really being accomplished. You can draw your own conclusions from the fact that I, a delegate, had been trying to get the problem of that cesspool solved since May 30 of last year and couldn't. What could we expect, then, for the ordinary citizen? Nothing, of course. No attention whatsoever. Those people were simply a bunch of good-for-nothings. We have dwelt on this problem at some length so you can see what can be done with people like these who thought problems raised by the delegates were not really worthy of attention, who think that people's problems can be ignored, who use public resources incompetently, and who take advantage of official vehicles just to carry on and party it up. Thus tremendous pressure had to be applied to get anything done and the image of People's Power was suffering, because it took a delegate to follow up the simple question of an open cesspool, when such a problem should have been taken care of through the regular channels. This problem we encountered in the Buildings Department is not a general problem. The problem simply seemed worse there because of the people we just removed. Again, I wish to emphasize that I've explained this in detail because I want you to realize the problem-solving possibilities that now exist, and that we can take measures as severe as these when the actual power resides in the people."

The People Don't Want Answers—They Want Solutions

"We must follow Fidel's example. He seeks out and identifies with the ordinary citizen to a terrific degree. I remember that not too long ago a

Granma article focused on the Caujeri Valley, in Oriente. And Fidel learnt, somehow, that the peasants there had shown a drop in productivity. So what did he do? Cross his arms and just chase after some data? No, he went straight to the peasants and talked with them. He gave us a good lesson in what socialist democracy is all about. That doesn't happen, unfortunately, with most of our officials. They don't go down to the trouble spots. They just try to discharge their jobs from behind their desks, applying scant attention to the struggle against bureaucratism waged by our country at the beginning of the Revolution.

"They thus obstruct the path to solutions because bureaucratic attitudes are just as much of a hurdle as anything else, a question of not meeting your responsibilities properly."

There is a reason for these harsh words by Comrade Jesús Fernández, a production assistant with the "Otto Barroso" cigarette processing plant. Since 1969 he has been fighting red tape, first with the old Local Power authority and now with the management of the People's Power Department of Buildings, to obtain the materials to repair some cracks and leaks in his apartment house in Miramar. And while his building is on the priority list, he has yet to get his hands on the materials. Recently, the straw that broke the camel's back was, as he declared in the district's accountability assembly, a bureaucrat's telling him he needed to refile his application, since administrative procedures had been changed.

"We have certainly done everything we were ever required to do, and we have the documents to prove it," Compañero Fernández says bitterly. And he adds, "And when we don't have documentary evidence, we have personal witnesses, especially the interviews we've had with the comrades formerly attached to Local Power, and now with People's Power. We have exhausted all remedies of a personal type. So we think there's no excuse for this type of situation. Why? Because the order giving our building priority is there, issued by People's Power, not Local Power; because the person who gave the order to go ahead was the director of the multiple dwellings unit, and People's Power was already in operation, even though it wasn't yet housed in its present quarters. So, a compañero from People's Power came down to check the situation, and *he* gave the OK, and the construction permit was processed as per his instructions. The only remaining difficulty at that time was the lack of manpower, but we said we'd take care of that. In other words, we don't have any problems with the procurement of the materials themselves; the materials are already on hand."

"Since when?"

"On January 25, 1977, we had a talk with the head of the Housing Department," says Jesús Fernández, looking for some papers in a file where he keeps all the details of this application. "He sent us down to see the director of multiple dwellings. I wasn't able to go down until March 23, 1977, that is, two months and two days later. I had an interview with this fellow on March 23, at their provisional quarters in a house on Twenty-fourth Street; the number is 4302. So these two steps should be regarded as taken before People's Power. The director told me that he didn't even have to come down in person because at the time of painting and renovation of buildings for the First Party Congress, he had seen the conditions of the house and understood the situation perfectly, so he was going to put the building on the priority list. But he recommended I go see the director of the buildings maintenance unit, who was and still is responsible for the materials and labor for all projects. He's the person who actually okays the work. So on May 7 he came to see me to advise me that the materials had arrived and that they could be picked up at the housing unit. But on the nineteenth I talked with the man in charge there and he said to me: "I'm going to give you the materials, but first I'll have to send out an inspector to verify your claim." On May 24, five days later, the inspector came and informed me that I should pick up the license in fifteen days. On May 30 I was granted authorization number 23031, folio 681, dated May 19, 1977." He is reading from the papers in his dossier.

When they ask you to get the license, you'd think everything was finally in order, that you're actually getting to the point of making repairs, right? But here's where the difficulties begin, and the situation becomes simply exasperating, explosive. On May 30, with permit in hand, I go see the director of buildings maintenance at 510 Twenty-eighth Street. And he confirms that the building we inhabit had top priority. Please note the date: May 30, 1977. Priority Number One, confirmed by the top official in that unit. But he tells me that he's had some trouble with roof tiles, shingles, etc., and that he had a requisition order open for forty thousand roof and siding tiles, and that as soon as he gets them 'he'll take care of our needs.' We only need 6,120. These tiles will be used to give the building the exterior finish it still lacks. So, as I was telling you, the fellow requests that I keep in touch with him. That I did, but the tiles are still to be allocated. Unfortunately, we are convinced that the materials did come in, although we can't specify the quantity. . . .Our interest stems from our aggravation at the fact that while we do know that materials came in, we were still passed over once again.

"On February 27, 1978, we went down again because we had firm information to the effect that tiles and siding had arrived and that, consequently, there was a possibility of getting the supplies. But what exhausted our patience was that that same fellow, with astonishing aplomb, advised us that we had to start the papers all over again because of some administrative reshuffle. That is totally unacceptable. In fact, it's an insult. Even he recognized that, and told me: 'Yes, I do remember you, I have the priority permit for your building, but you must now file for it again.' I said no, that that couldn't be, as the papers were already filed there. Procedural and organizational reshuffles should not affect a process already completed; they may delay the solution, but they can't nullify what has already been done. Can you imagine? Our process is revolutionary, and our organizations are continually evolving, and that should not injure the population. That's where my patience ran out, because we thought this problem was up to him. If a priority order has been assigned, it is they who have to find out if it is to be honored under the new system, and if not, to advise the person who filed the papers. But the hardest thing to swallow was that the person telling us all this was the very person who was acquainted with everything we did. This is internal negligence. A lack of sensitivity. If we fought such a hard battle against bureaucratism once, we shouldn't have to be dragged into it again at this late date."

"And the delegate didn't raise these issues at the municipality?"

"What happens in these accountability sessions? I have noticed that quite a lot, that many organizations give a reply but offer no solutions or claim to be having difficulties. I'm not saying difficulties don't exist, just that it's not a good enough excuse to leave problems alone. There's a lack of sensitivity. . . . We still don't have maturity as voters because, I tell you, there were plenty of answers that were wholly unacceptable. One of these concerns the Dionisio Roman school. It's hard to believe that in our country, with all the shortages of manpower, this school should have a repairs brigade totally paralyzed for lack of materials. I tell you that brigade should be at work eight to ten hours a day, as they work in construction, without stopping. For if the Ministry of Education doesn't have the materials, then another ministry must. Because, look, they are telling us they don't have roof tiles and other materials, but in this depot at Seventeenth Street and Forty-second there are more than ten thousand roofing tiles waiting for someone to pick them up. Who they belong to, I don't know for sure, I think People's Power. How can we have materials warehoused on one side, while the school is paralyzed because of shortages on the other?

"Another reply that was given during the session concerned a CDR complaint against chauffeurs smoking at a service station. The administrative reply: It can't be helped because the drivers don't have a place to stand. The solution should have been a no-smoking order strictly enforced. . . .

"So you begin to see the lack of sensitivity on the part of some officials! There's a school falling apart and they offer you an excuse. Their replies are often rationalizations. They are justifying why things are stymied. I think that revolutionaries should not stand for this, because they're walking by the spots in question, seeing how materials are misallocated, materials going to things outside their immediate social needs. So let's be clear about this! They're offering rationalizations, but I'm convinced these arguments should not be given, because the people have already heard them all. And that's why they turned to the People's Power assembly, to raise the issue. What they should do is look for solutions in the medium and long run. This is a revolutionary process that makes international agreements for the medium and long runs—so why can't we do the same at home? Why can't we tell the people the situation is going to be resolved by 1979, and keep our word? . . . It's time we started getting organized at different levels. We've had enough red tape, the people being asked to make the same arrangements over and over. The institutions in question , within reason, must assign completion dates for their plans. This jazz of reporting tomorrow, the day after. . . . At the highest levels our economy is sufficiently well planned. The ATM knows how much it's going to receive because those are economic calculations that deceive no one. Math is not poetry; three and two are always five. We have a system of planning in which we include all relevant factors, meaning that People's Power knows what it's going to deliver and when. So let the deadline be the twentieth and the delivery occur on the twenty-third . . . fine, at least there's satisfaction. A few days either way, but the delivery is made. For this reason we must ask these agencies to set a 'solution target date.' We are not going to go on telling the people there's a scarcity of materials. Just because a scarcity exists doesn't mean we can't do our best. The materials arrive at a given moment. Let's see how we allocate them."

"Do you think that if the managers had been present at the accountability session the meeting would have been more productive?"

"I think they should attend the meetings. Not too long ago something was published to that effect. And there was a reply, I don't recall who gave it, that the managers didn't attend in order to avoid confrontations. I think, nonetheless, that it's very important for them to attend these meetings, not necessarily to offer answers but to sensitize themselves to the problems of the ordinary person. Because, I insist, it's quite hard to sensitize themselves to the problems of the masses behind a desk. The manager should visit the crisis spots, where serious problems fester. Unfortunately, we have quite a few who don't go down to the schools, the housing units, where the real problems usually linger forever."

Erratic Service

"Once when we got there at eight o'clock in the morning to catch an early spot in line, we saw this compañero smoking downstairs. We were told the fellow we were supposed to see was not in yet. But this fellow turned out to be the very person we had seen earlier on."

These are the words of Josefina Sánchez, a social worker with the Calixto García Hospital, and a resident of an apartment house located at 4201 Seventeenth Street, in Miramar. The building is seriously affected by leaks. Right after we get to her apartment to conduct our interview, she shows us the state of dilapidation of the place, and she begins to fill us in on the kind of red tape she has been fighting.

"At this point the secretaries took a coffee break. Well! So an army comrade and I set about organizing a queue. So when I see this fellow walking past us, I say to him: 'Say, weren't you the person we saw downstairs?' 'Yes,' he said, 'but I start working at eight.' He didn't even stop to say, well, wait a minute, get organized, which is the least he could've said. In that place anyone could do whatever he pleased. He didn't help us at all, so I had to go back once again to see the director, but that Saturday the compañero, very gallantly, was not seeing the public because he had an appointment with the barber!"

"How did you learn he had to go to the barber's?"

"Because I overheard it. I stayed on, along with another compañero. I stayed because I like to see the outcome of dramas and melodramas, and I kind of like donnybrooks. So we stayed to find out what was going on. At approximately 11:30 A.M. the comrade arrived. We knew it was he because he looked like a person with a new haircut. On a hunch I walked up to him, but then he said he had to leave for a meeting. So I just put my foot down. 'Look,' I said, 'you haven't finished waiting on the public yet. Or is it that the People's Power assembly elected you just to look after your personal affairs?' He couldn't answer that, so he sent me to see another compañero. I told him I couldn't go on waiting and that I'd inform my delegate, Angela, about the matter.

"Another day I went back and saw the head of the Housing Department, and he, too, 'wasn't in'—but he was. I used to be a secretary at the Central Planning Board, and I can tell very well when a boss is or isn't around. Since I'm very outspoken and tell it like it is, I asked: He isn't in or doesn't he want to be in? We had worked together before, so I asked the secreary to tell him it was a compañera he knew. Finally I saw him, very courteous, but he told me he couldn't do a thing for me. 'Look,' I said, 'I don't want you to do anything for me. I'm raising a legitimate point: what are you here for? Because I'd like you to tell me why we've done all this, because I've wasted countless Saturdays here. I've been a witness to the disgust of the people. You're not receiving the people. You do as you please.' We'd seen it right there, how they'd take care of some people right on the street, without these individuals even having to come in. 'Look,' I said, 'I'm not going to waste another working day, but in the next meeting of People's Power I'm going to raise a complaint about what I've seen happening here. The secretaries come in at eight, and that's putting it politely; they sign up, and you don't know from Adam when they are off again for a snack, take their lunch breaks, etc. The last thing they do is pay attention to the public.' That's why Compañero Fernández and I decided to present this problem in the assembly, and I was going to write Compañero Machado Ventura a letter explaining the situation. He's the district's deputy in the National Assembly.

"And the explanation will be that there's an actual shortage of materials?"

"Marta, if I talk to a certain fellow and the materials suddenly appear—where are they coming from, if only bureaucrats have access to the people's property? I tell you that if I shell out three hundred pesos, I can get anything I need, sparkling new. For if the materials really don't exist, why can you find them in the black market? How come we can't get them easily the legal way?

"There's an Office of Multiple Dwellings that meets every twenty-four minutes to pass a resolution. If they met to hammer out solutions, it would be far more productive. We know that our nation has resources. This Multiple Dwelling unit doesn't function very well. Because it doesn't want to or because it can't? Simply, if it can't be done, let the administrative procedures change. Let the manager be honest and admit that he's not capable of handling the situation . . . ."

"Do you think the bureaucrats should attend the accountability sessions?"

"Yes, they should, because in that manner they'll be better equipped to meet the demands of the people. We can't equate a memo with a live, spontaneous debate on an issue."

"And what if the presence of the managers should give rise to ugly incidents?"

"If you didn't have confrontations, battles, even name-calling, would the struggle for people's power be worth the trouble? Isn't it precisely a battle where the people go to stand up for their own rights, which is the right of the people to have their own government? We must be capable of self-criticism, for if we can't practice self-criticism we can't be analytical, and then we can't get at the root causes of anything. I read Che all the time, and if we really remembered his example, we might not make so many mistakes, because Che engaged in criticism and self-criticism twenty-four hours a day. It's a question of adopting this outlook. The problem is not to read about Lenin and the October Revolution, but to carry Lenin's spirit into our everyday affairs. Similarly, it's not enough to listen to Fidel with the sound turned up so that the entire block can hear, it's a question of making an effort to practice what he recommends . . . ."

Irresponsibility and Runarounds

Compañera Abelenda went without a drop of running water for six months because her plumbing was stopped up. She has a son in Angola. So when the MINFAR commission came around for an inspection, she told them about it, and they came to see me. I explained that I had already presented her problem to the Multiple Dwellings Office but no solution had been found. So then the commission got in touch with that office, and a fellow was scheduled to come up and unclog the pipes.

"The day this fellow showed up, he said to me: 'I'm here from the multiple dwellings unit to remove the stoppage in a compañera's house.' 'Look here,' I said. 'Don't you also have instructions to check the entire building at the same time? Because the number of leaks and water waste is enormous.' 'Compañera,' he replied, 'I'm here to fix the whole thing.' 'Delighted,' I said to him. 'So why don't you begin with our friend whose son is in Angola?' 'All right,' he said, 'but first I'll have a look into each apartment to determine what I need in terms of wrenches, water tanks, float balls, fixtures, and so on.' He checked three or four apartments on the right side, made some notes, and the next day another fellow showed up with a toolbox full of bolts, wrenches, nuts, and so on. I was delighted, because I thought they were going to fix several apartments. But the next day the compañera with the son in Angola told me that while they had fixed her problem, they had created another . . . they'd obstructed the pipes of the apartment right below her. They'd drained the pipes to her apartment by pushing the stuff into the other fellow's plumbing lines. I asked her: 'But didn't the pumber realize what he did?' 'No,' she said, 'and he's already left. Besides, an inspector came up and told him that only one apartment was to be fixed and that the rest were not to be touched.'

"So I went down to the plumbing unit to see the head of the section. As I came in, I ran into the inspector, and he explained to me that his order only specified the home of our compañera. 'Fellow,' I said to him, 'I'm happy to see that you took care of her problem, but the woman below, the one whose plumbing you stopped, also has a son in Angola. The woman next door has two sons in Angola. A woman below has a son in Angola too. And Compañera Chela has her own husband in Angola. So if we are going to fix the apartments of people serving abroad, which I support and approve of, let them fix *all* the apartments, then. Now, I think the correct thing to do is what the plumber was going to do, that is, fix her apartment, then check the other apartments and get the whole place in working order. Because it's been three years I've been after you to get this done.' 'No,' he said to me, 'the instructions I have tell me different.' And he showed me the list with only the compañera's name on it."

The speaker, Iraido Cartaya, a retired accountant and now militia leader and Party member, is also chairman of the residential council representing an apartment house on Nineteenth Street, Miramar, which is rapidly deteriorating as a result of leaks. He has filed many applications to get the Multiple Dwellings Office to fix the place, but to date he has been successful in only one case, the one he mentioned at the beginning.

"Talk about red tape!" he says, "Here's the way the compañeros are treated: If I go down to one bureau, it's certain I'll be referred to another and yet another. I'm bounced around like a ball. I go down to this particular office and the director is not in—the deputy director is not in either—so I ask a fellow at the information desk: who *is* available? 'I am,' he says. 'But who are you?' I ask him. 'Are you the president? The director? The delegate? Are you a department head?' 'No compañero,' he says to me, 'but so and so is not here today, so and so is out of the office, this other fellow hasn't showed up yet, and—' 'So there's no one here? No one's in charge? If the people come here to ask for a report, who gives it to them—you? Are you the person to handle these questions? Because I happen to have this problem; let's see what you can do.' 'No,' he replies, 'I can only help you with the application.' 'But what have I to do with an application,' I reply, 'if I've had an application on file since 1975' "—he produces the application—" ' and I have one dated 1976, another 1977,

and yet another from 1978.' So what do I need an application for? What I
need is a solution to my problems."

"So this unit functions poorly,"

"No, it doesn't function poorly; it functions atrociously."

The Work Review Boards: The People's Advocates

"The problems with the administrative divisions constitute the bulk
of our case load, the ones which cause most aggravation to the population. For example, the problem of an overflowing cesspool is a nuisance
not only to the person who brings it up at a meeting, but also to every
resident who has to walk by the spot. Anyone can have an accident there
and fall in, to say nothing of the stench it spreads, which is endured by
the entire population. And in fact, it could cause an epidemic in the area.
And there's housing. In our municipality the problem is extremely
serious. We have 2,181 multiple dwellings and 343 rooming houses, all
in an appalling state of disrepair inherited from capitalism, the places
where our poorest citizens had to live.

"In the future, all these problems will be eliminated by the construction of new buildings. Of course, standing buildings also have their
problems—from the grave to insignificant, with only a minority in good
shape. The lack of maintenance of these properties has also aggravated
the situation. We also have in our municipality two rundown neighborhoods, right next to what used to be the bourgeois residential quarter. In
these areas everyone put up his house any way he could, some with wood,
others with wood and canvas. . . . As we are gearing up to stamp out these
shantytown conditions, the policy is to make all repairs with the materials originally used. Besides, within our jurisdiction we have two
squatters' settlements, Jaimanitas and Santa Fe. These are also in pretty
sorry shape. With this I want to emphasize that the population's needs
are way beyond the People's Power's present capabilities. We just don't
have the resources to meet the current needs."

The preceding evaluation of the housing situation in the Playa municipality was supplied to us by Emilio Aguilar, a professional member of
the municipal assembly executive committee. Compañero Aguilar is in
charge of the two most sensitive departments in the municipality, those
whose resources fall far short of the population's needs—the Department
of Transportation and the Department of Buildings & Housing. The
latter also includes the Office of Maintenance and Construction; the
Office of Water Supply and Sewers; the Office of Multiple Dwellings; the
Office of Housing and Urban Renewal; and the Office of Public Lodg-

ings. During the conversation he reveals to us that the executive committee has decided to remove several managers connected with these activities, namely the municipal director of Housing, and the head of the offices of Water Supply and Multiple Dwellings, and the technical deputy director of the Office of Maintenance and Construction. We inquire about the reasons that led to these measures, and how People's Power operated to reach its decisions.

"Was the scarcity of resources the main reason for the managers' lackluster performance or was it really a case of poor administration?"

"The objective shortages of materials are very real, and each delegate must be capable of explaining this to the population. Besides, the country's top leaders have talked about this subject at length. However, as the executive committee knew of some irregularities, and several delegates had registered complaints with the April assembly, it decided to appoint a special board of inquiry to look into the matter. This board, composed of six comrades elected by the municipal assembly, worked for thirty-one days and reached the conclusion that these managers were doing a poor job. In a nutshell, they were incapable of giving serious and thoughtful answers to each citizen's inquiry. At times they'd give vague, banal answers and make false promises. They have given the people the runaround. The multiple dwellings unit would send the applicant to Maintenance and Construction; this unit would ask him to file with another office, and that office would advise the person an inspector was to be sent, but this inspector would never come to any decision. If the problem was not susceptible to a solution, the person should have been told that, and a time estimate given—say, a year, four months from date, whatever. But they should have told the truth."

"The problem was limited, then, to poor responses to the population?"

"No, but this is a very important aspect of people's government. We have to insist on good treatment and the absolute truth for the population. But quite aside from the material shortages, these offices had also shown organizational deficiencies. Even with scanty resources much more could have been done. Another major area of poor performance was their inability to set correct priorities for the solution of problems raised by the public, even though it's obvious that each and every problem raised in the assemblies can't possibily be handled satisfactorily."

"Was it necessary, then, to plan more carefully?"

"Yes, that's correct. For example, Multiple Dwellings has to reach an agreement with the Office of Maintenance & Construction according to the budget established. Multiple Dwellings must find out how many buildings the maintenance people can service during that fiscal year.

"Thus, of the forty-five children's facilities in the municipality, it must be decided how many can be repaired this year, and for the schools, the same thing. An agreement must be worked out among the offices, taking into account the materials and the workforce available to each. One agency, for example, must decide which schools are to be repaired. And all these decisions must in turn include the delegates' requests, which obviously, also reflect the population's needs.

"Of course, there are delegates incapable of supplying correct information and constituents still shy of their delegates."

"What about that construction brigade left high and dry in that school?"

"Well, that's an example of poor organization. If we dispatch a brigade to a school, it should be because we already have the necessary materials. Lacking these, the brigade should be sent elsewhere. These leaders failed to utilize human and materials resources to the hilt. They definitely could've accomplished more than they did. . . ."

"As a member of the municipal executive committee in charge of administrative departments, what do you think of the work review boards set up to assist you?"

"I think the work review boards must be the fundamental weapon of the municipal executive committee. I think, and this is a personal opinion, that the job done by the Housing Review Board was excellent. It's going to set a precedent, it already has, for the way a board should proceed. We have yet to utilize the boards to the fullest. They are the principal supporting body of the executive committee. Each member of the executive committee supervises an administrative area, shares in the policy-making, confers with the top officials, but can't possibly oversee everything or get to know in detail the problems the way a review board can. The executive committee report on that department, with the benefit of the inquiry conducted by that board, is going to be fairer, more accurate, more serious. That's why I think we must develop these boards further, seeking out more ordinary citizens, people of integrity, unencumbered by obligations to other people, to other departments, so that they can act freely as people's advocates. The work review boards must be the people's defenders and a reliable source of support in the work of municipal government."

"Is it advisable to staff these work review boards with people knowledgeable in the respective fields of inquiry?"

"Undoubtedly. The Housing Review Board should include, for example, an accountant, because it's a question not only of seeing whether a problem has been resolved, but also of discovering how the resources were utilized. For this reason we should also have specialists on the labor force who can advise us and help us organize whatever is available, as well as compañeros with experience in hygiene and safety on the job. For example, any worker who's working in the sun should have access to fresh, pure water, because this problem doesn't require much in the manner of resources to be handled. It's just a question of a clean bucket full of water. A little thing like this helps productivity and lightens the burden of the worker. It's also important to find workers for these boards, because workers can be very analytical and profound in dissecting the problems of fellow workers. They know what jobs really entail. In short, we need as complete a spectrum of people as possible, ordinary people clashing and struggling daily with the problems, and, fundamentally, people with true compassion."

"Don't you think that among the very people who have formulated criticisms of an administrative department you could find one qualified to sit on this work review board?"

"Certainly. Any citizen, any revolutionary who expresses himself critically and constructively should be considered for inclusion. That's why I said that we're going to enlarge our work review boards. We are in need of critical people, responsible people, people with human sensitivity, people capable of tackling the problems and finding solutions."

What a Work Review Board Does

What exactly is, the role of a People's Power Work Review Board? There's no one better to answer the question than the head of one of them. Accordingly, we interviewed Pedro Rodríguez, a technician with the Construction Materials Ministry and president of the Playa municipality Housing Review Board. The commission also includes Ramón Esquivel, a military officer and delegate from a special district; Nivaldo Almarades, a college student who works at the Sugar Ministry and also a delegate; and two members who are not delegates José Ortega, head of the ICAIC Maintenance Department, and Laureano Sendin, an electrical engineer. The board began work in mid-1977, holding its first meeting with the municipal Housing Department in October. At that time they discovered a series of problems which were included in the executive committee report to the municipal assembly in April of the following year, facts also mentioned by several delegates. It was this assembly that ordered the Housing Review Board to conduct an inquiry into the matter. Resolution 18 of that session reads: "It is hereby agreed unanimously that the Housing Review Board prepare a report to be submitted at the forthcoming session; that the Board, on the basis of this information and other data it may gather or possess, analyze the existing situation in this department and advise the executive committee of the matter so that it may adopt whatever measures it deems necessary."

"We were not going to evaluate just one quarter's work, but a year and half, and they were told that," says the head of the board. "As skillful a report as possible. Yet when we had it in our hands, we realized it wasn't what we wanted and that it did not meet the requirements specified by the assembly."

"You collected the problems the population had with this board?"

"Yes, we conducted interviews, collected the views of the people. For example, we came across this fellow who has been trying to complete his septic system for four years and still has more than two meters to go to tap the main sewer lines, the whole thing being well known to the municipal authorities. We also discovered inefficiencies in the area of teamwork. We sat down with a group of delegates and a guide to learn about the problems they had with the Housing Department. There were ten to fifteen of them."

"How did you pick them?"

"At random. We found them in the waiting and consultation rooms the delegates keep in the departments, so we knew who had the most problems. We also tried to pick delegates from each zone. We did a tour of the entire municipality to get a feel for the overall problem. We verified a series of inefficiencies. For example, this fellow with the sewer problem has visited the department five or six times and still gets no satisfaction. We also learned about the poor performance of a manual drilling brigade that visited Buena Vista and took all of twenty-eight days to finish just one job. We also learned, through the testimony of a compañero on the block, that although he had all the papers he needed to get his well repaired, the department had failed to do the work. Indeed, the brigade told him that they couldn't do the job, that he had to apply to the department. He went to see the department but they still said no. We learned about deliveries of supplies to parties who no longer needed them. And we also found resources not being properly utilized. We therefore focused on their managerial methods, their attitudes toward discipline, tardiness, improper methods of conducting hearings. We saw that scant attention was being paid to work in progress, like little or none at all. That also came out clearly in our analysis. There was improper intervention by the director in matters outside his authority. In the maintenance division it was found that jobs were begun without license or budget.

"We met first with the municipal authority, beginning our work there. We took a look at the budgetary controls. These were inadequate;

the projections didn't balance out. We met with the Office of Water Supply and observed the bureaucratic centralization that prevails there, which is a very significant defect, because one person can't know everything. We saw at first hand how the replies given the delegates were inadequate. We thus came to the conclusion the department lacked the organizational ability to run things properly. We met with the Office of Maintenance & Construction and with the three other units—Water Supply, Multiple Dwellings, and Urban Housing. We realized that the municipal Department of Housing left much to be desired in its ability to organize teamwork. There was absolutely no follow-up or verification procedures between the municipal director and the departmental chiefs. No consultations with the economic sectors, which is crucial. At Multiple Dwellings we also met with the director, whom we advised of the deficiencies we had observed in the areas of work supervision, delegate information, and problem ranking. As you mentioned in relation to the case of the roof tiles,"—he is talking about Compañero Fernández's case—"if they don't have them, supposing they're not available, give him the other materials. But this man remains number one on the priority list, and when tiles arrive, we must give them to him."

"The board's work must've been very intense."

"It was. They worked thirty-one days at all hours—dawn, morning, afternoon, nights. It was a big job because of the amount of data to be examined. And the worst thing about all these deficiencies is that the people may wrongly conclude that things are as bad as before. But the deficiencies we learned about through the testimony of the people, and the administrative flaws we verified ourselves, convinced us that a real problem existed.

"The major deficiencies spotted by the board were, among others, the misallocation of resources, a grave charge; a general lack of discipline, equally serious; a lack of effective over-all coordination at the top: there were no work plans, no progress checks, and a pervasive feeling among the workers that resources were being poorly utilized."

"Could you elaborate a bit on how the board actually conducted the inquiry?"

"Well, we're six comrades, all workers, and some of us have national responsibilities. We all worked equally hard. At least three of us were going at it at any given time. We would have periodic meetings with the rest of the board to advise the other members of the progress of the inquiry. We interviewed ordinary people, people in other divisions, for example, people attached to the Office of Buildings Maintenance—we called them to ask for advice. From compañeros who had had some responsibility in the administrative apparatus, and who no longer worked in those departments, we asked for suggestion for improvement. We sought out people having a broad range of experience."

"What happened once the report was completed?"

"The final report was analyzed by the executive committee of the Playa municipality, and the major points were taken up later with the concerned administrative officers. That meeting was attended by twenty top officials from the Department of Housing, the president of the municipal assembly, the executive committeeman in charge of that division, a party representative from the municipality, and all the members of the Housing Review Board. A wide-ranging debate took place. This is one of the finest examples of democracy in operation. We debated, point by point, from nine in the morning till three in the afternoon. The report was approved unanimously, with some points to be clarified later, which they were. For example, the figures presented by the Department of Commerce did not jibe with those introduced by Housing; Commerce had, for example, twenty-five, and Construction had forty. But here inputs and outputs had to be balanced, the figures had to match. Other things concerned the excess of luncheons and meals in certain voluntary work operations: there was a discrepancy between the level of participation and the quantities. Well, all these facts underscored grave deficiencies, especially in materials, deficiencies later recognized by the director."

"Before we go any further, could you tell us how the bureaucracies reacted to your report?"

"Even though I'm no psychologist, some things were pretty obvious. The reaction, in our minds, was not one of outrage. When one can't justify the unjustifiable, the best thing is to quickly become part of the solution. As the evidence was everywhere, the report stood practically unassailed. Only a few points were contested."

"And these comrades, did they engage in any self-criticism?"

"Yes, even though they tried to justify a few things. But when the vote on the report came up it passed unanimously, as everyone could see that it summed up the truth about the problem."

"And the top administration officials also endorsed the report?"

"Yes, of course. They had no choice. With so much work behind the findings, there was only one thing left: to recognize the facts or to deny them. And not to recognize them would have been tantamount to a rejection of the report's findings. So no point was seriously questioned because the report was telling the truth. Some things they tried to justify and couldn't: improper use of cars, financial abuses, projects launched without a budget, inadequate replies to problems raised by delegates, red tape, and lack of respect for the population whenever citizens would explain their problems. All these things are a matter of record, concrete things, real things. The excessive centralization in the area of water supply, wells and sewers; the shortcomings of the director of the multiple dwellings unit. All these findings were not lies, they were the truth. The report was approved by everyone, thus admitting they were doing a poor job. We think we have used the best approach. Our intention was to search for ways to solve the problems of the population."

"And what happened after this meeting?"

"The board participated in a regular session of the executive committee because, as agreed, the role of the work review boards is to assist the executive committee. With all the facts in hand, we provided all the materials so the executive committee could decide on a course of action. Our job ended there.

Summary

At each level the agencies of People's Power rely on work review boards for their information. These boards, organized by branches and sectors of services and production, are entrusted with the task of counseling and assisting People's Power assemblies and executive committees in the management and supervision of their subordinate units. There are, for example, boards for education, health, construction, commerce, and services.

Boards must also be set up to oversee fundamental activities in a particular area, even when these may not be subordinated to the local People's Power but to a national administrative agency (see preceding chapter). Thus the sugar mills, given their national importance, are subordinated to the Ministry of the Sugar Industry, but this fact alone does not exempt local agencies of People's Power from supervisory responsibilities.

On the contrary, because of the role they play in the national economy, they have to be cared for in a very special way.

Thus the work review boards must ascertain whether or not the administrative department and the production and service units subordinated to them, as well as the national enterprises, comply with the methodological and normative guidelines laid down for them by the national bureau.

Accordingly, they must secure the information to evaluate the work each of these performs. To this end, they can, from time to time, conduct field inspections: the Education Review Board, for example, pay a surprise visit to a school, attend classes, see whether or not teachers discharge their duties adequately, whether the school satisfies the necessary health requirements, and so on, They are also empowered to summon officials from various bureaus, and to request from them any pertinent information, seeking, when advisable, the direct testimony of people affected by the recorded deficiencies.

In addition to all this they must see to it that work is correctly planned for, that the managerial councils function as they should, that financial matters are carefully recorded, that equipment and supplies are utilized to the limit, that all completed work is inspected, that official cars are used for business and not pleasure, and so on.

Furthermore, work review boards are to watch the manner in which the administrative units receive and process the problems raised by the people directly or through their delegates. This often entails support for the officials in question in the form of counsel, constructive critiques of their performance, determination of whether they are capable of correcting mistakes, and so on. In the case of officials who demonstrably fail to live up to their public responsibilities, the executive committee, basing itself on the report of the work review board, may recommend their removal.

On the other hand, the work of the boards is not to be restricted to the task of supervision over local and national administrative bodies. They must also conduct studies and develop projects that may permit improvement in the production and service units within their respective territories. They therefore assist the executive committees and the assemblies in making decisions. It's not enough, for example, for an assembly to decide to build a school in a particular municipality; it's necessary to know whether adequate resources exist. Thus the opinion of the work review board is indispensable.

There are two types of boards. Permanent boards are charged with inspecting and supervising the functioning of administrative, production, and service units in the municipality or province (as in the case of local agencies of People's Power) and the ministries, committees, and institutes in the case of the National Assembly. The second type is represented by the temporary work review boards created around a problem to be resolved in a relatively short period of time. These are ad-hoc or special boards. They study, for example, the way to rebuild a bridge damaged by a cyclone.

But who serves on these boards?

In the case of the National Assembly, they are made up exclusively of deputies. At the level of the local agencies of People's Power they are made up of delegates and ordinary citizens under the chairmanship of a delegate. Every effort is made to use delegates with experience in their respective fields, even though the boards are also assisted by specialists who are not delegates.

The work of the boards makes it possible for an ever larger segment of the population to become involved in matters of self-government, while enhancing People's Power through the contributions of many intellectuals and professionals who, because of their professional activities, might otherwise remain isolated from the problems of the people. Their expertise, usually superior to that of the delegates in various technical areas, is critical to the performance of People's Power.

These boards also endeavor to involve workers and technicians who, because of their daily work experiences, are able to make significant contributions to the success of the idea.

As noted earlier, the work review boards require their members to be free from allegiance to any outside person or institution. Members are expected to judge the performance of all kinds of units assigned to their care, resolutely and without fear. The boards are one of the most critical mechanisms attached to People's Power for the control of the state apparatus.

To sum up, through the work review boards the administrative sector has come under the direct scrutiny and supervision of the masses, a development which has contributed greatly to elimination of bureaucratic inefficiencies.

On the other hand, as has been shown, administrative officers used to be free of pressure. They could promise solutions and deliver nothing. Now they cannot act in that fashion, as they are held directly accountable to the People's Power assembly, and the assembly retains the power to remove them.

The pretext of kicking problems upstairs has also largely vanished. Before, even to move an air conditioner from one office to another, or to transfer a cleaning person, the Minister himself had to be consulted. Now such decisions are left to the local assembly. With People's Power, bureaucratic arrogance and contempt for the public have come to an end. And residents can and must report poor service or incorrect attitudes observed in different units of production and service. And to this, as previously explained, the work review boards add their own supervisory contribution.

Because of People's Power the bureaucrat no longer has the last word. He can no longer take refuge in the glib excuse for his poor performance that he was following the Ministry's policy. For now the last word rests with the local assembly of People's Power.

13 THE ARMED FORCES AND PEOPLE'S POWER

Anatomy of a Working-class Army

"I had been a member of the 26th of July Movement from 1956. And, before that, of the Orthodox Youth,* the same unit our commander in chief came from. During those years I fought in the underground, sending men to the mountains, gathering weapons, carrying out sabotage, distributing propaganda, and I was imprisoned. But come to think of it, I did nothing compared to what other compañeros did."

Several colorful buildings rise amid green gardens. Only the basketball courts introduce a splash of gray into the landscape. And it is only the olive green uniforms worn by the hundreds of young men that reveal to us we are on the grounds of a military unit. The speaker, blessed with an engaging smile and a lanky build, is Major Ricardo Prieto Meilian, the director of the Camilo Cienfuegos Military Academy, in Matanzas.

"These schools exist in all the provinces," he explains. "They were set up in 1967 with the purpose of assisting the national education system, moulding kids between twelve and thirteen. Here they get secondary and precollege education, in addition to certain basic military instruction. Upon graduation as cadets, they enter the higher military academies, from which they graduate as officers of the Revolutionary Armed Forces. Here we also prepare future teachers who will eventually practice as such in civilian life."

---

*Orthodox Youth was the youth arm of the Orthodox Party, a left wing formation dating from Batista days. It no longer exists.

"How did you become a soldier?"

"Well, I belonged to the 26th of July Movement, as I said earlier. When the Revolution triumphed, on January 1, 1959, I took part in the assault on a town in the province of Camaguey, and we occupied several police stations. Those days I went around with my knapsack everywhere, as the police were looking for me to kill me. After the triumph of the Revolution I stayed in the police, but I was transferred to Havana, where I stayed for two years. In 1961 they transferred me to the police battalion, which was a quasi-military unit . . .designed to fight in wartime . . .not exactly concerned with catching pickpockets. When Girón came about, I was with the battalion. After that we were transferred straight to Army supervision, and that's how I became a soldier. . . ."

"And before the triumph of the Revolution, what kind of occupation did you have?"

"Well, I was a hatmaker. . . .With needles and things, I sewed hats. . . ."

The present Revolutionary Armed Forces (FAR) have as a direct forerunner the eighty-two-man contingent which, led by Fidel Castro, disembarked from the yacht *Granma* on Playa de las Coloradas, Oriente Province, on December 2, 1956. They follow in the heroic tradition of the Mambí Army, which fought long years for the freedom of Cuba from Spanish colonial rule, and of the young men who, also commanded by Fidel, assaulted the Moncada Barracks in Santiago de Cuba on July 26, 1953.

Their olive-green uniform received its baptism of fire in the streets of Santiago, on November 30, 1956, when the combatants of the 26th of July Movement donned it for the first time to support, through a general uprising and assaults on military installations, the landing of the *Granma*.

Yet after two years of a fierce civil war, it was that popular army, with the disheveled uniforms, born in the very midst of the people, which triumphantly entered the capital of the Republic with the head of the Revolution at the fore. Of the bearded guerrilleros not one had studied in a military academy. The victory of the Revolution sounded the death knell for the corrupt Batista army, which lacked principles and patriotism; it was a puppet army that the United States had created at the end of the struggle for independence to replace the Mambí Army.

It was the beginning of a new era.

On October 16, 1959— ten months after the entry of the Rebel Army into Havana—the Revolutionary Council of Ministers dismantled the old Ministry of Defense and substituted in its place the new Ministry of the Revolutionary Armed Forces, appointing as its head Commander Raúl Castro. The Ministry of Defense disbanded on that occasion was, in prerevolutionary Cuba, a den of bureaucratic politicking, reactionary plots, and intrigues, and its principles and methods were so out of tune with the reality of the emerging body of armed forces, diametrically different form those existing prior to January 1, 1959, that the creation of a new organization was unavoidable.

"The Rebel Army merged with the national Revolutionary Militias, established that same month and composed of hundreds of thousands of workers, peasants, students, and professionals, who, in their spare time and in brief courses, acquired a basic miltary training." This is the way the weekly *Verde Olivo* described the birth of FAR in the issue of October 20, 1974.

The first regular division began to be formed in mid-1961, right after the Rebel Army, the National Revolutionary Militias and the Revolutionary Police—the people in arms—beat back the mercenary invasion attempted at Playa Girón, beginning on April 17. Their troops were entirely drawn from the first two organizations, which would henceforth become the nation's standing army.

"The road traveled to this day was not easy," *Verde Olivo* added. "From the first day of revolutionary exhilaration, following the fall of the tyranny's last bastion, the Rebel Army had to mature quickly, passing from the phase of organizing guerrillas and columns, whose chief active contingents still remained deployed in the provinces of Oriente and Las Vilas, to a phase of consolidation of squadrons, regiments, divisions, and armies."

Today, the Revolutionary Armed Forces are the nucleus around which the entire Cuban people can be mobilized to protect the nation's territorial integrity and the conquests of the Revolution.

Every Soldier a Workingman

"I am a an officer, a lieutenant, and secretary of the Communist Youth at the school besides. My parents live in one of the most remote areas of Las Villas, where the main focus of the counterrevolution was sown after the Revolution's victory . . . right in the heart of the Escambray Montains where the bandits roamed. Our whole family is what you might call . . . real hillbillies."

"I am a second lieutenant, head of the general preparedness faculty of a battalion here at the school. I am of working-class origin. My father was a bus driver, my mother a grade school teacher."

" I am a worker, like my parents. I hold the rank of lieutenant, and I'm also a delegate for our district to the Matanzas municipal assembly."

"I'm a first lieutenant . . .the son of a peasant."

"I'm a first lieutenant, too, the son of a worker . . .a sugarcane worker."

The group is dressed in olive-green uniforms, a part of the officers' contingent at the Camilo Cienfuegos Military Academy in Matanzas.

Lieutenant Mariño has just finished a report, as a delegate to People's Power, given minutes before to hundreds of youths—"Camilitos" and "Camilitas."* After listening to him with great care, they are now breaking up into small groups and dispersing throughout the courtyards and gardens. The group here, composed of elements from all over the island, of proud peasant and working-class background, typifies the new officers and Army.

An Army of Workers and Peasants

In the words of Fidel, on December 30, 1973: "Every single one of these men, and every single citizen of this country able to bear arms, is not simply a soldier of the Army, Navy or the Air Force: He is, above all else, a soldier of the Revolution! And when the time for combat comes, they will be resolute and heroic, not primarily out of formal discipline or from the habit of obeying the orders of superiors. They are above everything else the defenders of a great cause and a great idea; defenders of their motherland and defenders of the revolutionary cause of Marxism-Leninism; upholders of the great cause of the international revolutionary movement, firmly convinced of the significance of their extraordinary historical mission."

A huge portrait of Camilo Cienfuegos hangs behind the director. His office is small and spartan. There are no luxuries or frills of any kind. Nothing superfluous. And, especially, nothing to indicate that this is indeed the office of the director of the Camilo Cienfuegos Military Academy.

"Look, what distinguishes our armed forces is their ideology. We, the military, live in a society of workers, in a proletarian society of communists. We have not reached communism, which we strive to build, but our ideology, our world view, is communist. And therefore I am a worker, with a uniform and a rank . . .and with the military knowledge to defend the motherland. The same as a technician who repairs a public bus . . .I am a soldier, but I'm a worker, too."

---

*"Camilitos" is affectionate name given to students at junior military academies. Such as the Camilo Cienfuegos Military Academy. Cienfuegos, one of the Revolution's outstanding military leaders, died in a plane accident soon after the victory of 1959.

Back in the yard, after we leave the director's office, First Lieutenant Alberto Acevedo discusses with us and fellow officers the new situations created by People's Power in Matanzas: "The capitalists would like you to believe, quite self-servingly, that the army is apolitical . . .yet they keep it as one more repressive instrument to use against the people. To what class do the members of the capitalist armed forces belong? To the very class they are busy repressing. The overwhelming majority of the soldiers of Chile, Bolivia, and other countries, for example, belong to the class they keep down. They belong to the working class, or they are peasants, but they oppress those of the same class because they have been indoctrinated to believe that the army is above politics and that they have to obey the orders of their superiors."

"The capitalists," Second Lieutenant Miguel Barceló adds, "take advantage of the problem of political indifference. But I can tell you that we don't. We are a part of the people, of the people in uniform, as Commander Camilo put it. We defend our class interests, the interests of the working masses. Look here . . .I am a worker dressed in uniform and got to be an officer in the army, like all these compañeros"—he points at the group—"like those who are also the sons of workers, of peasants. And the youths studying here . . .the 'Camilitos' . . .are studying to join the military academies tomorrow and serve in a crucial task such as the defense of the homeland. They are aware of the role they play, because we Cuban soldiers cannot be ordered to invade another country, to go and fight against another people if we haven't been attacked, to go into the factories to repress the workers. . . .No, we are not going to go because we know our duty and our functions well. . . .We are politically conscious."

Cuba at present has armed forces technically equipped with a generous array of modern weapons, thanks to the assistance of the Soviet Union, and her army boasts men who display a tough discipline. The reason for the FAR's military might can be easily understood. As mentioned earlier, the Revolution was attacked from the very beginning by saboteurs and counterrevolutionary actions, the infiltration of weapons and agents, the development of armed counterrevolutionary bands which would later surface in practically all the provinces, and the training of mercenary troops that eventually launched an invasion through Playa Girón. But the gravest danger lay in the possibility of direct confrontation with the U.S. Armed Forces. Hence we can affirm that the FAR are principally a defensive apparatus.

In his speech of December 30, 1973, marking the completion of the war games on the fifteenth anniversary of the revolutionary triumph, Fidel himself defined the main feature of the Revolutionary Armed

Forces. They are "possessed of a profound political consciousness, possessed of a true revolutionary culture, possessed of a political ideology, the political ideology of exploited and oppressed classes, the political ideology of the proletariat, Marxism-Lenism and Internationalism."

"Our armed forces," he added, "possess specific traits which set them apart. They are first, and above all, a part of the people. Their roots can be found in the humble roots of our people: in their workers, their peasants, their students, their intellectual workers."

The Military and the Party

"I'd like to give you an analogy that, however artificial, reflects what we think of the Party."

The speaker is Second Lieutenant Miguel Barceló. The rest listen attentively.

"The Revolution is like a train. In a train the most important part is the locomotive. Without the locomotive the train goes nowhere, neither backwards nor forward. Our locomotive, though, has no reverse gears, only forward. . . . To us, the Party is the locomotive, the force that pulls the whole Revolution, all its activities . . . to our people in general, since the people and the Revolution are the same thing. Therefore, being a part of the locomotive is supremely important."

The process of building the Party among the military ranks began on December 2, 1963, seven years after the *Granma* landing, on the eve of the fourth anniversary of the revolutionary triumph, within a unit of the Army of the East.

Since then, in addition to the achievements in the area of military and political preparedness, the strengthening of military discipline, the raising of military morale, the institutional development and the fulfillment of all missions assigned to the troops, we find the growing political-ideological work elaborated by the grassroots organizations of the Communist Party of Cuba (PCC), and the Union of Communist Youth (UJC).

Precisely because Cuban soldiers understand that their armed forces are *not* apolitical, they think like a black officer, a member of the political section of the Camilo Cienfuegos Military Academy. He says, "The Party is everything to us. In our lives it is the principal goal—reaching it, joining it, becoming a member of it. As the political organization in a revolutionary process such as ours, it guides all the activities of our society. We are, within the Party organization, the followers of the doctrines and principles propounded by Marx, Engels, and Lenin."

The conversation picks up momentum. The group exudes enthusiasm and interest in the topic at hand. Eyes focus on the lieutenant, the secretary of the UJC at the school, when we raise the following question: "What is the procecdure for joining the Party or the youth within the armed forces?"

"The same as in the civilian sphere. . . . There's only one procedure for both. . . . Here in our unit there are members of the Party and Communist Youth, and we have a high percentage of the latter. You can see that a youth can enroll here when he is still a child . . . at twelve or thirteen years of age. At that time he joins the Red Brigades, where the UJC finds its members within the military schools. At fourteen they are eligible to be elected model youths. After that they follow a procedure to be admitted to the Youth; they are interviewed and an analysis is made. Later they are introduced to the masses as members and given a membership card. And, of course, there are other avenues. For example, in the battalions which already have members, we have a monitoring program according to which a compañero is kept under scrutiny for a few months and entrusted with a variety of tasks, from ideological and political viewpoints. He is also subject to an inquiry. We study his discipline, his attitude toward study, his performance in the fulfillment of duties. But he also goes through a meeting of model youth and is presented to the masses. And it is the Youth Commitee which eventually grants him membership."

"And is it possible for an officer to join the Party without first going through the Youth?"

"It might happen," the Lieutenant replies, "but according to the current Party statutes, in order to be admitted to the Party the candidate must first spend no less than three years as a member of the Youth. Previously, we did have what used to be called the 'Direct Step' . . . which was a direct passage for those compañeros who couldn't participate in the organizational phase of the Party owing to a variety of problems . . . because the organizers didn't do a good job where he worked, because the compañero didn't have a good record at a given job, or because he evidenced errors that barred his admission at that point and that the Party later, in the process of recruitment, enabled the compañero to overcome, while acquiring the virtues he should have as a member. So on that basis he could gain membership status."

He then adds: "Officers and noncoms participate in the grassroots-level command committees, which also admit other personnel who exercise command. Two variants may be found: There may be a committee of officers only, having eight to ten officers, or you can have a committee composed of instructors and officers, if the minimum quorum of officers to form the chapter is lacking. . . .there are many teachers who are not soldiers, but civilian employees of the FAR."*

The first lieutenant speaks up again: "Right here in our school you can see that the officers who have military rank, well, they also serve in a grassroots organization together with civilian comrades, We have cases in which out of ten militants, four are officers and six are civilians."

At present, around 85 percent of the FAR officers belong to the Party or to the Youth, and the percentage in some units is as high as 90 percent.

Military Discipline and Party Disicpline

"Major, to become an officer, it is necessary to be a Party member?"

"Not really, although a high percentage is. In combat units, for example, 90, 99, and even 100 percent are Party members. But being a member is not a prerequisite to reaching the higher military ranks."

"In other words, there are top-ranking officers who are not members?"

"I personally don't know of any. It's possible, though. It may happen. . . .An officer can lose his Party status and continue to serve as an officer. I, myself, a field officer, could lose my Party membership and still keep my rank, even get promoted."

"So what is the relation between military discipline and Party discipline? Don't you get into problems when you bear the military responsibility in addition to that of the Party?"

"Not at all!. . .Look, I'm going to give you an example. I, a major and the director of this academy, am a Party member, but not a Party official, just a plain member . . .but as the director of this school, I can give an order to Lieutenant Mariño"—he is sitting beside him and nods in agreement—"and he has to carry it out. If he doesn't, he gets himself into a real jam . . .because that's the way military discipline is, right? Now, it so happens that Lieutentant Mariño is a Party leader, and I'm not. So if we are in a meeting or at any Party activity, I have to sit there as a simple member and follow what he says."

---

* A worker who discharges his duties within Revolutionary Armed Forces (FAR), either in production or services, with the same rights and duties enjoyed by the rest of the Cuban working class. Essentially, they are connected with the technical complex which guarantees the defense of the country. They are devoted primarily to instruction, health, and construction, but they also participate in combat training and the political preparation of soldiers, and in recreational and sports activities.

In Cuba we encounter the singular situation of finding unions within the Armed Forces, the National Union of FAR Civilian Workers, created in September, 1971, and affiliated with the Confederation of Cuban Workers (CTC).

Emphatically, Lieutenant Mariño declares: "In the Party there's only one discipline: Party discipline. . . .Everyone is a member of the Party, and if someone makes a mistake he gets criticized for it."

The major reiterates:

"Look, as a soldier, Lieutenant Mariño has to obey me if he wants to avoid headaches. . . .He has to salute me in a military manner, request my permision to withdraw, and so on. Now, as he is also a Party leader and I am not, I have to comply with all the Party orders he may give me. . . .I am under an obligation to fulfill them and to heed his authority because he's a Party official."

"What is the difference between the discipline of a bourgeois army and this one?"

"Come now!" Lieutenant Mariño says. "You know that discipline of a bourgeois army is imposed, because the personnel complying with the orders don't know what they are fighting for . . .so orders have to be imposed. For example, the capitalists, to send their troops to Vietnam, had to impose it. . . .'Get on that plane and get over there! If you get killed, tough!' With us, discipline is of another sort. It is *conscious*. Here we know why we have to defend the motherland."

"The compañero gave you an example of ordering people to get on a plane." the director interrupts. "We have a difference in ideology. Using this example our soldiers get on the plane because they are convinced of the legitimacy of the cause they serve. Now, if we say, 'Get on that plane!' they have to get on it, because they can't disobey. But because of our ideology they know *why* they must obey. They know why they go. Look, that combination has to exist, military discipline and moral discipline, in everyone's conscience. That is precisely what the bourgeois armies lack."

The Armed Forces and People's Power

"I was aksed by a citizen what I thought, if I didn't think it was extraordinary that armed forces personnel were also casting ballots. I replied, no, I didn't think it unusual, I thought it was logical and natural, because in the Revolution and under socialism there is a total interpenetration of the armed forces and the people, and we are all armed forces.

"In peacetime, a number of compañeros bear arms, they have to keep watch in defense of the Revolution, but in wartime all the citizens become the armed forces which defend the nation."

Thus Fidel Castro explained to the journalists who were covering the Matanzas elections, on June 30, 1974.

"So the most natural thing is for the soldier to participate, just as he participates in productive activities, in civic activities, because it is inconceivable not to allow the soldier the right to vote. It is absurd. It would be to deprive him of a right enjoyed by all citizens in a workers' society."

The Revolutionary Armed Forces, as an integral part of the nation's life, also share in the process of setting up agencies of People's Power.

One of the chief tenets of socialist democracy is the participation of workers, peasants, students, and other social strata in the affairs of the state. Consequently, the military—workers and peasants, by and large—can also enjoy this privilege in a country such as Cuba.

The Soldiers Cast Their Ballots

"We set up two polling stations, one at the social club and another underneath the theater. We also set up our own ballot boxes. We elected a president for the polling place, and a secretary, who had the list of the compañeros eligible to vote. So we gave them special cards to be presented on election day. The compañeros eligible to vote were those sixteen years old or over, and who had no impediment from a penal standpoint. We opened the polls at eight A.M. We checked the voters off a list and gave them a ballot with the names of the candidates on it. Next they went into the voting booths, which we had set up with sheets . . . very private, very confidential, and registered their preferences. They put a cross besides the one candidate they supported out of a slate of five."

So voted the "Camilitos" and "Camilitas" of Matanzas, according to Lieutenant Mariño, the delegate to the municipal assembly of Matanzas elected by the officers, noncoms, classes, and soldiers of the Camilo Cienfuegos Military Academy.

A clause inserted as Article 9 into the provisional by-laws for elections to agencies of People's Power governed the form of military participation in the management of the state: "In FAR military units and the units of the Youth Labor Army (EJT), composed of members who, totally or partially, reside permanently in said units and in student boarding schools, special voting districts will be created, one for each unit or school."

This measure was necessary in order not to eliminate from participation in People' Power those segments of the people who, owing to circumstances of work or study, follow a regimen of internship that prevents their normal participation in everyday affairs in their neighborhoods.

"Well, it was a new thing for us," Lieutenant Alberto Acevedo explains, "a new thing for us who had never participated in this kind of massive vote . . .and new, too, because for the first time in the history of our country the military have the right to vote. Yet there is a difference with regard to the elections held before the Revolution. In Latin America you see the army, the militia, naked force, controlling the ballot box, and they have the gall to claim they are apolitical. But who watches over the ballot boxes here? You go to a polling station here in the province of Matanzas, or any municipality, and the people watching the polls are the Pioneers; children between nine and ten years old were running the balloting that day."

"Yes," Lieutenant Mariño agrees. "We saw something different here in these elections. It was the Pioneers who handed out the ballots and ushered us around. And in the specific case of our school, it was the "Camilitas," the compañeras of thirteen, fourteen, or fifteen years of age who, because of this, were not qualified to vote."

"We posted the biographies of the five candidates all over the place . . .throughout the school, the battalions, the mess halls, everywhere. So all the personnel had plenty of time to study them and learn about each candidate and later freely cast a vote for the person they thought would best represent them before People's Power. About nine hundred people voted. . . .The truth is I don't recall the exact figure," Lieutenant Miguel Barcelo says.

"And how many votes did you obtain, Lieutenant Mariño?"

"I got 856 of those 900. . . .I think they invalidated fifteen or twenty."

Lieutenant Mariño was elected on June 30, 1974, during the first round of voting. Thus he did not have to undergo a runoff election, scheduled for July 7, set up in case none of the candidates got the majority in the first round.

Why did Lieutenant Mariño obtain so many votes? We put this question to the officers at the academy.

Apparently, it was the outstanding character qualities of Lieutenant Mariño that produced the landslide, the secretary of the school's UJC explains. The lieutenant elaborates: "In the first place, he is a young compañero with an extensive career. Compañero Mariño participated as a strecher bearer at Playa Girón at the age of fourteen, an early involvement in the activities of the Revolution in defense of the homeland. And besides this, he has a fine educational background that allows him to handle this post. The compañero has completed his second year of law, and also has spent two years with our unit. Of the five compañeros in the race he was clearly the one with the most impressive qualifications."

"And you, Lieutenant Acevedo, did you vote for Lieutenant Mariño? . . .We know the vote was secret, but since it's been almost a year. . . ."

Laughter greets Lieutenant Acevedo's mild embarrassment.

"Yes, we voted for him."

"Why?"

"Well, it would be repeating what the compañero has already said. . . . Anyway, what we must always bear in mind is that the compañeros we elect must be capable of collecting the viewpoints, the concerns, the grievances of the people, as we have seen tonight. . . .They should be adept, too, at transmitting problems through the proper channels, and capable of suggesting solutions. We saw in Compañero Mariño a fellow who had the right qualities to fill the office of People's delegate. And that led me to vote for him. I also voted for his experience, of course, for his revolutionary qualities, but . . .in reality, all five candidates were quite good."

The functions of the military delegates are identical to those discharged by their civilian counterparts. Consequently, they act as spokesmen for the problems affecting the population where the district is located, and even the city in general. Accordingly, the units are regarded as the legal domicile of members of the armed forces.

An Officer Reports

"I have attended the municipal assembly meetings of May 7 and June 14; I have, therefore, a one hundred per cent attendance record. I have participated in order to present our problems or to seek explanations. . . .I have set aside two days a week for political consultation, but they haven't been sufficiently utilized.

"With regard to our petition to relocate the bus stop nearer the main gate, it has been turned down because there is already a bus stop in front of our unit, and another facing the grocery store, and ours can't be moved because the spot is dangerous.

"The other proposal we made—but which must be channeled through the proper administrative authorities—is that the women students graduating on July 2 get a chance to obtain some fabric for the graduating ceremony. The reply is still pending."

The immense majority of Lieutenant Mariño's constituents are ado-
lescent students at the academy. The delegate himself, twenty-eight
years old, looks barely older than the students when he finishes reading
his report from the podium to the almost 900 "Camilitos" assembled on
the wide esplanade of the school.

"Any proposal, any suggestion you care to make, you can do it
now. . . ."

In this special district there is a special relation between the delegate
and most of his constituents, because Lieutenant Mariño is not just a
delegate, he is also a superior officer to the "Camilitos," a teacher at the
school, and an adult among youths. This does not deter the students,
however, after some initial hesitation, from offering criticism and suggestions.

The first to approach the microphone is a mulatto youth with a
dignified appearance: "I think the report corresponds to our concerns,
but perhaps because we did not express many, the report had to be brief.
After saying this I want to take this opportunity to mention a particular
concern. On rainy days we have some transportation problems here. On
Routes 4 and 6 they have put new Girón buses, but on our route the old
vehicles have been kept. And when it rains, they can't come out, and we
are left there waiting for the rain to let up. They have no windshield
wipers, and water leaks in through the broken windows. I think in these
cases, when it rains, they should put the new buses on this route."

"I think the compañero's motion is quite valid and will therefore pass
it on in writing to the executive committee. As soon as I receive a reply
I'll advise you of it, Lieutenant Mariño says.

Another compañero, who had been practically shoved by the others to
the fore, takes the floor: "There are technical deficiencies with regard to
the TV sets. In all out units we have TV sets, but on days of recreational
activity they cannot be used because they are broken. What I suggest is
that People's Power bring a technician here to fix them."

Amid a wave of applause Lieutenant Mariño registers the complaint.
He then adds: "We had thought of that. Beginning on Monday I'm going
up to the administration of commercial industries to see whether we can
have a technician assigned to the school, and whether we can get the sets
that can be serviced here repaired on the grounds, and the rest taken away
to the shop. I think your request is very reasonable. Anyone else want to
suggest something? Some compañera student?"

A "Camilita," buoyed by the applause of her compañeras, strides to
the front and declares: "Nearby there's a pizza parlor . . .but, what happens? When the counter is full, we are told to go in the dining area where

there are seats. . . .I did, and it turns out that the pizza costs more in there than at the counter, and I was carrying just the exact amount of money. . . .You can imagine!" Laughter. "It would help if they put up a sign with both prices."

"This problem goes beyond the pizza parlor. That's why the municipal assembly has proposed that consumers be given all the information they need," Lieutenant Mariño points out.

The assembly continues with a series of other speakers, both the "Camilitos" and the "Camilitas," and also teachers at the school.

The enthusiasm with which the soldiers participated at the Camilo Cienfuegos Military Academy in Matanzas can also be observed in all the special districts of the province, which serves as headquarters for the units of the Central Army.

The First Delegate

"The Compañero Sergeant," First Lieutenant Juan Montelongu is saying to a Cuban magazine, "became a historical figure, I'd say, because he was Latin America's first military representative to People's Power. That is because, of all the Latin American countries, Cuba happened to be the first where fighting men came to enjoy this great civic right: to elect and be elected to the agencies of the state. What happened is that we were the first in the province to finish the elections, so Pablo became the first People's delegate to the Cuban Republic."

Sergeant Pablo Pérez Hernández, scarcely twenty-three years of age, a Party member, and head of the maintenance and repair detail of a tank unit attached to the Central Army, was a chauffeur before joining the Revolutionary Armed Forces. He was born in Cienfuegos, a city in the adjacent province of Las Villas. His father, José Pérez, was a sisal worker. Now he is seventy-two and retired.

"He looks upon himself as a old communist, despite the fact he doesn't have a Party card," says Sargeant Pérez Hernández. "Do you know why?" He does some figuring on a piece of paper. "See whether he's right. Just with our family you could found five organizations, both political and social. The old man has eight sons, four daughters, and twenty-three grandchildren. Of this total six are Party members, three are in UJC, thirteen in the Pioneers, and five in the FMC, including Mother. All the adults are *cederistas*, and Father is a CDR coordinator for his zone. We have workers, employees, students, and grade schoolers. Four are in the armed forces. Three fought against the counterrevolutionary bands and took part in the action at Playa Girón. . . ."

The case of Sargeant Pérez Hernández is not unusual.

The members of FAR were eligible for election either in their special districts, if they lived inside military compounds, or in their own neighborhoods, since there they enjoy the privileges all Cubans enjoy: that of worker and resident.

"We would like to insist again, finally, on what you think, officers of the Camilo Cienfuegos Military Academy, with regard to the right of soldiers to vote. . . ."

Lieutenant Miguel Barceló provides the answer: "There is one thing that in my judgment defines the whole thing with respect to the right to vote enjoyed by the armed forces of our country. Camilo declared that the army is the people in uniform. Then, since the army is people in uniform and the people have the right to go to the polling booths, we also go to the polling booths. . . . There's nothing else to explain."

Indeed, there is nothing else to explain.

As Fidel Castro once said: "It is not tanks against the people. . . . it is the people riding the tanks."

14 UNDERDEVELOPMENT: AN IMPEDIMENT?

Fidel Castro referred to the problem in a speech on July 26, 1974: "...
we have a few debts to settle with underdevelopment. And we have a few
unsettled debts with the suffering of the people: when we find a mother
declaring that she has twelve children in a single room, and she is
suffering from asthma, and from this or that; when we see people suffer,
ask for things—would one be a magician to produce them out of a hat,
out of one's pocket! But we have to face reality. And reality is here
determined by the fact that we need one million dwelling units so
families may live decently—one million!

"And we must work hard to have a million dwelling units! Beginning
with sand, cement, stone. . . ."

People's Power Is Not a Magic Wand

Despite the fact that since 1970 the economic development of Cuba
has registered impressive gains, the effects of underdevelopment have yet
to be eliminated.

The Matanzas experience with People's Power consequently starts
with this reality. In his speech to the people of Matanzas on that July 26,
1974, Fidel wanted to make clear that People's Power is not a magic
wand capable of solving every single problem.

"Now you will objectively encounter many dificulties. There are many
needs, of every type: a need for housing, aqueducts, cinemas, grade
school buildings, children's centers, everything. If you take stock, you'll
see the needs are many everywhere. Hence we cannot start out from

utopia, the ideal believing that all of a sudden, just because the institutions of People's Power have been created, these problems are going to be solved overnight. The country's resources are very scarce; building materials in particular, are in short supply.

"We know very well what you would be capable of building, with the community's energy, if only the resources were there."

But Cuba's underdevelopment, won't it be an impassable obstacle for the agencies of People's Power? What can they accomplish if the scarcity of material resources prevents them from counting on the minimum required to confront their tasks? Won't they be discredited before the masses on account of their helplessness in dealing with the many problems raised by the people?

Here are the experiences of two members of the Cardenas executive committee.

The correspondent addresses Laureano: "What are the main difficulties you have faced?"

"Principally I'd say it is the shortage of certain resources, especially those connected with the housing problem."

"And how do you feel about the responsibility you bear when you are well aware that, in view of the present reality, numerous problems presented to you won't have a solution, not for any lack of commitment on your part, but because they stem from underdevelopment?"

"Look, the new delegates elected now, the first thing we told the people, with revolutionary honesty, was that we would not be able to solve many problems. There is moral strength in being forthright, and this helps. When the situation arises, people are more likely to believe you if you tell them that there is no solution to their problem. My personal experience is that the voter largely accepts the problem as defined by the delegate. When they bring up housing problems, for example, and we explain why these questions can't have a ready solution, they react with trust in what the delegate says, so we don't feel under pressure. Moreover, the tact and politeness with which the people present their problems to the delegate, their humility, their lack of arrogance, their respect for all things, makes one feel confident. Actually, we are gratified that the people understand."

The question has put Alexis in a thoughtful mood. He adds: "There's no pressure from the people, but there's another kind of pressure, coming from within, because we feel obligated to the people. It is difficult for us being unable to solve all the problem because we, too, come from the people. So we are pained by all this. For example, these days, it's been raining hard, and we know there's a danger of slides and cave-ins, and we're thinking that any moment we may be advised that someone's house has been swept away, caved in, whatever, and we lack the necessary materials to meet this situation. However, a peculiar thing happens: very few people come here to request housing, to ask for construction materials. Some do come, though. And you say to them: 'Look, I'm not going to give you a solution, but I'm going to give you an explanation. This is this way or that way, so your case has no solution. I'm not going to ask you to come next week, saying I'm going to see what happens in the future. Because what I have to say to you is that what you are asking is reasonable, but for the time being it simply cannot be done.' Then the person says: 'The truth is, they haven't solved my problem, but it is no less true that no one ever spoke to me this way before. So I have to wait." We suffer because of this, but, really, we can't say anything else.

"In connection with this very question, here at the regional bureau there's an economic commission consisting of forty persons that couldn't be comfortably accommodated in this place. So we looked around and found a house in the back, and we were going to assign it to them for their office. But in these rainy days the housing problems become more serious, so the executive committee decided that the economics compañeros had to fit into smaller quarters. The committee turned the dwelling over to the municipality so it could assign it to the neediest family. We can't lick all problems, but by acting in this manner we are at least satisfied that if we demand an effort from others we have shown the way by our own example. Of course, it is obvious we can't give this building away, since it is our headquarters, but other things can be managed. . . . The housing problem is the toughest, but we have explained to the people here that this is a national problem and that we are not going to make ourselves look good by blaming the higher-ups. That would be real easy, but not too revolutionary.

"The people know we get everything the country can afford, and that whatever is available is distributed according to the people's most pressing needs. We cannot ask for what doesn't exist. We have to talk straight, and when they claim a functionary has deceived them, we ask them to file a complaint against him. We are not here to excuse the faults of any bureaucrat. A lot of years are going to pass, and many problems will evade solution, but the people have confidence because the compañeros who are in power today are all the more or less like Laureano. The people have seen their work over the years, tested their integrity. People say, 'So and so I elected him. He can't fool me.' "

Alexis continues: "Many times the delegate must explain to the people why a particular problem can't be solved.

"For example, the problem of running water in Cardenas is such a situation. A delegate incapable of giving the public a good explanation of such an important problem influences the way the populace perceives People's Power. It may happen that this individual, because of his inability to understand the problem of government, may fail to guide the people properly. That wouldn't be the fault of People's Power, or of the municipality. Fidel said that there wouldn't be any magic wand to lick all problems. And that's when a delegate proves his worth. For it's not only a question of resolving problems but, often, of correctly interpreting them for the people.

"That's why I say that a good delegate is the kind of person who can interpret the central directives to the people, explain them well, so that the people can realize the possibilities of People's Power."

The Just Distribution of Scarce Resources

Alexis adds: "When construction materials arrive, the municipal assembly immediately reports the number of sacks delivered and decides in a democractic fashion how they are to be allocated to each district."

This reply reminds us of something Fidel said in his speech to assembled cadre, on July 26, 1970: "Let me warn you about something: When some repair work is in order, don't you decide what must be done. Let the residents speak up. Let them, with their sense of justice and fairness, have the say as to who is in direst need. Because as long as the decision is administrative, it will always be subject to a lot of contradictions and opinions, and may even run the risk of favoritism.

"Let us protect the cadre from this peril. Let us establish that it is they [the people] who must decide. And if the residents make a mistake, let them make a mistake. It's their privilege. . . ."

Fidel's words have come to life in the Construction Materials Distribution Commissions organized by People's Power at the block, district, and municipal levels throughout most of Cuba's provinces.

How do these commissions work? How do they determine who is most in need? How is favoritism avoided? How do delegates look upon them? All these questions were answered in a conversation we had with some of the members of a commission attached to District 12 of Santi Spíritus, whose delegate is Compañero Héctor Pentón.

The group included Francisco Espinoza, manager of the municipality's funeral home; Pedro Rodríguez, a dairy worker; Gilberto Fernández, a microbrigade leader with the food division, and the delegate himself.

For balance, we also tried to discover the people's true opinion of the matter, talking with both satisfied and dissatisfied citizens about housing.

"The block trusts us. The people elected us because we are responsible comrades, revolutionaries dedicated to conscientious work, people determined to avoid cronyism," Francisco Espinoza affirms. "The needy comrades on the block fill out an application for materials; then the commission visits the houses to check the claims and picks the neediest cases."

"What do you do with these most urgent cases?"

"They are put on a priority list, a sort of ranking according to need," Pedro Rodríguez says. "The district commission also checks the cases and determines which is most pressing. In this district we have fourteen CDRs, and in each one there'e a commission, in addition, of course, to the district commission I've already mentioned. In my CDR, for example, we have ten residents in need; of these three are really urgent; that is, they require a budget on the order of 500 pesos; others need only about 50 pesos. So the municipality gives us guidelines: we can indertake X number of repairs costing 500 pesos; X number costing 350 pesos; and X number at 50 pesos. In that way the most urgent cases are gradually cleaned up. For its part, the CDR commission assigns priorities to a number of households, say five. Then we go CDR by CDR, house by house, to verify where the most pressing needs are."

"When the block commissions are formed, three comrades are chosen, with one being chairman. They determine the most serious needs according to a descending scale, from 1 to 12," Gilberto explains. "After the cases are picked, the municipality analyzes the quantity of construction materials it has on hand and says: we can allocate to each district five repairs at 500 pesos; eight at 350 pesos; and ten at 50 pesos. Then each CDR determines the top candidates for each budgetary level and passes this information on to the district commission. So if we have five at 500 pesos for the entire district and there are fourteen CDRs, we have fourteen instances with the highest priority, and we are obliged to pick the neediest five among these fourteen. During our inspection tour we check the state of the dwelling, whether it's falling apart, how many people use it, whether any sick people live there, and so on. It is by using such criteria that we select the most urgent cases."

Gilberto continues: "Once the job is done, the commission chairman visits the house and checks on the the use of the materials. After the ranking is worked out, there's a district meeting to tell the people of the selection. The people are invited to cross-examine the choices, to satisfy themselves about the rankings, to see whether their case or someone else's is more urgent.

"Is the entire district welcome or only those affected?"

"Everyone, but, in general, only those affected and a few others show up. I think that's the most reasonable and useful way to distribute the materials, and up to this point we haven't had any problems. We have licked quite a few cases. Cronyism has no place here. It's a block commission elected by the residents themselves, and if that commission should make the mistake of giving materials to a comrade out of favoritism, someone may get up during assembly and say: 'I'm not in agreement with such and such distribution, for I live on the same block and am twenty times worse off than he is. Besides, there are plenty of checks, and an inquiry can revoke any arrangement and reshuffle the whole thing."

"As members of the commissions, you must be subject to a great deal of pressure from your peers. . . .Some people try to persuade you that their cases are more urgent. How do you handle this?"

"When we run into one of these cases we tell the compañero: If you want to see for yourself, come and accompany the commission on its rounds," Francisco replies. "We ask the person to go visit some cases. That way he can see why his is less serious than others. This instance concerns a family with five kids, this one a couple having only one; this house is larger, that one smaller; this one has sanitary facilities, the other has none. So we show the complainant the conditions of those on the list and on his own, because we have evaluated both. That way he can see for himself that his case, bad as it may be, is not the worst. The person then is satisfied that a more critical problem has been solved. We really haven't had any problems with the system in this district."

"And you, Comrade Delegate, what do you think of the commission?"

"For us the commissions are a great help. If it weren't for them, we'd be overwhelmed by the pressures for construction materials. Formerly, the distribution was done in a more bureaucratic way; afterwards, an office for distribution of materials was set up. But this way was no good. We always had problems, and the distribution wasn't always fair. In my view, this system is well suited to present conditions. This is a very old city, and we have great needs, There's a lot of rundown housing because of the years . . . ."

This reminds us of what Ramón Piloto, delegate and president of the executive committee of the Tahuasco municipal assembly, said to us: "These commissions have solved a tremendous problem for us; they have relieved us of a tremendous work pressure, because the most common problem in every district is the one connected with housing. The residents know already that the delegate is not supposed to tackle these problems, as there's a special commission for this purpose." "Have you had any problems with stubborn cases?"

"No," Gilberto replies. "I'm an old hand in matters of construction. I have thirty-odd years of experience in construction, and ever since the distribution of materials began, I've been involved with it. When you are appointed to one of these commissions, you accept the job as a revolutionary and try to do it as well as possible. We haven't had any problems because the process has been fair.

"The cases have been taken to the assembly and they have been approved. There has been a consensus. When a comrade takes the floor and says, as we mentioned earlier, 'Look, I'm worse off than this other fellow,' he's invited to check the circumstances for himself, to go ahead, to satisfy himself. Let him judge for himself. He's urged to do just that. I think this is one of the fairest ways to distribute materials."

We wanted to verify the commissioners' assertions in the field. So, we interviewed two comrades in the municipality of Sancti Spíritu. One of them, Lila Rodríguez, was not chosen by the district commission; the other, Manuela Fernández, was. Here is their testimony:

"Compañera Lila, why did you apply to your block's construction materials distribution commission?"

"Well, we requested materials to build what we call a suspended bedroom alcove. Below, we'd have the living room, eat-in kitchen, and hall, and above, the bedrooms. Right now, we're living very tight; there are four of us: myself, my husband, and two children. But although the commission agreed with my request and approved my application, they also approved Manuela's, who's in even worse shape than I am. She didn't even have a bathroom."

"And when you learned that Manuela had gotten the allocation, what did you think?"

"We thought it was okay because we knew the situation. She used to live with her sick husband—he's dead now—and she didn't even have a toilet. She was just living in worse conditions than us."

"What do you think of these commissions?"

"They're wonderful."

"Wonderful?"

"Yes, because those most in need get the materials. It's the best way. That way you avoid privileges, giving materials to others on account of favoritism, do you understand? This way I know my turn will come."

We visited next Manuela Fernández, a winner in the allocation of materials, to hear her views.

"Well, I had filed for materials with Local Power a long time ago and never got them. Now, with People's Power, when I least expected them, the CDR informed me that I could go and buy the materials, that my case had been selected first. I was really in need. My house was literally falling apart. . . ."

Objective and Subjective Problems

To sum up, we can say that People's Power is able to confront the problems of underdevelopment principally through a system of better priorities and allocations of scarce resources. They can determine clearly, for example, which buildings are to receive the cement and other materials delivered to the municipalities.

Second, People's Power is committed to giving a convincing explanation to the population when needs cannot be met at once. When the people are told honestly about the shortfalls affecting certain consumer items or materials, they accept it. Of course, People's Power must not only explain the reasons why some needs must be deferred; it must also set up a plan for the distribution of resources so that the people can be given, whenever possible, a concrete target date for the solution of their problems.

Last, People's Power can solve a great many problems unconnected with the availability of material resources which affect the daily life of the population: it can improve the operation of services in units such as grocery stores, supermarkets, restaurants, cafeterias, barbershops, dry-cleaning establishments, and so on.

Speaking to the National Assembly in June, 1978, during its first session, Fidel Castro remarked: "Everyone must be able to distinguish between problems rooted in objective conditions and those issuing from subjective conditions. Only in this way will each delegate and voter be able to tackle in earnest the problems caused by subjective conditions, problems like hygiene in a restaurant, poor service to the public in a store, or unmotivated committees, assemblies, delegates, or bureaucrats. For all these problems can be overcome by improved attitudes and a commitment to serious effort, and they should never be confused with objective problems that can only be solved by the process of development.

"The whole series of calamities: we don't have this, we lack that; we are short of steel and things with which to fix our houses, tubing, lead, and plumbers—all these things," he continued, "have an economic origin, and that origin is underdevelopment. And if there's something the Revolution cannot be accused of, it is its genuine desire to solve these problems, because, in a way, one of the 'flaws' of our Revolution has been, all along, that we have tried to bite off more than we could chew . . . .

"The fundamental problem facing the country today is that of under-development, the accumulation of the necessary investments for growth, because without true development the string of calamities we call poverty, far from going away, will only multiply, and it would be utopian, truly utopian, to imagine that our essential, objective problems can be resolved without development."

Further on, he added: "I believe we need to make a serious effort to educate the electorate, but, to do this, we must first strive to educate the people's representatives, because if they don't have the facts, the information, the expertise, it will be impossible to educate the voters.

"If the delegates don't have a clear picture of the situation based on solid information, if the constituents don't have it, then everything degenerates into chaos . . .because any constituent can come up with impossible requests . . .

"We are facing human beings with a lot of expectations and needs, and we are limited by reality. Now, it must be said that the capacity of our people for understanding is enormous—they have demonstrated this during these years of Revolution—but, essentially, problems must be explained properly, taking good care to avoid confusing the set of objective factors with that other set issuing from subjective circumstances."

15 TOP STATE ORGANS

Institutionalizing the National Assembly

On December 2, 1976, in his inaugural address to the National Assembly, Fidel Castro welcomed this new stage in the revolutionary process with these words: "With the historic act we are witnessing today the provisional character of the revolutionary government comes formally to an end, thereby opening the way for the adoption, by our socialist government, of permanent institutional forms. From now on, the National Assembly is to be recognized as the supreme organ of the state, assuming all the functions assigned to it by the Constitution. It has been both a duty and a great triumph for our generation to have reached this goal."

Next, addressing the 479 representatives in the audience, Fidel said: "Unlike the bourgeois world, we find here no differences between military and civilians, whites and blacks, young and old, men and women, because we all enjoy equal duties and rights. Luckily, there are no differences between rich and poor, exploiters and exploited, the powerful and the powerless, because the Revolution has stamped out the political power of the bourgeoisie and land-owning classes to build a workers' state. And this means all our workers: manual and intellectual, men and women, young and old, soldiers and civilians, all those who devote their lives to the service of the country and the Revolution, or study to inherit our ideas, our efforts, and our struggles.

"In our Revolution the professional politician has been eliminated, because now we are all politicians, from the grammar school to the retired elder. Thus the Party and the state are served, not by those who would make a career out of this type of service, but by those the Party and the people have chosen for specific tasks. Under socialism, office is not sought, and candidates do not blow their own trumpets.

"Here neither wealth, nor social connections, nor the family, nor publicity or propaganda, as happens in bourgeois society, can have any power to determine the role a person is to play in social affairs. It is only merit, personal merit, ability and modesty, total devotion to duty, to the Revolution, and to the cause of the people that determines the trust society bestows upon any of its children. . . .

"These representatives of the people receive no monetary compensation for their efforts. And they do not discharge their office beyond their fellow citizens' purview. Their mandate is subject to termination at any time by the will of the same people who elected them. No one can be above the law, or the rest of his fellow countrymen. Their office does not entail privileges and perquisites, but duties and responsibilities. And under our system the government and the administration of justice are directly controlled by the National Assembly. There's a division of functions, but not a separation of powers. The power is one, indivisible, and of the working people, who exercise it through the National Assembly and the government agencies subordinated to it. Our kind of state takes into account both the experience accumulated by other peoples who have traveled down the road of socialism and our own practice. And as befits a genuine revolutionary concept, we apply to our concrete conditions the basic tenets of Marxism-Leninism."

Later on, he pointed out the profound institutional transformations the country had gone through before the process could culminate in the National Assembly.

"A year ago the first Party Congress convened. And, since then, in the fulfillment of its resolutions, a significant amount of party and state activity has taken place. The socialist Constitution was approved in a model referendum. All the measures required for the success of the new political-administrative arrangement have been adopted. We have completed, in excellent and enthusiastic manner, the nomination of candidates and the election of delegates to the municipal assemblies, and that formed the basis for the ensuing steps: the election of provincial delegates and of deputies to the National Assembly, and the formation of People's Power at the municipal and provincial levels. Also, the new provinces were established last November 7. At the same time, after months of intense work, the blueprint for a new central state was hammered out, in accordance with the principles of the Constitution, the new political-administrative structure, the introduction of People's Powers, the economic plan in operation, and the necessary search for a maximum of efficiency and uniformity at a minimum cost in the central administration. Even though it is a field where one can and must continue to advance in the coming years, it was possible to define with satisfactory precision the function, structures, and organizational blueprints of all the central government agencies, an accomplishment embodied in an important piece of legislation called the Act for the Organization of the Central Administration of the State, approved by the Council of Ministers in one of its last acts as a legislative body. Through this law a total of forty-three central agencies were established (with thirty-four at the level of national committees, or ministries). The heads of these ministries, enjoying the rank of ministers, are to constitute the Council of Ministers, a body which also includes the President of the Republic, the appointed vice-presidents, and the Council's Secretary. Through this blueprint, and the elimination of regional divisions, the number of central bureaucrats will be reduced sharply, with redundant employees to be reassigned to other services or to productive activities. Obviously, they will not be abandoned to their fate, or simply "laid off," for the government will adopt, as it has always done, appropriate measures to find them new employment.

"A great administrative decentralization is now also overtaking all government functions. From now on municipalities and provinces will be entrusted with important duties. The closest coordination among all the country's communities, and between these and the central government, is more necessary than ever. Any manifestation of local or regional egoism must be combatted resolutely, while it is also incumbent upon each and every province to strive in an appropriate manner, both fair and rational, for its own development, provided the interests of the whole nation are never lost sight of.

"It's easy to appreciate that profound institutional transformations have taken place in a short period of time. With establishment of this National Assembly, the election of the State Council, its President, Vice-President, and the appointment of a Council of Ministers, the fundamental part of this historic process of revolutionary institutionalization has been completed. . . .

"No one can deny that the process which culminates today represents an advance we can all be proud of, a settling of accounts with history and our revolutionary consciences, the happy fulfillment of a sacred duty that issued from the Moncada itself, and which is incontrovertible proof of our loyalty to our Revolution and its principles. Now it is up to us to adapt our minds to the changes we have made, work with enthusiasm and confidence in the new conditions, observe the norms in a disciplined fashion, and struggle relentlessly so the new institutions may function in an optimal manner."

"Now we have only one step left before us," concluded the Cuban leader, "to announce that at this precise moment, the revolutionary government transfers to the National Assembly the power it has discharged up to this day. In this manner the Council of Ministers puts into the hands of this assembly the legislative and executive function it exercised for almost eighteen years, the period of the most radical and profound political and social transformation in the life of our nation. Let history judge this period impartially!

"For my part, I am, dear comrades, a tireless critic of our own creations. Everything could have been done better from the Moncada till this day. The light indicating the best option is experience, but that, unfortunately, is not usually possessed by youths undertaking the hard and difficult road of Revolution. Let that remind us, however, that we are not know-it-alls, and that before each decision, one may perhaps find yet another that is better.

"You, with great generosity, attribute great merits to your leaders. I know that no man has extraordinary merits, and that every day we may receive great lessons from the humblest comrades.

"If I had the privilege of living my life all over again, I would do many things differently, but I can assure you that I would fight with the same passion for the same objectives I have fought for till this day."

The Deputies

To begin with, it should be pointed out that 55.5 percent of the deputies in the National Assmebly are also delegates chosen directly by the people in the 169 People's Power municipal assemblies scattered throughout the country.

Of the 481 elected deputies, 107 are women, that is, 22.2 percent. Some 29.9 percent are workers directly tied to production, services, or teaching; 1.5 percent are peasants; 7.9 percent are technicians in the agricultural, industrial, and service areas.

Further, a total of 12.3 percent work at the national level in the social, political, and economic activities; deputies also entrusted with local leadership duties constitute a full 29 percent, and deputies in uniform are 7.3 percent.

When these figures are considered in isolation, without taking into account other factors such as social origin, type of work done before discharging the present leadership positions, and so on, they furnish a distorted vision of the assembly's class composition.

A very sizable portion of the deputies come from very humble social backgrounds. Many have been ordinary workers who, because of their talents or commitment, in addition to their spirit of self-improvement, very quickly attained positions of leadership in both the government and Party systems. Thus only 28.5 percent of deputies can boast a higher education; 59.7 percent have only a secondary education, while 11.8 percent exhibits only an elementary education.

In addition, 441 deputies are Party members or candidates for Party membership, while 24 are with the UJC (Union of Communist Youth), that is, 91.7 percent and 5 percent, respectively.

More than half of the deputies are under forty, and only 15.8 percent are over fifty. The average age of deputies is forty-one.

As Fidel affirmed in his speech, deputies in the Cuban socialist state enjoy no personal or economic privileges, as was the custom during the capitalist era. On the contrary, save for rare exceptions, they continue to carry out their usual job routines. State duties take only a fraction of their free time. This, together with the fact that more than half of the delegates are delegates elected directly by the people, ensures that the representatives of the masses will keep in touch with the people and their problems.

When the duties of a delegate so require it, for example, when a work commission to which he may be attached is conducting a rapid and intense inquiry, he may request a leave of absence without pay. In such a case he receives a stipend equivalent to his normal salary, plus expenses.

The deputies are expected to maintain constant and close relations with their constituents, to listen to their complaints, suggestions, and criticisms, and to process them appropriately. They must also be ready to explain government policies on various matters and, just like the delegates, submit a performance report to their constituents, that is, to the municipal assembly that elected them, the body which reserves the right to recall them at any time if a majority finds they have fallen short in their assigned duties. The deputy, however, cannot be recalled by the municipal assembly without its first requesting an opinion from the National Assembly or the Council of State, depending on which is operating at the time. Only after the report is received from one of these bodies can the recall process start.

The National Assembly

The People's Power National Assembly is the supreme political body of the Cuban state, and the only one with legislative and constitutional powers. Only the National Assembly is empowered to amend the Constitution, to approve, modify, or repeal laws or to submit them to a public referendum when appropriate. It is also the sole institution empowered to revoke executive orders of the State Council, or orders and directives issued by the Council of Ministers, if these fail to conform to the Constitution or to existing law.

Among other things, the National Assembly is also empowered to elect the presidents of the Assembly and the State Council; to appoint the top central executive body, or Council of Ministers, and to select the members who serve in the top judicial institutions at the national level: the attorney general and the justices of the Supreme Court.

The National Assembly discusses and approves the national plans for economic and social development; the state budget; the principles that are to guide the planning and management of the economy, and questions of credit and monetary policy. The assembly also approves the general guidelines that will govern both foreign and domestic policies, reserving to itself the right to declare war in cases of military aggression and to conclude peace treaties.

On the other hand, the National Assembly is the institution charged with appointing permanent and temporary work commissions to aid in its supervisory and support tasks. These are made up exclusively of deputies, in contrast to work commissions at the municipal and provincial level, which, while presided over by a delegate, can always have members who are not themselves delegates.

Lastly, the National Assembly is expected to learn, evaluate, and adopt whatever necessary action is advisable as a result of performance reports filed by the agencies elected or appointed by it, including those of the provincial assemblies.

The National Assembly is elected every five years in contrast to local assemblies, which must be replaced every two and a half years.

The Assembly is in ordinary session twice a year, and may hold extraordinary sessions when at least one third of its members request it, or when it is convened by the State Council.

The Presidency of the National Assembly and the State Council

The presidency of the National Assembly is composed of a president, a vice-president, and a secretary selected by the Assembly itself. Their principal duties involve the convening and conducting of assembly sessions, the supervising of such activities as the workings of the special work review boards, and the relations between the Assembly and its counterparts abroad.

The State Council represents the National Assembly when the latter is in recess, carrying out its resolutions and wielding supreme power within the Cuban state for all national and international purposes. It is composed of a president, or head of state, a first vice-president, five vice-presidents, a secretary and twenty-three other members. In all, the Council has thirty one members picked by the National Assembly from among its own ranks.

Among the prerogatives of the State Council is the power to summon the National Assembly into special session, and to set a date for the periodic elections of the same body. As an executive organ of the Assembly it can, during a recess of the Assembly, promulgate laws and decrees; issue a general order of mobilization if the defense of the country requires it; and remove, upon the recommendation of the president, members of the Council of Ministers.

The head of the State Council is the chief of state, head of the Council of Ministers, head of the government, and supreme commander of the armed forces. In this manner the Cuban Constitution combines in one person the leadership of the state, the government, and the Revolutionary Armed Forces.

The Administrative Apparatus at the National Level

Three types of organizations can be distinguished in the central administrative apparatus: the state committees, the ministries, and the institutes.

At the national level the state committees fill the role played by the administrative departments attached to People's Power at the local level. They deal with questions that affect all the activities and all the organizations and institutions of the state and have, therefore, a decisive leadership role in all those areas. There are eleven organizations with these characteristics, although not all of them are called committees. They are: the Central Planning Board; the state committees for the Procurement of

Technical Materials, Science & Technology, Economic Collaboration, Construction, Statistics, Finance, Norms and Standards, and Labor & Social Security; and the National Bank of Cuba.

Under the new approach to the mangement of the economy, the role of these committees has become significant. They provide the central economic guidelines to the various ministries and institutes and, in general, to all agencies and institutions of the state.

The ministries are the equivalent, at the national level, of the various administrative departments subordinated to local agencies of People's Power. They are entrusted with the administration of one or several branches and subdivisions of the economy, culture, education, security, defense, and so on. There are twenty-three ministries: Agriculture; Foreign Trade; Domestic Trade; Communications; Construction; Culture; Education; Higher Education; Revolutionary Armed Forces; Food Industry; Sugar Industry; Electrical Industry; Light Industry; Building Materials Industry; Fishing Industry; Chemical Industry; Steel Industry; Interior; Justice; Mining and Geology; Foreign Relations; Public Health; and Transportation.

The institutes are charged with divisional tasks, but of lesser importance. There are nine organizations of this type: the Cuban Academy of Sciences; the Cuban Institute for Domestic Market Research; the Cuban Institute of Hydrography; the Cuban Institute of Radio & Television; Institute for the Care of Infants; National Institute of Sports, Physical Education and Recreation; National Institute for the Development of Forest Resources; National Institute of Cybernetic Systems & Computer Techniques; and the National Institute of Tourism.

As mentioned earlier in this book, owing to the decentralization brought about by People's Power throughout the country, the functions of most of these organizations in the central administrative apparatus have ceased to be primarily executive, tending today toward a guidance role, laying down directives, standards, and methodological guidelines for the use of local People's Power administrators and the service and production units subordinated to them.

Other tasks left to the central organs involve the functions of technical assistance, the formation of specialized manpower, and the location of scarce technical personnel, plus problems of investment and research in various areas connected with their main field of interest.

The Council of Ministers, the nation's top executive and administrative body, is picked by the National Assembly upon the recommendation of the head of state, who presides over it. It also includes a first vice-president, several other vice-presidents, a secretary, the heads of state committees, and the ministers.

The president, first vice-president, and vice-presidents of the Council constitute its executive committee.

The Supreme Court and the Attorney General's Office

The Supreme Court exercises the highest judicial authority in the nation, and its decisions are not subject to appeal. Through its governing council, it exercises legislative initiative and rule-making powers; it adopts decisions and establishes norms to be observed by all people's tribunals, and on the basis of that experience, it issues compulsory instructions guaranteeing uniform judicial practice in the interpretation and application of the law.

The Supreme Court includes a president, a vice-president, the heads of various courts, and the judges, both professional and lay.

The structure of the Supreme Court is as follows: plenary council, government council, penal court, civil and administrative court, labor court, national security crimes court, and military court.

To hear a case, the courts attached to the People's Supreme Court require the presence of their presidents or legal acting presidents, two professional judges, and two lay judges.

The Supreme Court is chosen by the National Assembly and must report to that body, which reserves the right to recall its appointees if it deems this to be necessary.

The courts represent a system of state organs structured as autonomous units independent of one another and only hierarchically subordinated to the National Assembly and the State Council.

The judges, in their role as administrators of justice, are independent and owe obedience only to the law.

The nation's attorney general's office has, as its primary objective, ensuring the application of socialist legality by the state agencies, the social and economic entities, and the citizenry. The attorney general's office is structured as follows:

- Attorney general's office
- Provincial offices
- Municipal offices
- Military office

The offices of the public attorney are organized vertically throughout the nation, and remain subordinated solely to the national attorney general's office, and are thereby independent of any local agency.

The central attorney general's office is composed of an attorney general assisted by two deputies and two public prosecutors, who serve at the pleasure of the attorney general.

Assessing the Performance of Local Agencies

As explained by Deputy Faustino Pérez, head of the Office of People's Power Evaluation, in his report to the first 1978 session of the National Assembly: "The tasks of the delegates and the people were clearly outlined by Raúl Castro at the conclusion of the Matanzas seminar when he declared—'the responsiblity of the delegates is not solely to act as conveyers of the complaints of the masses, but, more important, to study their solution, attempt to resolve them or suggeest possible courses of action. This is precisely one of the ways in which the people and their delegates can manifest their participation in the solution and disposition of public affairs. . . .' "

And he added: "The delegates and organizations of People's Power exist fundamentally not to explain problems to the people, but to resolve them. Indeed, the delegates are to strive, in the first place, not for explanations but for solutions, steering these solutions through the appropriate departments, authorities, or administrative units, the executive committee, the floor of the assembly or whatever, making suggestions, or promoting, whenever advisable, the mobilization of the electorate, the support of the CDRs and the rest of the political and mass organizations existing within the confines of the municipality. The delegate must have a combative and energetic attitude in the face of problems and difficulties which his constituents have raised or which he, on his own, has observed or detected.

"We know, of course, that some problems can't be resolved at once, and that the solution of some may even take a long time. Confronted with such problems, and only after exhausting all possible remedial channels, may the delegate explain to the people why these problems cannot be resolved at the present time, giving the public all the pertinent reasons and not mere replies to get himself off the hook. We must bear in mind Comrade Fidel's words. On July 26, 1974, he said 'What cannot be omitted is to offer an explanation to each citizen who may come to request something, explain with honesty, with sincerity, whether a solution is feasible. No one must ever be deceived.' "

Further on, Pérez touches upon the question of executive committees and assemblies: "The municipal executive committee must look upon each district problem as its own, must react with the vitality and sensitivity that each case requires, and must provide the delegate with the closest and most direct source of assistance for the success of his office. In the municipal assemblies the most important problems affecting the grassroots must be discussed, the problems which are hitting the population hardest. They must discuss the concrete problems most frequently brought up in the districts so the voters may see, so the people may feel, that the problems they raise are the object of attention, concern, and analysis in the very heart of the assembly they elected. In other words, we must try to select the most pressing problems detected in contacts with the people, those defying solution even by the executive committee, and turn them over for debate by the entire municipal assembly. That way the people's interest in the assembly is bound to grow.

"So that must be the idea which should prevail in the provincial assemblies, to make sure that formal aspects or statistical reports do not drown out the possibility of open and direct debate in the profound treatment of the most urgent problems affecting a given territory. Sometimes we have seen a contrast between the operation of some provincial assemblies and our National Assembly, wherein its chief tasks, namely, the debate and passing of laws and national plans, have not become a hurdle to in-depth discussions of concrete problems affecting the population or even an entire community. We think that the development and operation of the National Assembly constitutes with the pertinent qualifications, a good model and a fine example for the other levels of People's Power."

In his closing remarks Pérez returns to the role of the delegates: "The agencies of People's Power came into being to represent the people in the affairs of the state, the delegates acting as their 'advocates,' as Fidel pointed out, so we must avoid reducing our role to that of mere 'messengers' for the explanations of the bureaucracy which, being often inadequate, would change our role to that of 'advocates' for the inefficiency of the administrative machine in the face of just demands by the people. The agencies of People's Power must be preserved as the basic organs of our socialist democracy."

Faustino Pérez's comments, widely acclaimed by the deputies, as well as the report filed by Deputy Luis Rodríguez on the "Net Results of Accountability Sessions by the Provincial Assemblies," which was eagerly debated, constitute proof of the manner in which the National Assembly meets one of the duties assigned to it by the Constitution; that is, to "learn, evaluate, and adopt all necessary decisions issuing from the performance reports filed by the . . . provincial assemblies which, in turn, cover the performance of municipal assemblies and delegates."

The phrase "the lackadaisical performance of the delegates" included in the document filed by Deputy Rodríguez, a clear insinuation that delegates had been less than energetic in the fulfillment of their duties, was rejected by the majority of the deputies, numbering forty, who participated in the discussion of these reports.

In defending their record the representatives who did speak, all delegates elected by the people, raised very serious complaints against administrative leaders who had failed to respond adequately or had given bureaucratic answers.

In this context, Deputy Sonia Rodríguez, in a much-applauded speech to the National Assembly, explained how her municipality handled the problems: "In our municipality, once the accountability session is over, the executive committee sums up all the problems connected with the various bureaucracies and proceeds to advise those districts which have filed specific complaints. This notification is accompanied by a deadline for the reply in question to the executive committee itself. In addition to this the delegates also know that they must press the case separately through the usual channels.

"In order to make this idea a reality, it was agreed during the assembly that the heads of enterprises and economic units would stay at their desks throughout the day on Fridays, as late as eleven P.M., so that they might accommodate visits by people who could not, on account of work, see them during the day.

"All the replies are analyzed by the executive committee before being communicated to the delegates, independently of the latter's efforts. If the executive committee agrees with the reply, it sends it down to the delegate; if not, it returns it to the agency, pointing out that it is a bureaucratic reply that cannot be sent to a delegate as it shows a lack of respect for him and the electorate. That's the way we do it, and we have returned quite a few replies.

"But, on the other hand, we also have meetings with all the heads of economic units and enterprises; we attend them as delegates together with the executive committee. And enterprise after enterprise, with the companeros from the various departments also present, we have conducted formal meetings wherein each director takes the floor to answer complaints raised by the people.

"The mechanics of the procedure is simple. For example, when the turn of the companero from the electric utility comes around, we ask the delegates if they want to raise any questions they may have on that subject. The companero is then expected to answer in full, and by area, if necessary, as the executive committee watches the proceedings.

"After that, it's difficult to go away with a bureaucratic answer, or to convey a bureaucratic rationalization to an accountability session.

"Besides, these explanations are checked between the sessions. We keep an eye out for the way problems are being handled.

"Now, however, one of our chief concerns was the course to follow with comrades who gave the public inaccurate answers. But, after all, it's the assembly that elects the director of an enterprise so, if he doesn't measure up to the job, let him be replaced. We have done this with a number of comrades. For example, the electric utility was not responding properly to the complaints brought by the public. This situation was then taken up in the assembly, which took the matter to the provincial executive, and he forced the compañero to resign. Another fellow in similar circumstances was also asked to resign.

"And if we have to throw them all out, we will throw them all out, but bureaucrats must be made responsive to the people's needs."

Work Review Boards and Inspectors of People's Power

A report recommending the creation of a corps of inspectors, introduced by the People's Power commission of Local Agencies, gave rise to an interesting debate. During this exchange, Deputy Humberto Pérez's views gained much attention and respect because of their depth and seriousness. (Pérez, who heads the Central Planning Board, was a prominent participant in the Matanzas experiment.)

Because of the significance of this analysis, in which the tasks of the work commission are carefully spelled out as fundamental instruments of People's Power—"the true district attorneys of the people"—we have decided to present most of the original text here.

"First we wish to declare that we agree with the concept of a corps of inspectors and, therefore, with the two opening paragraphs of the report, where it is stipulated that systematic control exercised by competent agencies is an indispensable activity to guarantee the socialist order and legality and ensure the observance of established norms. In other words, the first principle contained in the first paragraph demands a system of public inspection.

"The second paragraph reads similarly: popular control is implicit in the process of creation and perfecting of our socialist democracy, presupposing the active participation of the masses in the affairs of the state, and thereby rendering a system of popular or social control inevitable. . . .

"We are totally in agreement with the necessity of a dual system of inspection and, in addition, we recognize that this system has already been tested in other socialist nations. But we are also quite aware that the institutions of People's Power already possess built-in instruments of inspection, and that on this account the creation of a group of People's inspectors might strike some as a duplication of the work already envisioned for the work review boards. . . .

"We would like to stress here how, when People's Power came to Matanzas, and then to the entire nation, we always took pains to incorporate the experience of other socialist nations (especially the Soviet Union, where you find a vertical system of popular inspectors with a national authority in charge of over-all coordination) and how we tried to adapt this approach to our conditions, that is, state-sponsored inspections and popular inspections, working side by side on the job of supervising our institutions.

"On the other hand, speaking of the state inspections system, in Article 7 of the act that regulates the relations between People's Power agencies and the central government (approved in 1977 by the Council of Ministers), it is clearly stipulated that the national authorities enjoy the power to inspect and verify how the local units comply with standards and regulations set forth by the former. Similarly, the organic laws defining the provincial and municipal authorities allow for ample powers to inspect and oversee the performance of any administrative division subordinated to their legal purview.

"Now, how do we envision the system of popular inspections, the orderly participation of the masses in the different activities? Fundamentally, through the work review boards.

"In Article 33 of the organic code regulating the operation of municipal assemblies, of four points describing the responsibilities assigned to the work review boards, three are devoted to the activities of supervision. The three opening sections read as follows:

"(a) To assist and support the assembly and the executive committee in their respective tasks and in the supervision of municipal enterprises and administrative departments;

(b) To insure that the administrative departments and the managements of the municipal enterprises comply with existing provisions, as well as agreements and resolutions passed by ministries and other central agencies, the provincial assembly, or its executive committee;

(c) To secure the necessary data to evaluate the performance of the administrative departments, enterprises and units, conducting, when advisable, field inspection tours, or summoning pertinent officers to furnish the required information.

"The fourth point is the one that refers to the work review boards' duty to conduct studies, draw up plans, and collaborate in every possible way with the executive committee in the development of municipal assemblies.

"In the provincial assembly the same four points already mentioned (pertaining also to the work review board) are raised; the first three almost identical to those we read, but applied to their level, while the matter of direct inspections is also mentioned.

"We must bear in mind that these municipal work review boards are basically composed of persons who are not delegates. And not that there's a difference with the National Assembly, whose work review boards receive the support and assistance of people who are not deputies but whose members are required to be. In the case of the municipal and provincial assemblies the law requires only the chairman to be a delegate. This is done to facilitate involving the rest of the municipality's population, workers in particular, in the tasks if government, control and inspection.

"The same appears, of course, in the Constitution, Article 110, where the inspection and control repsonsiblities of these boards are clearly laid out in full.

"We assume that the proposal introduced here was inspired by the experience of other countries, notably the Soviet Union. In the USSR there are work review boards attached to agencies of People's Power and a network of inspectors. Now this soviet system of popular inspection has a vertical structure: from the national organization at the ministerial level, subordinated both to the Council of Ministers and to the Party's Central Committee, down to the tiers at the republic, region, and municipality levels. In each enterprise a group of People's inspectors is formed to oversee its activities. These inspectors operate within the collective ambit of each enterprise, helping to check on the management, the use or resources of all types—financial, material, etc.—and the quality of production. These are fulcrums for the system of municipal control, which is usually composed of only one professional and the rest nonprofessionals. In addition to this, in the rural soviets you also find outpost inspection stations empowered to conduct general inquiries throughout the municipality.

"In the USSR the People's Power review boards also have four functions stipulated in their by-laws, but, contrary to ours, they have only one that refers to inspections, while three are concerned with the passing judgments, the making of proposals, conducting studies, rendering assistance, and so on.

"In the USSR, and this was taken into account, the People's Power permanent boards did not materialize till 1936. And these auxiliary boards did not exist in the soviet organs of People's Power—they are not even mentioned in the 1936 Soviet Constitution. . . .Only in the 1977 Constitution, Article 21, are the People's Power commissions mentioned for the first time, this despite the fact that an inspection system existed already in 1918 to fill such functions, inaugurated as a system of government control and, later, in 1920, bolstered by one of popular control—the so-called peasant-worker inspections, and so on. This is the reason why in the soviet experience inspectors exist apart from the agencies of People's Power.

"Now, in our case, when we looked for ways to organize both systems of control, state control and people's control, which was the basic and legitimate departure point, we took into consideration the experience of other socialist nations and decided to try a different model from the one they had, for the reasons we are explaining here, opting instead to operate through work review boards at the national, provincial and municipal levels, all charged with tasks of control and inspection on behalf of the people.

"These commissions have been set up throughout the country. We now have an average of twelve per municipality (according to a report filed yesterday), including one connected with commerce and public dining facilities.

"This being so, and precisely because the review boards have not commenced operation till now, it seems to us redundant to create a parallel group of inspectors, which would further tax the time of the executive committee—it's certainly not very rational or efficient—until these boards have reached a normal operating level in the fulfillment of the duties assigned to them. Then, perhaps, if advisable, we might want to suggest a support mechanism for these boards.

"For this reason, I'd like to suggest that before we approve the proposal as advanced, we take stock of these elements and re-examine the question."

But the first session of the 1978 National Assembly was not devoted entirely to debating the merits of People's Power and the motions offered to ensure its refinement. A major portion of the three work sessions (June 28–30 at the Karl Marx Theatre) was taken up with debate on various other bills. Among these, for example, the new Code for Youth and Infancy (which had been submitted earlier) was finally passed after 140 amendments, the result of grassroots discussions and analysis.

16 CONSTRUCTIVE CRITICISM AND CREATIVE INITIATIVE

We cannot conclude this book without an account of an interview with one of the most prominent supporters of the process of institutionalization in Cuba—the president of the National Assembly and member of the Cuban Communist Party Politburo.

"The experience of People's Power is a new experience for Cuba, even though it already had an experimental run in Matanzas. How valuable do you think it has been? What kind of difficulties have you encountered?"

"It's natural that an experience so recently introduced hasn't matured sufficiently yet. The delegates and the deputies now are literally building the road over which others will travel, but inevitably finding the path full of underbrush and other obstacles, because there simply was no road before them. So they have to make the road as they go along: it's not an easy task. And the agencies of People's Power still often lack the resources to discharge their functions properly.

"Second, as always happens when a new institution is created, especially when the tasks previously were scattered through other institutions, there are functions that remain a bit up in the air, that no one knows who is supposed to tackle, and as a result begin to accumulate. This kind of thing will begin to vanish as we perfect the norms that regulate the relations between different agencies.

"But despite these difficulties, experience, on balance, has been extremely positive. Today we are far more aware of existing problems; we have learned about them through the participation of ordinary citizens, through accountability sessions, through the progress reports filed by the provinces with the National Assembly. So we are more aware of both the larger and the smaller problems, which, if forgotten, can transform themselves into big ones through the phenomenon of gradual accumulation.

"That's the unique advantage of the agencies of People's Power. Of course, knowledge per se is not the solution of a problem, but it is the indispensable step to the solution, for their study, to find the way to a workable solution. And we have already achieved that stage. On the other hand, the introduction of People's Power has coincided with an economic crisis in the capitalist world that affects us insofar as we maintain economic relations with these countries. One of the effects has been a drop in the price of sugar to levels well below the cost of production in any country, a situation which is aggravated by measures adopted by some countries, such as the United States, which put obstacles in the way of our marketing the commodity and set back out efforts to secure a price consistent with the costs of production.

"This affects our plans because the raw materials, machinery, and so on we must purchase in capitalist markets cannot be acquired when the sugar price drops and foreign exchange reserves are hard to obtain.

"This could be viewed, then, as hard times, but we're making headway. This year's sugar harvest has been the second largest in volume in the nation's history. The largest was in 1970. And the p ·ople are licking many problems thanks to their committed effort. Besides, many investments we have made are beginning to ripen, and although till now they have only represented expenses and produced nothing, very soon they may start contributing to the solution of these problems. For example. in the near future we will witness a dramatic surge in the production of cement, which is one of the critical elements for the population, as the need for construction materials is acute, to effect repairs, put up new housing, etc. This is one of the problems that keeps turning up in all accountability sessions, in all the letters we get from the deputies. . . ."

"I'd like to ask you something concerning the economic difficulties. Do you think that if the revolutionary leadership had foreseen the troubles to be encountered over this period they would have put off for some time the introduction of People's Power throughout the country?"

"No, I don't think it would have been put off, because the organization of People's Power stems from a general idea we have about the institutionalization of our revolutionary state, our socialist state. At certain moments all our attention had to concentrate on our defense against the aggression of imperialism. Not all these aggressions have vanished. The economic blockade continues, for example, but we have won. The question of who will conquer whom has been answered. Socialism won in our country. Our people prevailed in the face of foreign aggression. Today we are sufficiently strong not only to defend our revolutionary order, but even to extend assistance to other progressive countries in their struggle against imperialist attacks. We have reached the point where we can begin to perfect our institutional framework. During all these years we tried different institutions with the aim of finding those which, under the circumstances, would permit us the necessary maneuverability to carry on with our task while guaranteeing the most solid democracy for the people. We are always searching for ways to give the people an active say in the political process. Even congressional bills were submitted to the people for consultation and approval.

"Now the moment has come for us to pass on to a plane of formal representative institutions, whereby the constant and systematic participation of everyone can be insured. That's why the introduction of People's Powers was not predicated on an economic opportunity. We could not renounce these measures that are to be permanent, of lasting significance, because of a circumstantial problem."

"Faced with this situation of economic restriction, what is the role assigned to the agencies of People's Power?"

"There are things which do not depend on the economic situation. They depend on the organization, the education, the control one can exercise over certain specific facts. Courteous service to the public is something we all desire. And good service can be obtained whether you have three dimes or three million; it doesn't hinge on financial or economic conditions. It depends on the education you give people who must deal with the public. I have always stressed that we all find ourselves in need of some service sooner or later. A person can complain about the service she got in a cafeteria, but if the waitress herself goes to buy a shirt, then she may complain of (and is vulnerable to) the service she gets at the store. In similar fashion, if the store clerk goes out and must catch a bus, she may complain about the service she gets from the driver, and if the bus driver gets off the bus to enjoy the beach, *he* may have grudges against the services there. . . .So it's quite clear we all have an interest in good service. Good service is of benefit to all. It's a general problem. We are going to treat one another in a fraternal way, according to the socialist idea of human coexistence; we are all going to strive to do our level best for others. . . .That's the way to get the best from others, too. . . .For no one should expect decent treatment from others if she or he is not prepared to offer it. These are aspects that People's Power through its activities, its administrative powers, can improve day by day."

"You said that there's a long road ahead. What is the role assigned in this scheme to the creative initiative of delegates, municipal assembly, and the people themselves?"

"This is important. With initiative we can discover the most efficacious methods, the best. We cannot regulate everything in advance. It is life which teaches, and life teaches through experience. If one takes an initiative, it may succeed or backfire. If it works, we must disseminate it. If if backfires, we drop it. For example, we still don't have a regulatory code for the work review boards. This code could have been elaborated, but we have chosen instead to see how they develop, how they carry on with their work, how they really perform their duties and serve the cause of the building of socialism in our land. And when we see how they've done it, we'll put it into writing. We'll write the by-laws—that's the way it's going to be handled. That's the role assigned to initiative.

"In the recent elections we elected 10,725 delegates to the municipal assemblies, 1,115 delegates to the provincial assemblies, and 481 deputies to the National Assembly. These 10,725 delegates share a common trait. They are people who have deserved the appreciation and respect of the people, and yet they are different. Some are like this, some are like that; some work over here, others over there; some exhibit one level of development and others another; but all have something in common, and that is the desire to serve through these offices the people who elected them. However, since not everyone can give a good account of himself and not all behave in the manner expected of them, the masses have reserved to themselves the right to recall those who fail in their assigned duties. And they *have* recalled some. But the important thing is to see that, on the whole, these delegates, striving to resolve the problems in accordance with the prerogatives of People's Power, have done a magnificent job. They have contributed considerably to the progress of our society. They are connected with the whole of the country's population; they are the ears of the people, and they are also the voice of the same people in their search for a better life. Some display more initiative, but all must—and this is my opinion—endeavor to fulfill these two functions: receive information from the people and convey the voice of the people to the agencies that will make the decisions on the problems affecting them. Nobody has to keep anything inside him; no one must avoid his duty; no one must rest content with the first negative reply he receives. They must always be ready to insist, suggest, request a re-examination of the problem. And the point is not merely to come to raise a complaint or present a problem, but to show initiative and say: Look, comrade, this can be resolved with this, that, or that. We have these resources, we have these possibilities; this much can be done. In other words, not only to demand, but also to offer solutions."

"Concerning the people themselves, I've heard that some comrades withhold their criticism before the masses because this saves them headaches. . . ."

"That is certainly not something to be proud of. There are, of course, criticisms offered in a bad spirit, but there are also criticisms made in a constructive way, in the hope of correcting something that is wrong. That's the kind of critique we always regard as correct, and I suppose that if someone had some arguments for criticizing something, that something can't be all that perfect. One must never be afraid of exposing the facts in as precise a manner as possible. There's a common habit of generalizing. I've heard a compañero say, for example, 'Everyone is saying this,' and I've asked him, 'Where did you hear that everyone says that?' And he would reply, 'Well, I was on the bus and people were talking about this.' 'How many people were talking about this?' 'Three people.' So I said to him,' If three people are saying this on a bus, is that the whole world? Did you take care to find out what the opinion was in your own home? Your neighbors? Have you listened, really listened, before arriving at the conclusion that everybody is saying that? Because it may be a case of only three or four souls.' Another common generalization is to blame an entire profession or trade for the faults of one member. They're likely to say, 'All these fellows are alike; there are no exceptions.' But in that lot we can find those who give a fine account of themselves and those who do not. This kind of generalization is not good. The correct thing would be to establish the complaint in more precise terms: on such and such a date, at this time, in such and such a place, under these circumstance, such and such a thing happened. And, whenever possible, name the principals involved, so that the denunciation is not a blind shot, missing reality by a wide berth. If the comrades raised their complaints in this fashion in the assemblies, it would help enormously with the resolution of problems. So let's do away with generalizations because they are vague. Let's have precise criticism because it allows us to adopt concrete measures."

"What do you think of the role of the press in support of People's Power?"

"I think the press has three tasks in connection with People's Power. In the first place, it must disseminate the experiences, the work, and the activities of the agencies of People's Power. It's very important for the people to know what they did, when they meet, the topics to be discussed, the problems the system is zeroing in on, etc. Second, and related to the first, the press must collect the critical aspects of the question: where's the flaw, what wasn't done, what deficiencies exist, what problems are being neglected. . . . And, next, let the people be informed about the success, what has been accomplished, what has been resolved—the positive side of the question. Summing up, it must concentrate on the activities of People's Power, the criticisms, and the positive accomplishments, when these occur.

"Sometimes there is hyperbole in one aspect or another. Sometimes it is a case of positive exaggeration. Sometimes it's negative. But both are wrong. Sometimes it isn't exaggeration, but one's thinking that things were really worse than they were, a matter quickly set right through a reexamination of the problem, listening to new opinions. And sometimes the opposite occurs, and that kind of distortion is also a obstacle on the road to real solutions."

"And when you inform the assembly that twenty-nine problems were resolved, while six are still pending, but the licked problems were insignificant whereas the pending ones are major. . . ."

"They're the biggies. Maybe you can exaggerate a bit there on the positive side if you just look at the matter in numerical terms and neglect the actual magnitudes. . . .

"I think the process has a crucial task to perform, not only in the guidance it provides but in the information it transmits.

"I'd say we have seen very good works published on People's Power. But sometimes I'd say that little effort has been made to probe matters, and often what is said does not accurately reflect reality. I think that if I were a journalist, and were assigned to cover the agencies of People's Power, I'd try to read up on the subject, bring myself to date on the matter, for only this would allow me to really penetrate the jargon created by each activity as it develops, since only by bearing in mind these problems of communication can one really convey the facts to the general public in a satisfactory manner. And the journalist must be understood by everyone, for he is writing for the masses and must always be thinking of the average reader as he writes."

"The historical forces were on our side, the correlation of forces helped us. And that is why we have been able to see, have been able to reap the fruits of the effort of so many men who fought so hard and yet never saw their dreams come true. . . ." So spoke Fidel at the conclusion of the First Congress of the Cuban Communist Party. He added further on:

"What does history show? That men held power and have abused power. Even in revolutionary processes, some men acquire extraordinary power, especially during this phase, especially during the early years. But when processes are finally institutionalized, when there is already a party, when standards are already in place, when these standards practically become a culture for the community, then there is no longer any danger.

"We are now entering an institutionalization phase of our revolutionary process, a safe phase, a phase with great guarantees, because the guarantees come no longer from men, but from institutions. . . .we finally have come to feel like mere drops of water in this ocean that is the people."